The FLASH

VOL. 11: THE GREATEST TRICK OF ALL

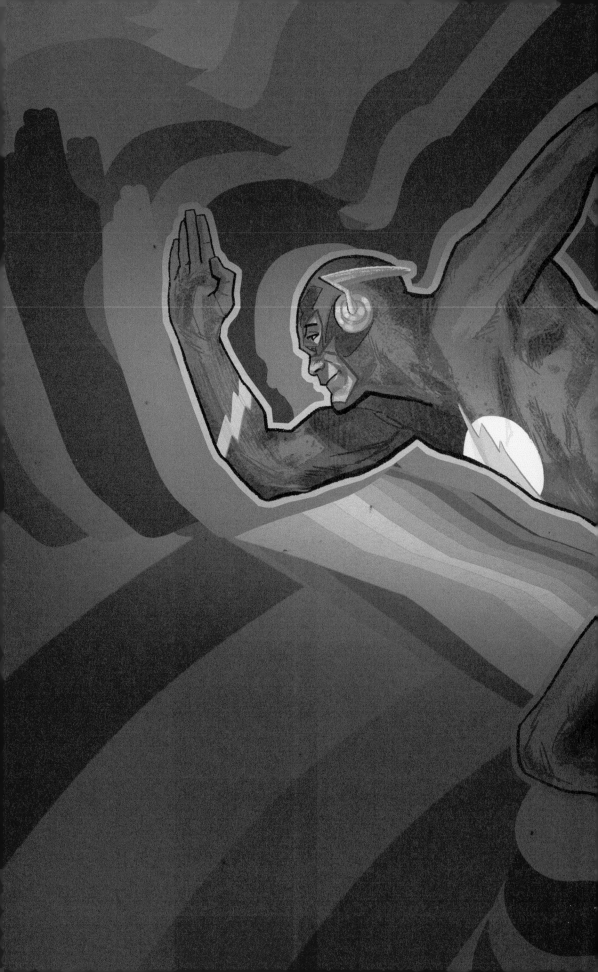

The FLASH

VOL. 11: THE GREATEST TRICK OF ALL

JOSHUA WILLIAMSON
writer

SCOTT KOLINS
artist

LUIS GUERRERO
colorist

STEVE WANDS
WES ABBOTT
letterers

RAFA SANDOVAL,
JORDI TARRAGONA,
and TOMEU MOREY
collection cover artists

SUPERMAN created by JERRY SIEGEL and JOE SHUSTER
By special arrangement with the Jerry Siegel family

PAUL KAMINSKI Editor – Original Series
ANDREW MARINO Associate Editor – Original Series
JEB WOODARD Group Editor – Collected Editions
ERIKA ROTHBERG Editor – Collected Edition
STEVE COOK Design Director – Books
GABRIEL MALDONADO Publication Design
TOM VALENTE Publication Production

BOB HARRAS Senior VP – Editor-in-Chief, DC Comics
PAT McCALLUM Executive Editor, DC Comics

DAN DiDIO Publisher
JIM LEE Publisher & Chief Creative Officer
BOBBIE CHASE VP – New Publishing Initiatives & Talent Development
DON FALLETTI VP – Manufacturing Operations & Workflow Management
LAWRENCE GANEM VP – Talent Services
ALISON GILL Senior VP – Manufacturing & Operations
HANK KANALZ Senior VP – Publishing Strategy & Support Services
DAN MIRON VP – Publishing Operations
NICK J. NAPOLITANO VP – Manufacturing Administration & Design
NANCY SPEARS VP – Sales
MICHELE R. WELLS VP & Executive Editor, Young Reader

THE FLASH VOL. 11: THE GREATEST TRICK OF ALL
Published by DC Comics. Compilation and all new
material Copyright © 2020 DC Comics. All Rights
Reserved. Originally published in single maga-
zine form in *The Flash Annual 2, The Flash* 66-69.
Copyright © 2019 DC Comics. All Rights Reserved.
All characters, their distinctive likenesses, and
related elements featured in this publication are
trademarks of DC Comics. The stories, characters, and incidents featured in this publication
are entirely fictional. DC Comics does not read
or accept unsolicited submissions of ideas,
stories, or artwork. DC – a WarnerMedia Company.

DC Comics
2900 West Alameda Ave., Burbank, CA 91505
Printed by LSC Communications,
Kendallville, IN, USA. 1/3/20. First Printing.
ISBN: 978-1-77950-032-8

Library of Congress
Cataloging-in-Publication Data is available.

PEFC Certified

This product is from
sustainably managed
forests and controlled
sources

PEFC
PEFC/29-31-337   www.pefc.org

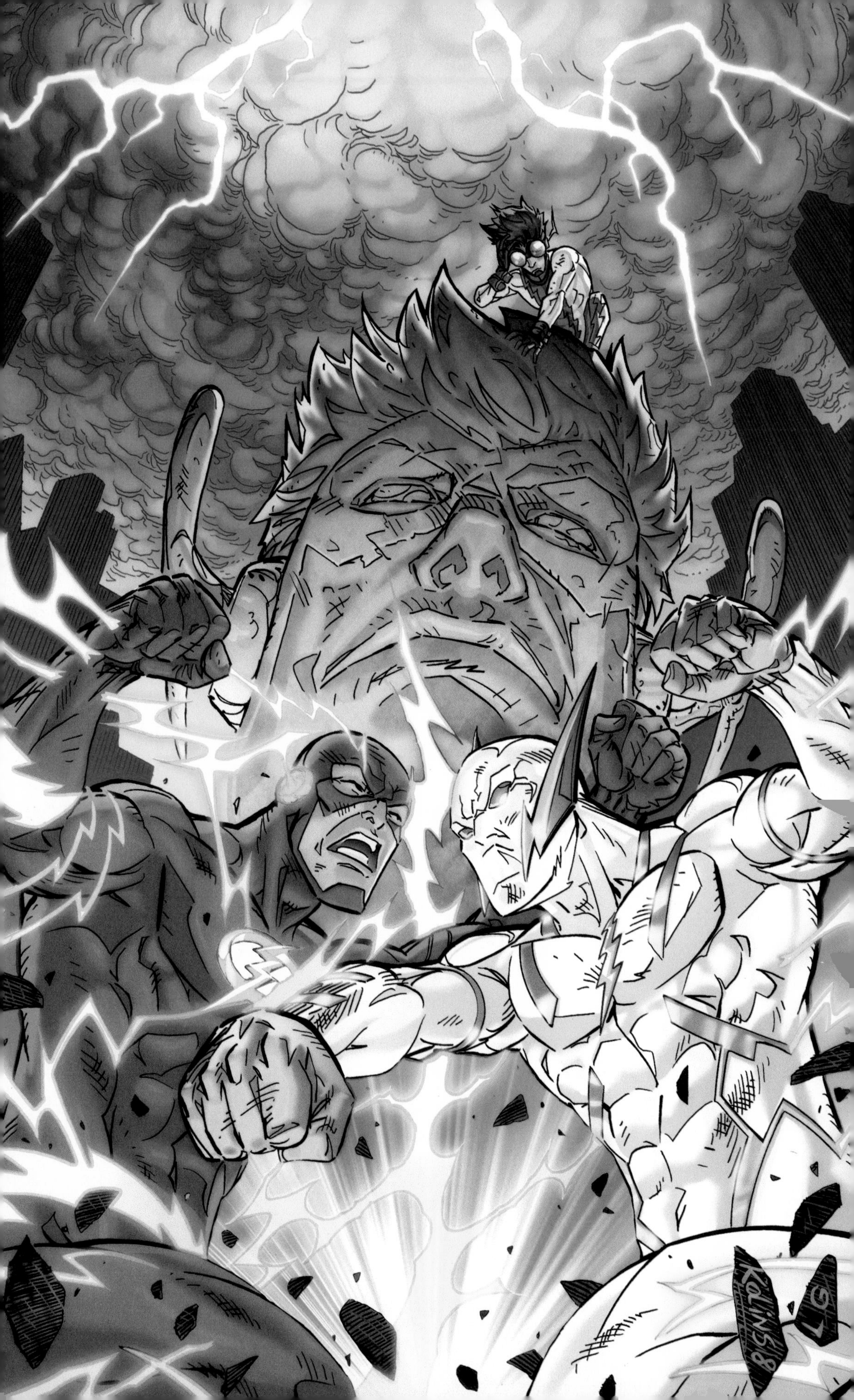

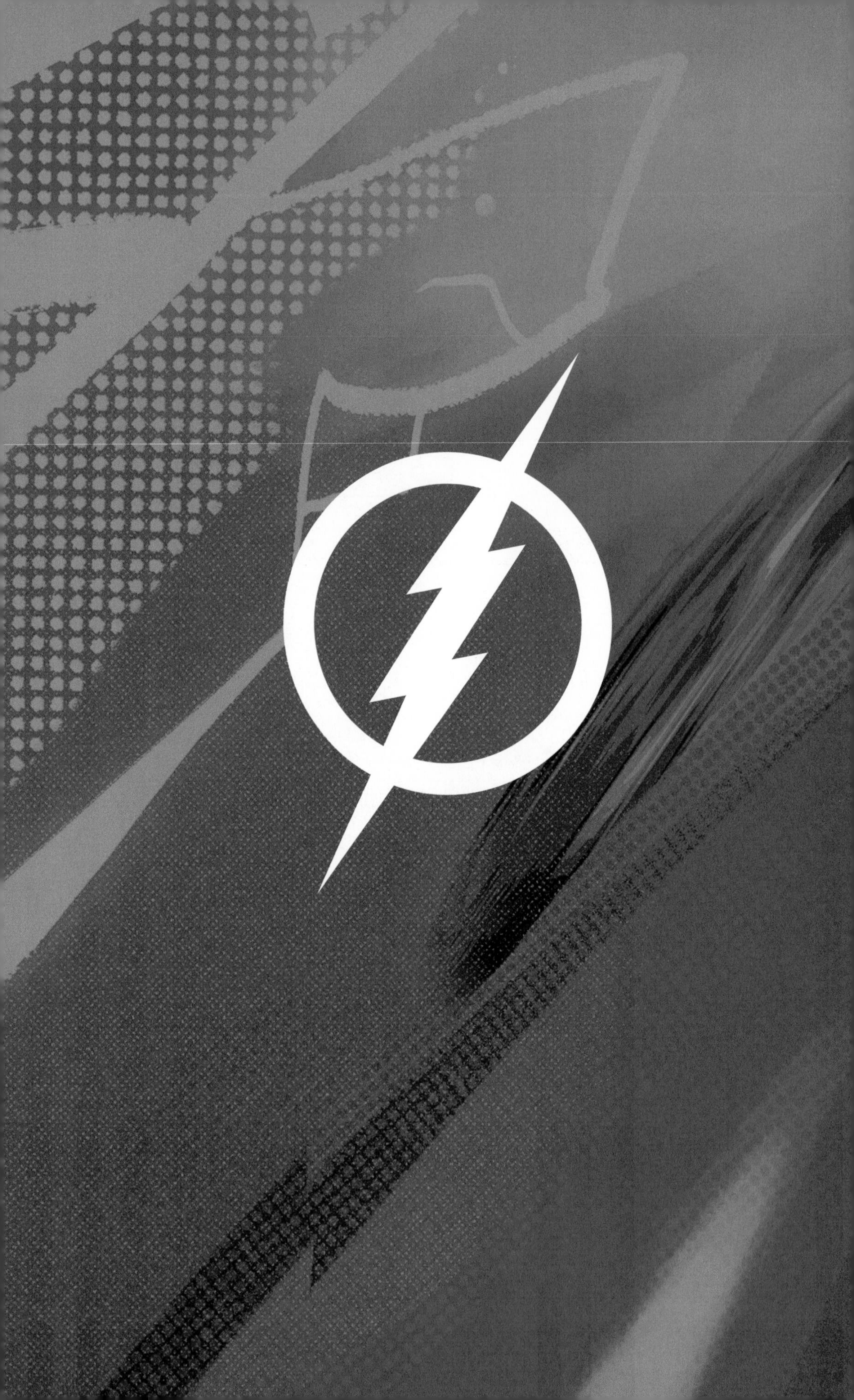

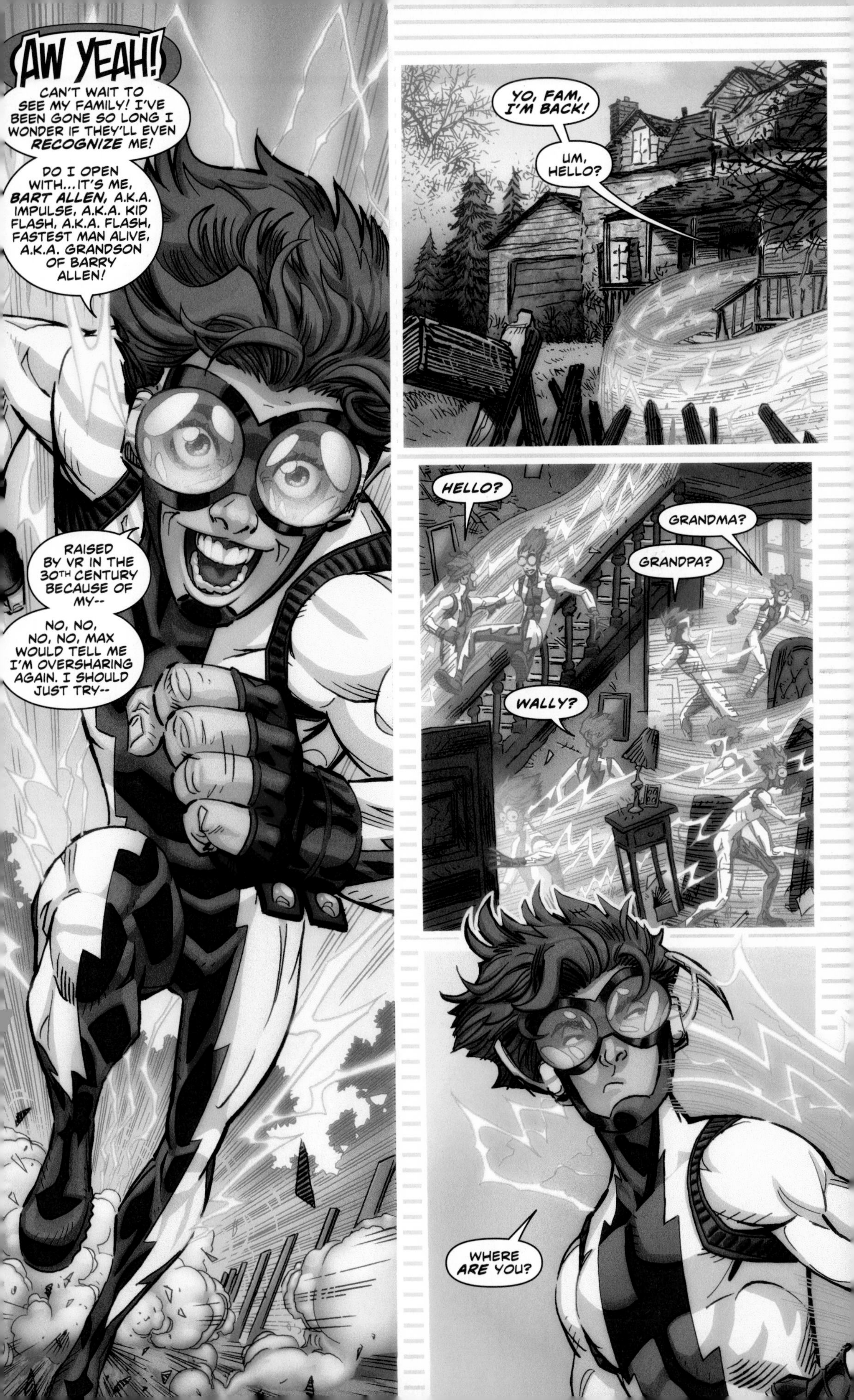

AW YEAH!
CAN'T WAIT TO SEE MY FAMILY! I'VE BEEN GONE SO LONG I WONDER IF THEY'LL EVEN *RECOGNIZE* ME!
DO I OPEN WITH...IT'S ME, **BART ALLEN,** A.K.A. IMPULSE, A.K.A. KID FLASH, A.K.A. FLASH, FASTEST MAN ALIVE, A.K.A. GRANDSON OF BARRY ALLEN!
RAISED BY VR IN THE 30TH CENTURY BECAUSE OF MY--
NO, NO, NO, NO, MAX WOULD TELL ME I'M OVERSHARING AGAIN. I SHOULD JUST TRY--
YO, FAM, I'M BACK!
UM, HELLO?
HELLO?
GRANDMA?
GRANDPA?
WALLY?
WHERE *ARE* YOU?

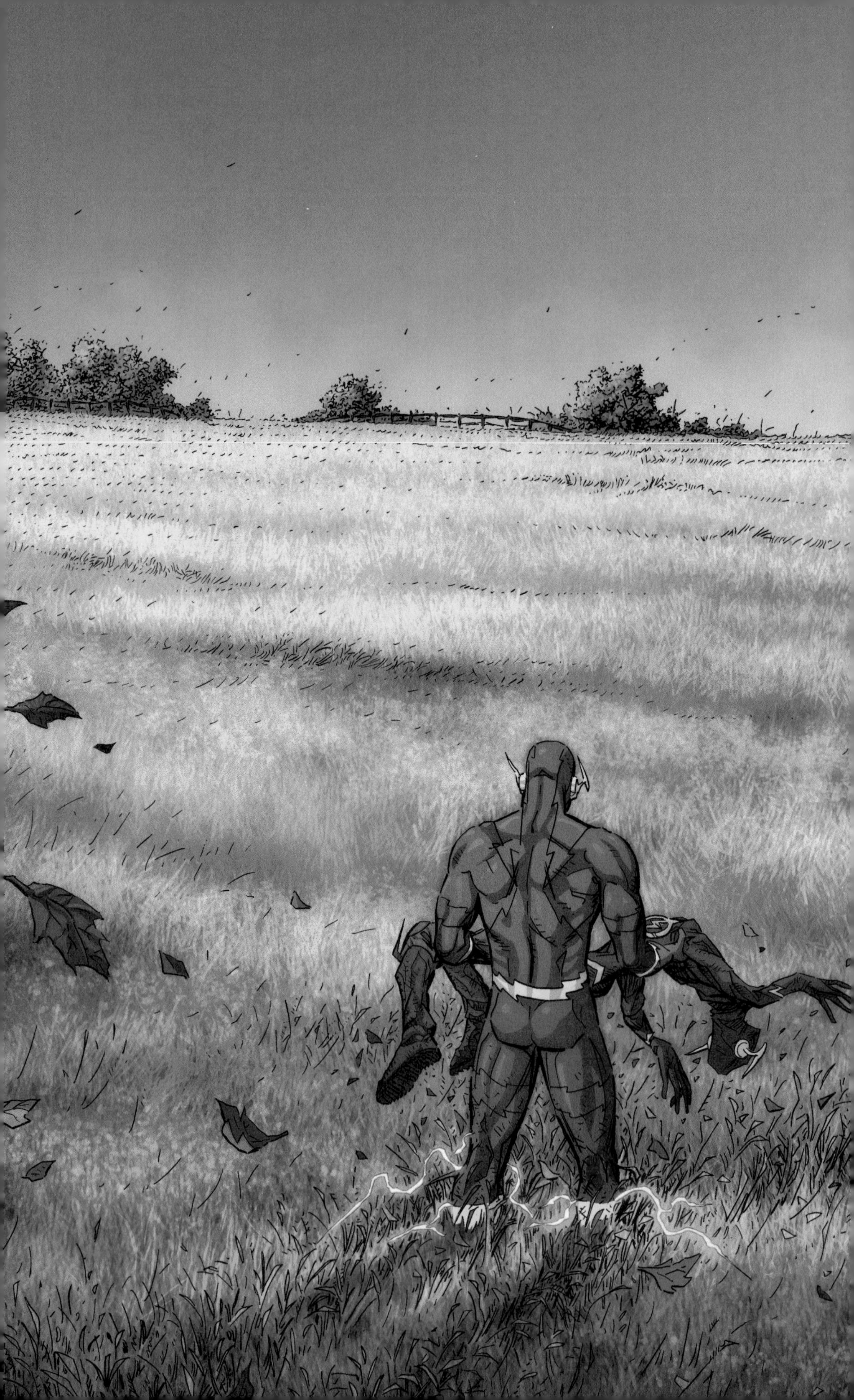

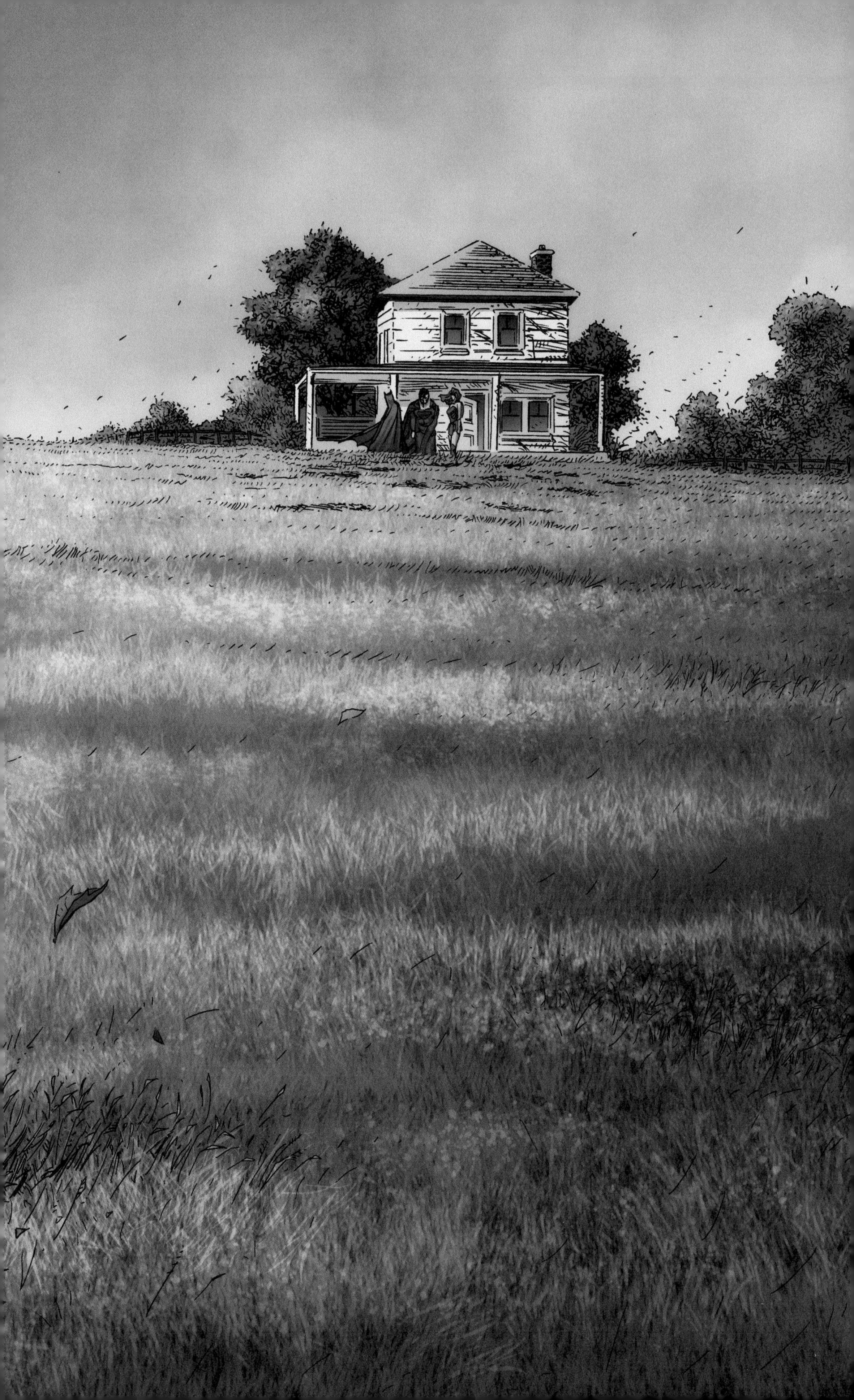

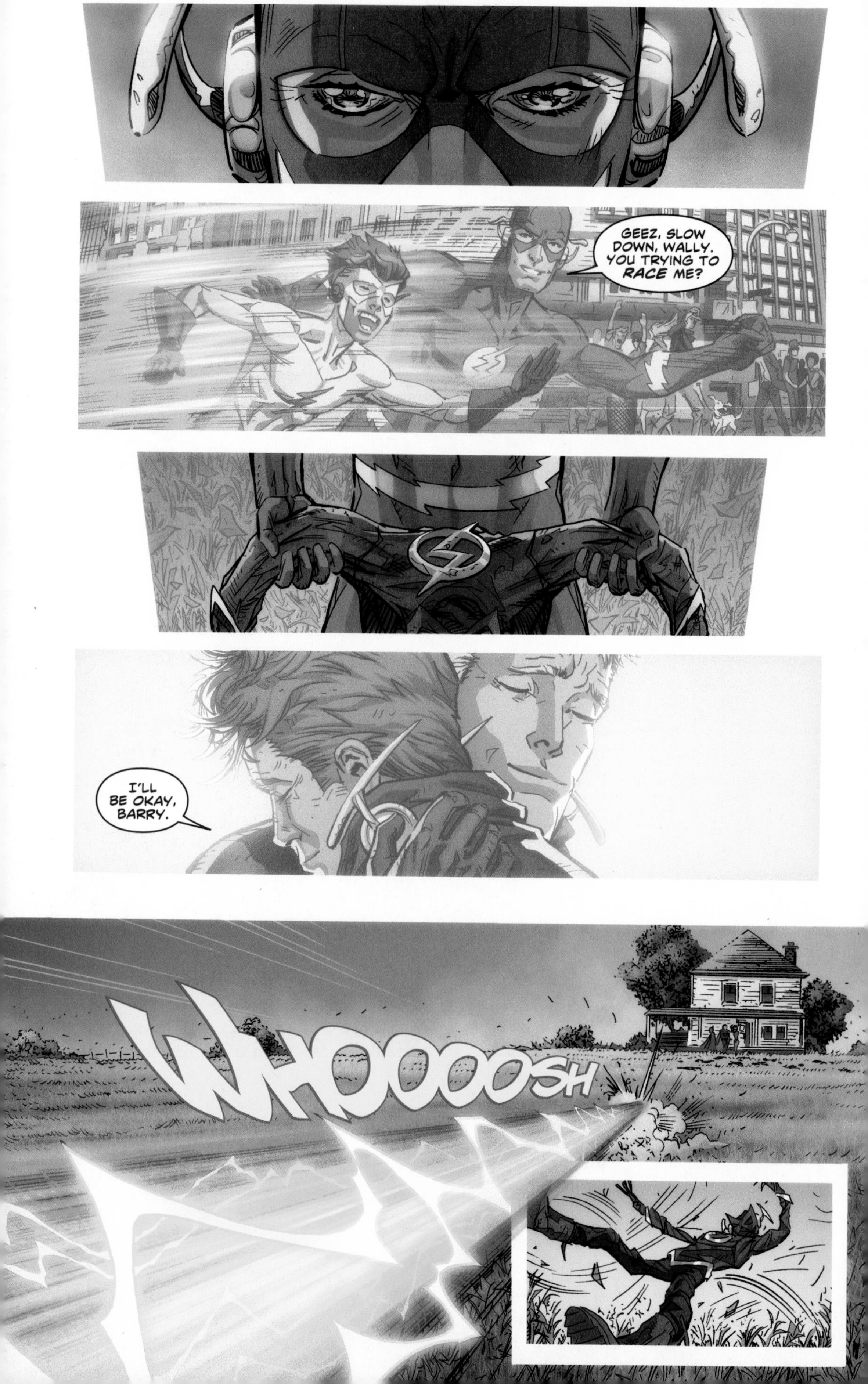
GEEZ, SLOW DOWN, WALLY. YOU TRYING TO RACE ME?
I'LL BE OKAY, BARRY.
WHOOOOSH

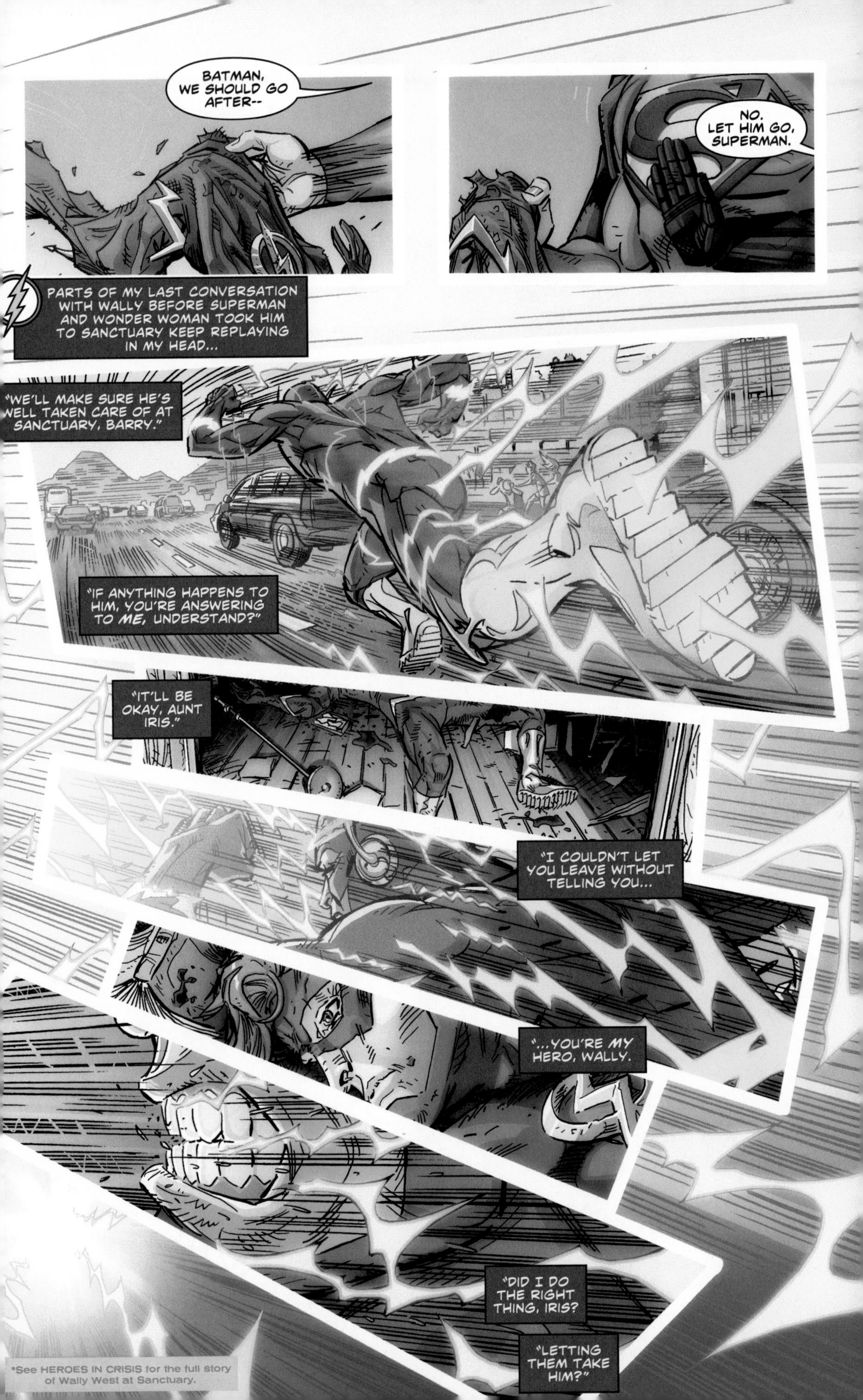
BATMAN, WE SHOULD GO AFTER--
NO. LET HIM GO, SUPERMAN.
PARTS OF MY LAST CONVERSATION WITH WALLY BEFORE SUPERMAN AND WONDER WOMAN TOOK HIM TO SANCTUARY KEEP REPLAYING IN MY HEAD...
"WE'LL MAKE SURE HE'S WELL TAKEN CARE OF AT SANCTUARY, BARRY."
"IF ANYTHING HAPPENS TO HIM, YOU'RE ANSWERING TO ME, UNDERSTAND?"
"IT'LL BE OKAY, AUNT IRIS."
"I COULDN'T LET YOU LEAVE WITHOUT TELLING YOU...
"...YOU'RE MY HERO, WALLY.
"DID I DO THE RIGHT THING, IRIS?
"LETTING THEM TAKE HIM?"
*See HEROES IN CRISIS for the full story of Wally West at Sanctuary.

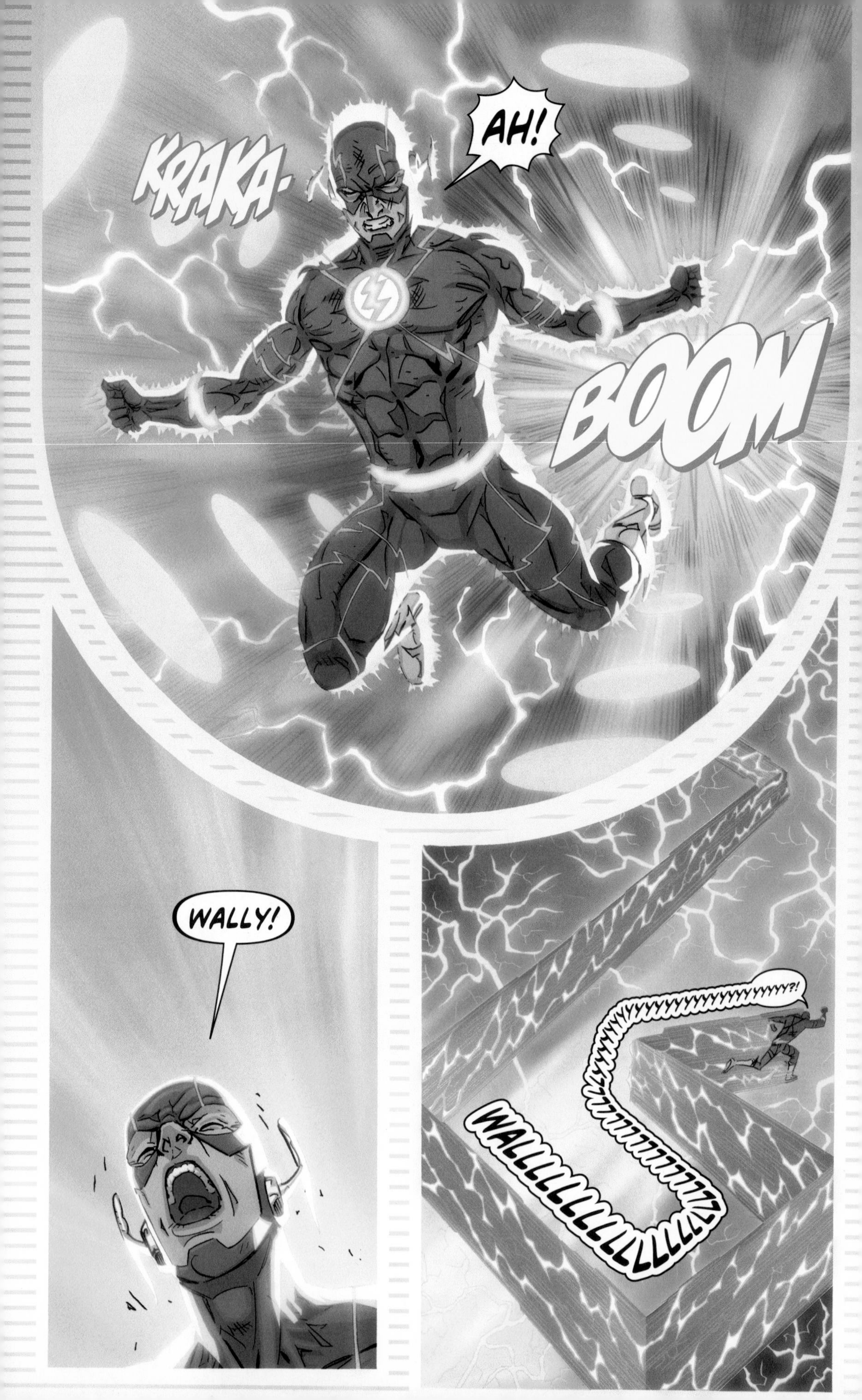
KRAKA-
AH!
BOOM
WALLY!
WALLLLLLLLLLLLLLLLLLLLLLLLLLLLLLLLLLLLYYYYYYYYYYYYYYYYYYYYYYYYYYYYYYYYYY?!

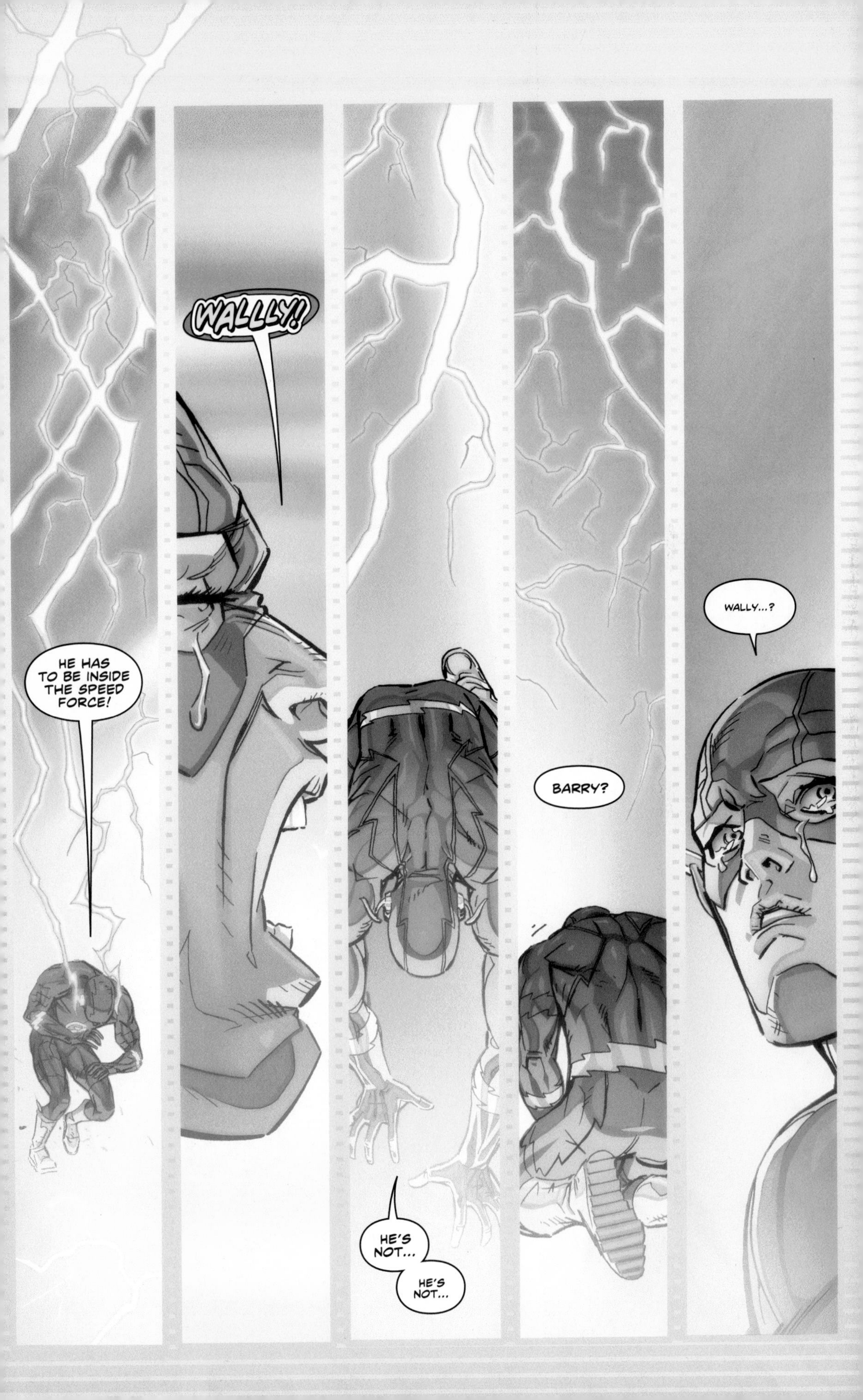
HE HAS TO BE INSIDE THE SPEED FORCE!
WALLLY!
HE'S NOT...
HE'S NOT...
BARRY?
WALLY...?

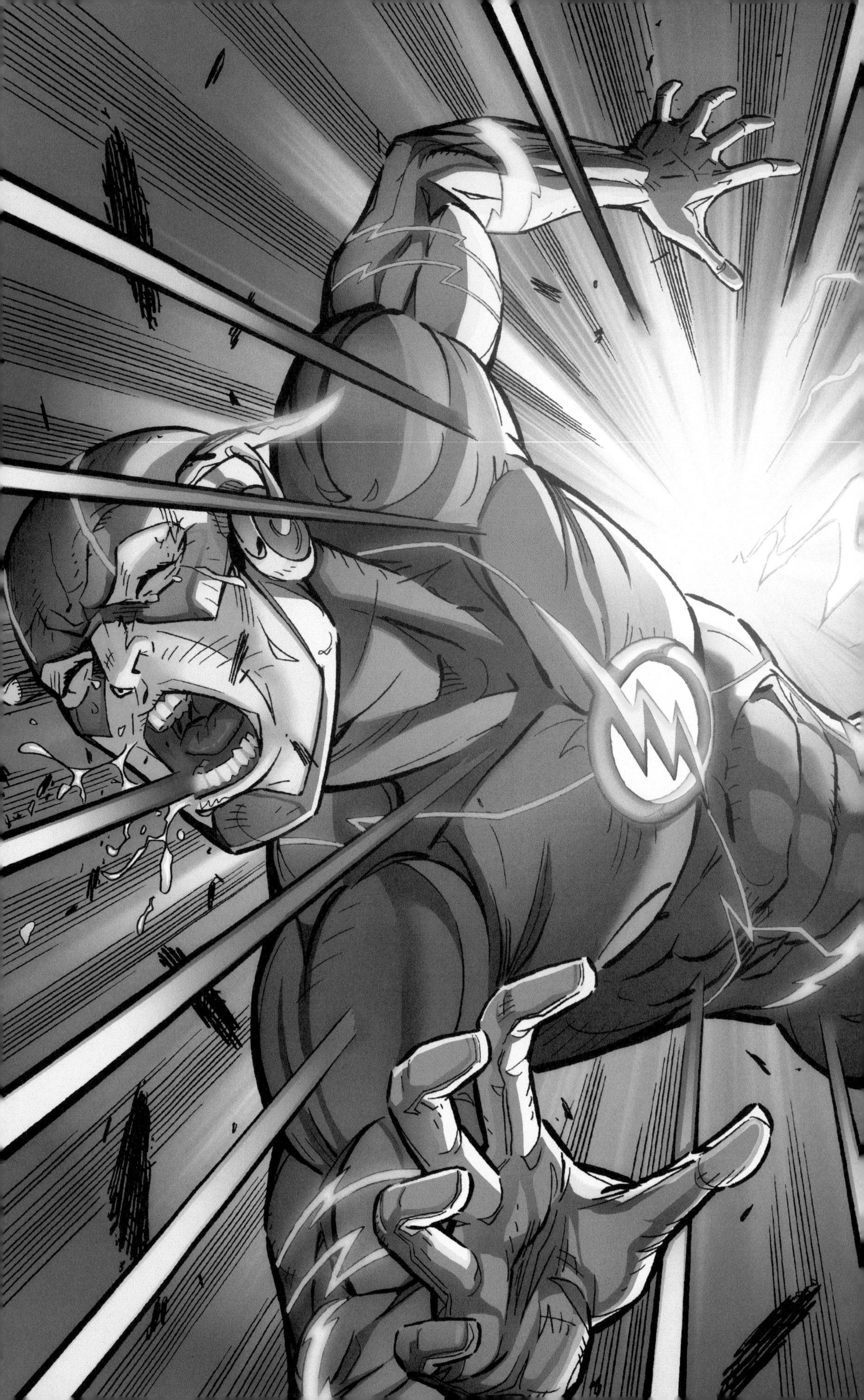

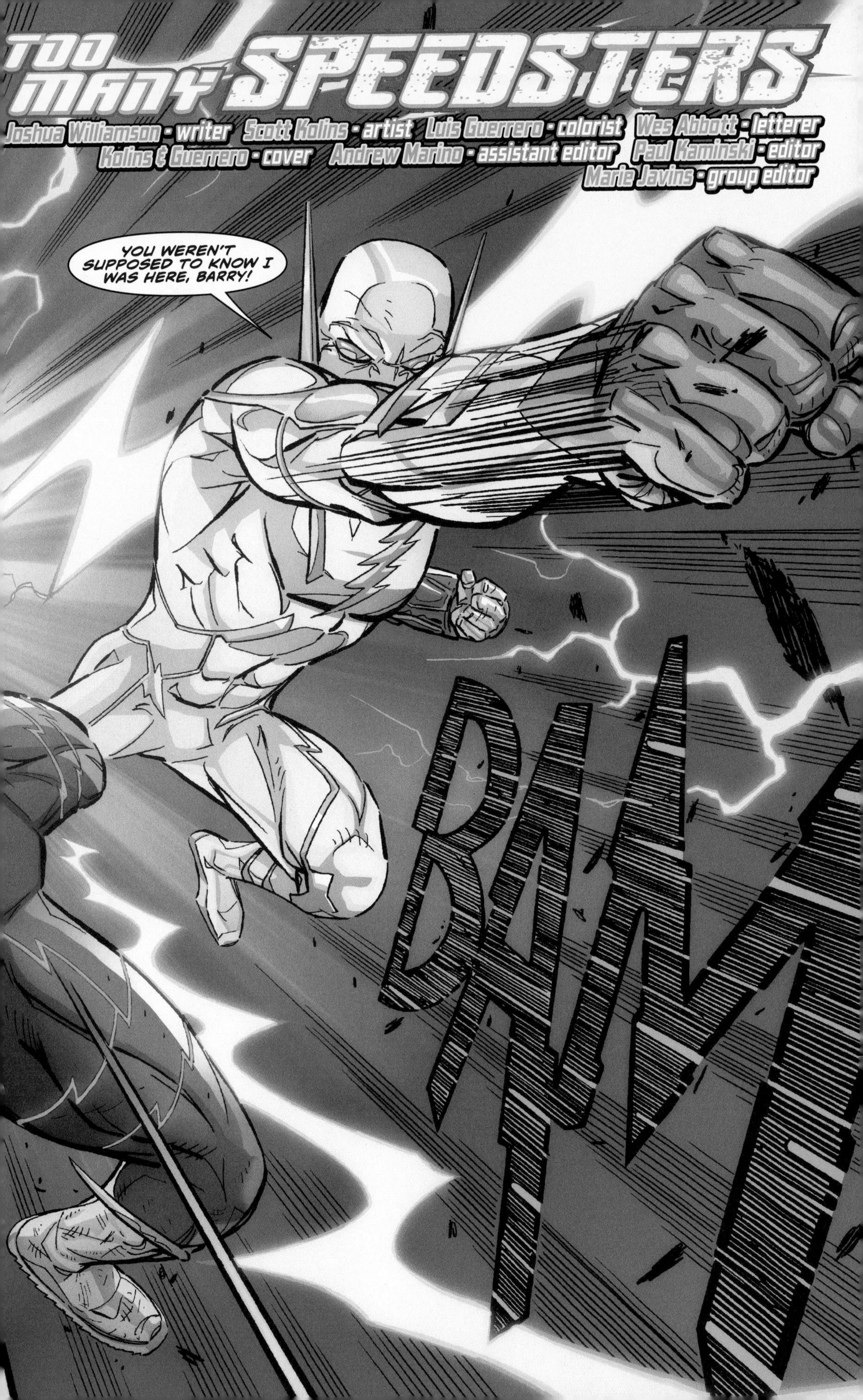
TOO MANY SPEEDSTERS
Joshua Williamson - writer Scott Kolins - artist Luis Guerrero - colorist Wes Abbott - letterer
Kolins & Guerrero - cover Andrew Marino - assistant editor Paul Kaminski - editor
Marie Javins - group editor
YOU WEREN'T SUPPOSED TO KNOW I WAS HERE, BARRY!
BAM!

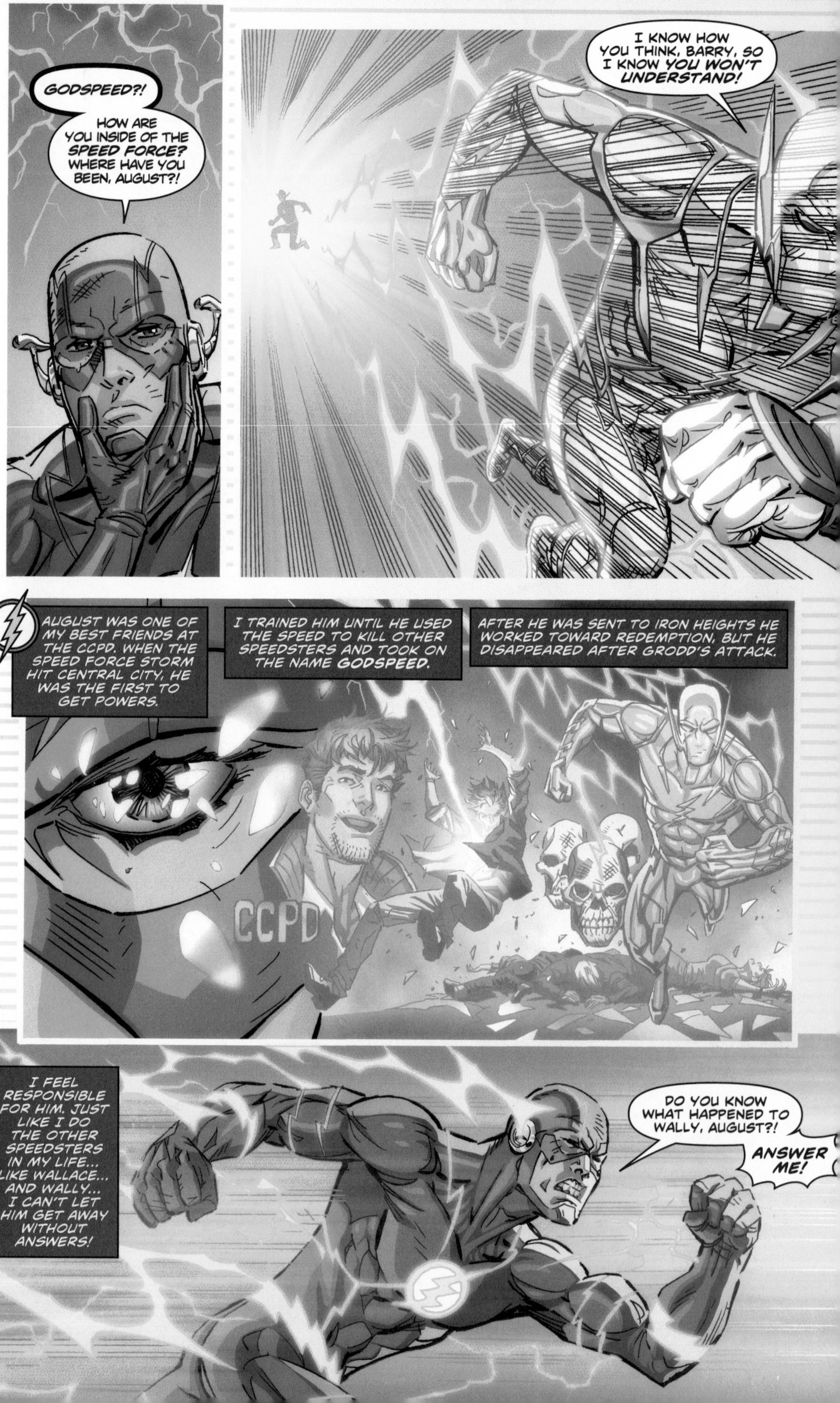
GODSPEED?!
HOW ARE YOU INSIDE OF THE SPEED FORCE? WHERE HAVE YOU BEEN, AUGUST?!
I KNOW HOW YOU THINK, BARRY, SO I KNOW YOU WON'T UNDERSTAND!
AUGUST WAS ONE OF MY BEST FRIENDS AT THE CCPD. WHEN THE SPEED FORCE STORM HIT CENTRAL CITY, HE WAS THE FIRST TO GET POWERS.
I TRAINED HIM UNTIL HE USED THE SPEED TO KILL OTHER SPEEDSTERS AND TOOK ON THE NAME GODSPEED.
AFTER HE WAS SENT TO IRON HEIGHTS HE WORKED TOWARD REDEMPTION, BUT HE DISAPPEARED AFTER GRODD'S ATTACK.
CCPD
I FEEL RESPONSIBLE FOR HIM. JUST LIKE I DO THE OTHER SPEEDSTERS IN MY LIFE... LIKE WALLACE... AND WALLY... I CAN'T LET HIM GET AWAY WITHOUT ANSWERS!
DO YOU KNOW WHAT HAPPENED TO WALLY, AUGUST?!
ANSWER ME!

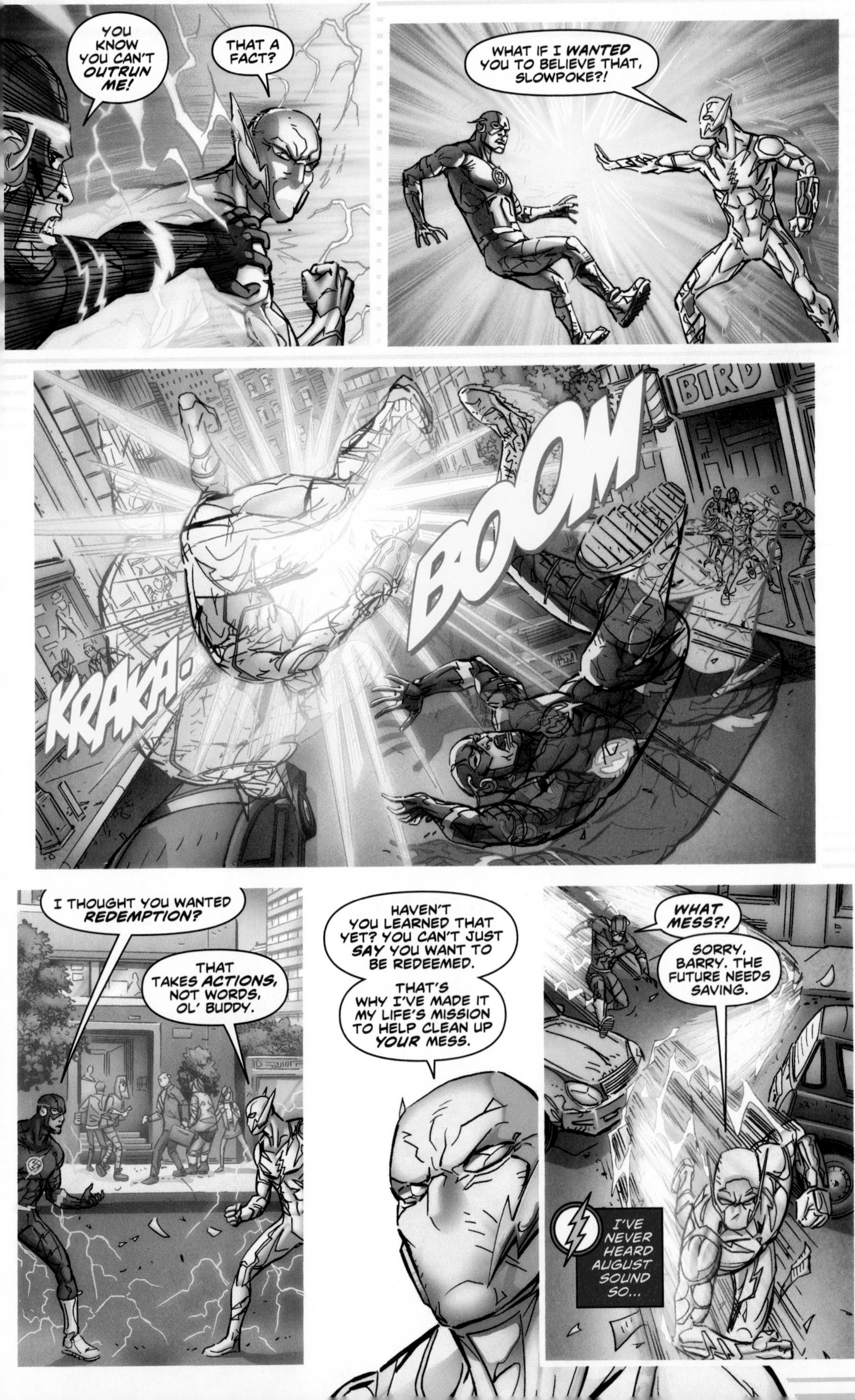
YOU KNOW YOU CAN'T OUTRUN ME!
THAT A FACT?
WHAT IF I WANTED YOU TO BELIEVE THAT, SLOWPOKE?!
BIRD
BOOM
KRAKA-
I THOUGHT YOU WANTED REDEMPTION?
THAT TAKES ACTIONS, NOT WORDS, OL' BUDDY.
HAVEN'T YOU LEARNED THAT YET? YOU CAN'T JUST SAY YOU WANT TO BE REDEEMED.
THAT'S WHY I'VE MADE IT MY LIFE'S MISSION TO HELP CLEAN UP YOUR MESS.
WHAT MESS?!
SORRY, BARRY. THE FUTURE NEEDS SAVING.
I'VE NEVER HEARD AUGUST SOUND SO...

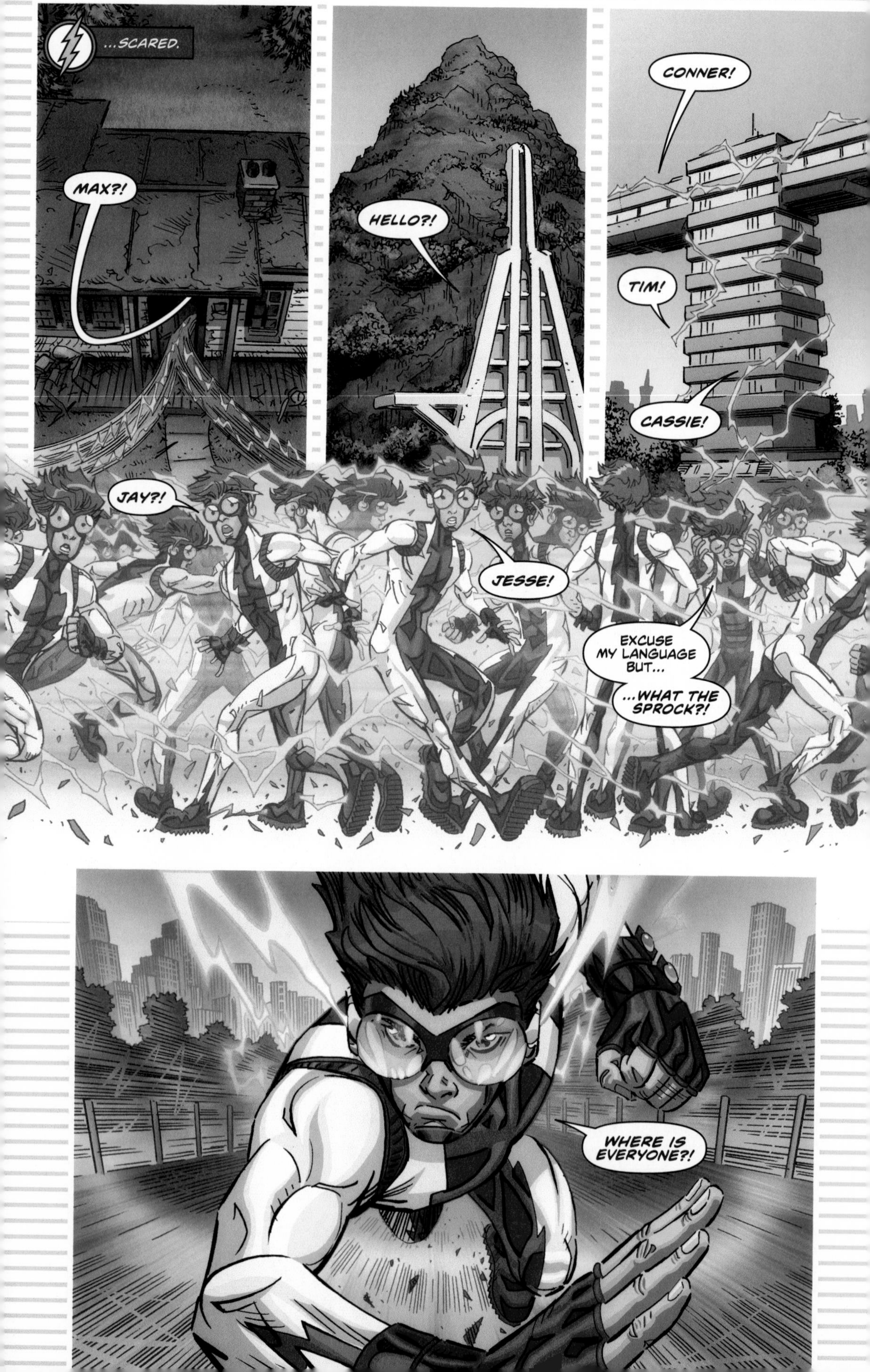
...SCARED.
MAX?!
HELLO?!
CONNER!
TIM!
CASSIE!
JAY?!
JESSE!
EXCUSE MY LANGUAGE BUT...
...WHAT THE SPROCK?!
WHERE IS EVERYONE?!

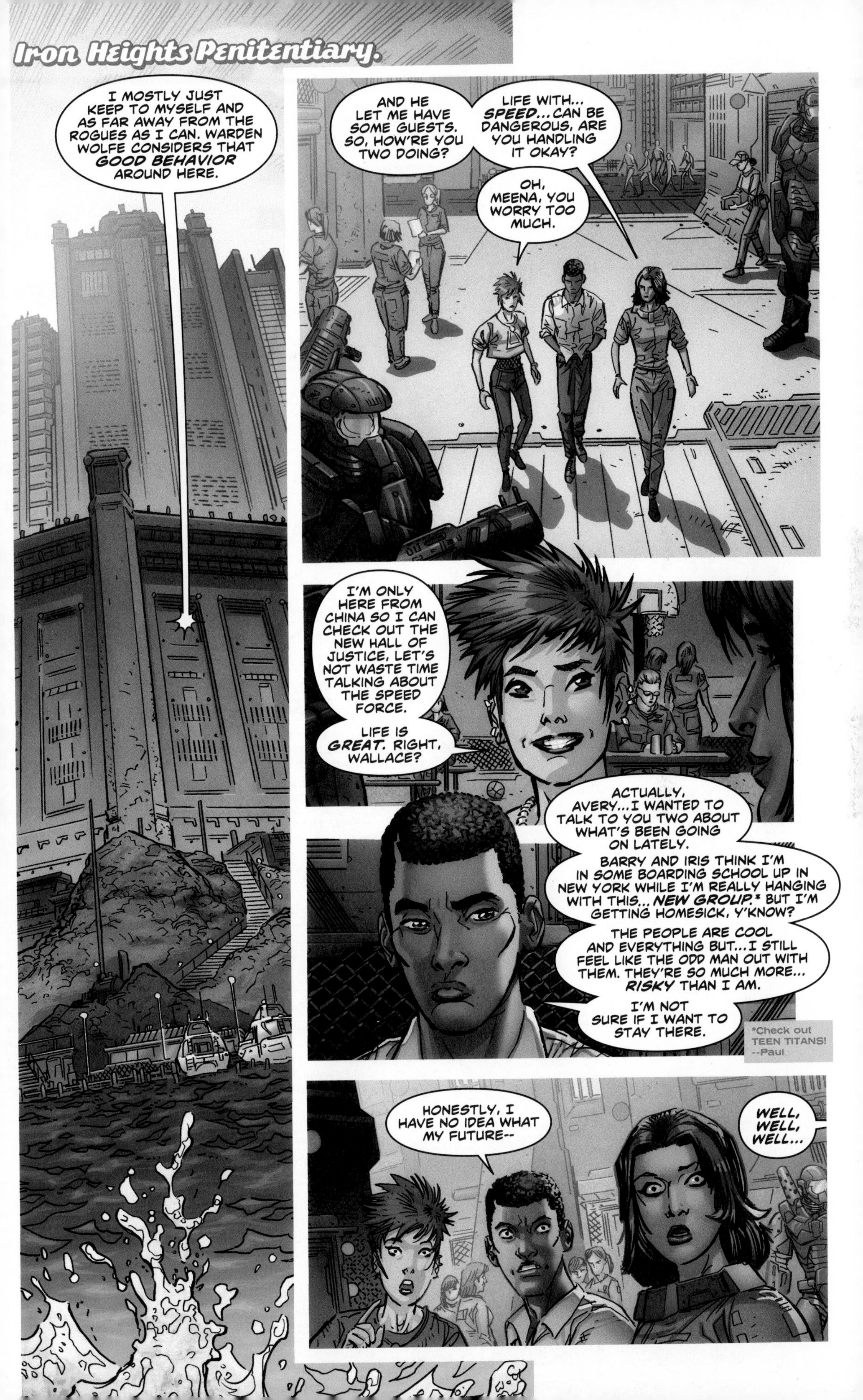
Iron Heights Penitentiary.
I MOSTLY JUST KEEP TO MYSELF AND AS FAR AWAY FROM THE ROGUES AS I CAN. WARDEN WOLFE CONSIDERS THAT GOOD BEHAVIOR AROUND HERE.
AND HE LET ME HAVE SOME GUESTS. SO, HOW'RE YOU TWO DOING?
LIFE WITH... SPEED... CAN BE DANGEROUS, ARE YOU HANDLING IT OKAY?
OH, MEENA, YOU WORRY TOO MUCH.
I'M ONLY HERE FROM CHINA SO I CAN CHECK OUT THE NEW HALL OF JUSTICE, LET'S NOT WASTE TIME TALKING ABOUT THE SPEED FORCE.
LIFE IS GREAT. RIGHT, WALLACE?
ACTUALLY, AVERY... I WANTED TO TALK TO YOU TWO ABOUT WHAT'S BEEN GOING ON LATELY.
BARRY AND IRIS THINK I'M IN SOME BOARDING SCHOOL UP IN NEW YORK WHILE I'M REALLY HANGING WITH THIS... NEW GROUP.* BUT I'M GETTING HOMESICK, Y'KNOW?
THE PEOPLE ARE COOL AND EVERYTHING BUT... I STILL FEEL LIKE THE ODD MAN OUT WITH THEM. THEY'RE SO MUCH MORE... RISKY THAN I AM.
I'M NOT SURE IF I WANT TO STAY THERE.
*Check out TEEN TITANS! --Paul
HONESTLY, I HAVE NO IDEA WHAT MY FUTURE--
WELL, WELL, WELL...

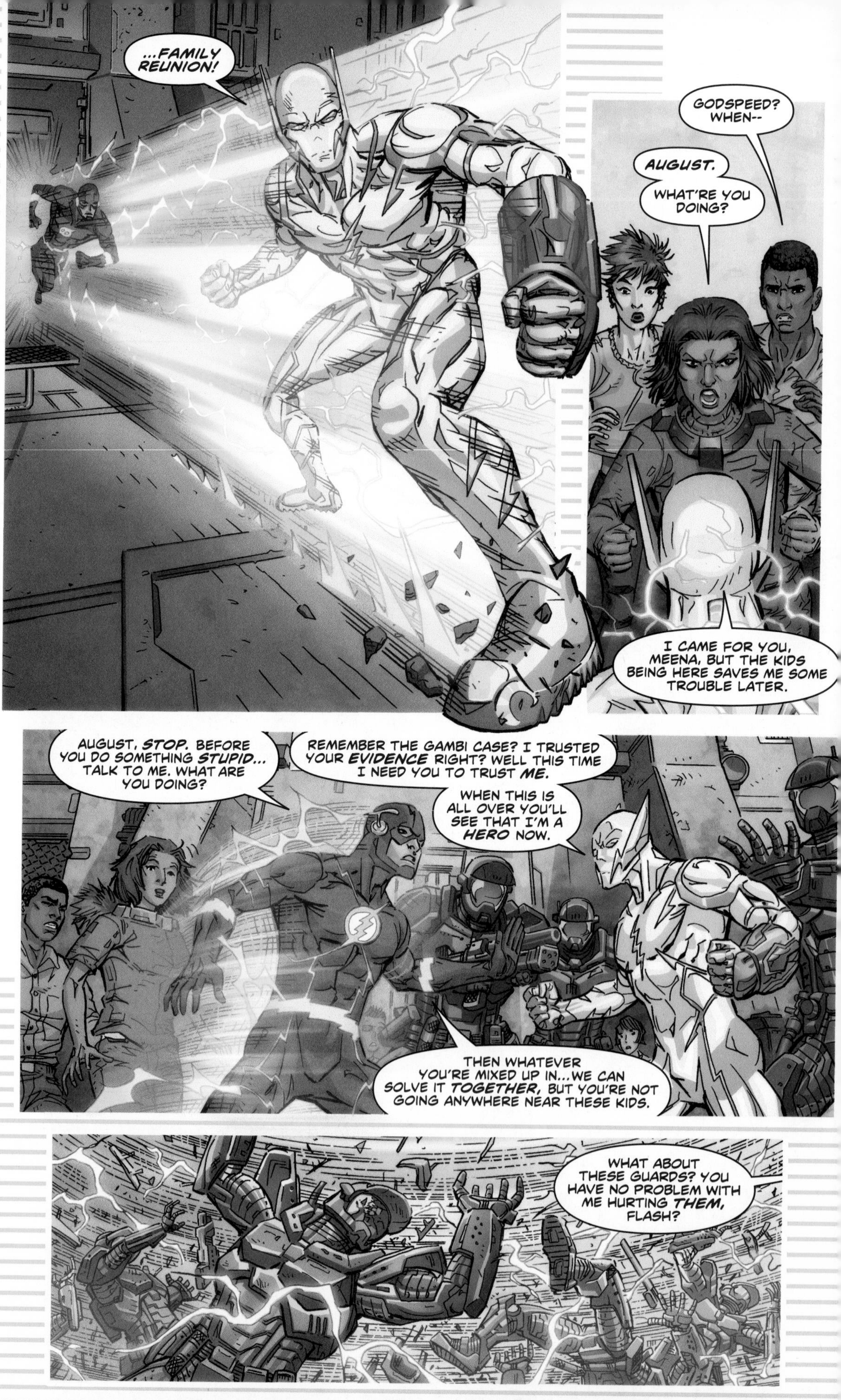
...FAMILY REUNION!
GODSPEED? WHEN--
AUGUST.
WHAT'RE YOU DOING?
I CAME FOR YOU, MEENA, BUT THE KIDS BEING HERE SAVES ME SOME TROUBLE LATER.
AUGUST, STOP. BEFORE YOU DO SOMETHING STUPID... TALK TO ME. WHAT ARE YOU DOING?
REMEMBER THE GAMBI CASE? I TRUSTED YOUR EVIDENCE RIGHT? WELL THIS TIME I NEED YOU TO TRUST ME.
WHEN THIS IS ALL OVER YOU'LL SEE THAT I'M A HERO NOW.
THEN WHATEVER YOU'RE MIXED UP IN...WE CAN SOLVE IT TOGETHER, BUT YOU'RE NOT GOING ANYWHERE NEAR THESE KIDS.
WHAT ABOUT THESE GUARDS? YOU HAVE NO PROBLEM WITH ME HURTING THEM, FLASH?

WHAT IS WRONG WITH YOU?!

WALLACE, AVERY, RUN!

WAM

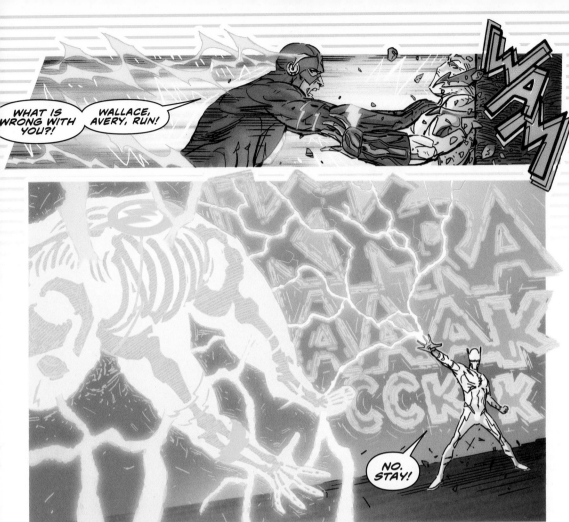

NO, STAY!

FLASH?!

UGH...

THE FLASH IS THE ONLY ONE WHO BELIEVED IN YOU, AUGUST.

IF I DIDN'T HAVE MY POWER INHIBITOR ON, I'D KICK YOUR ASS MYSELF, AUGUST.

IS THAT ANY WAY TO TALK TO AN OLD FRIEND?

YOU AND I WERE NEVER FRIENDS, BUT I'VE STUDIED THE SPEED FORCE AND I CAN SEE THERE'S SOMETHING WRONG WITH YOU.

IS SOMEONE IN YOUR HEAD?

I'VE NEVER BEEN MORE LUCID.

KKRACKK

I'M DOING THIS FOR YOUR OWN GOOD, MEENA.

AAHHHH!

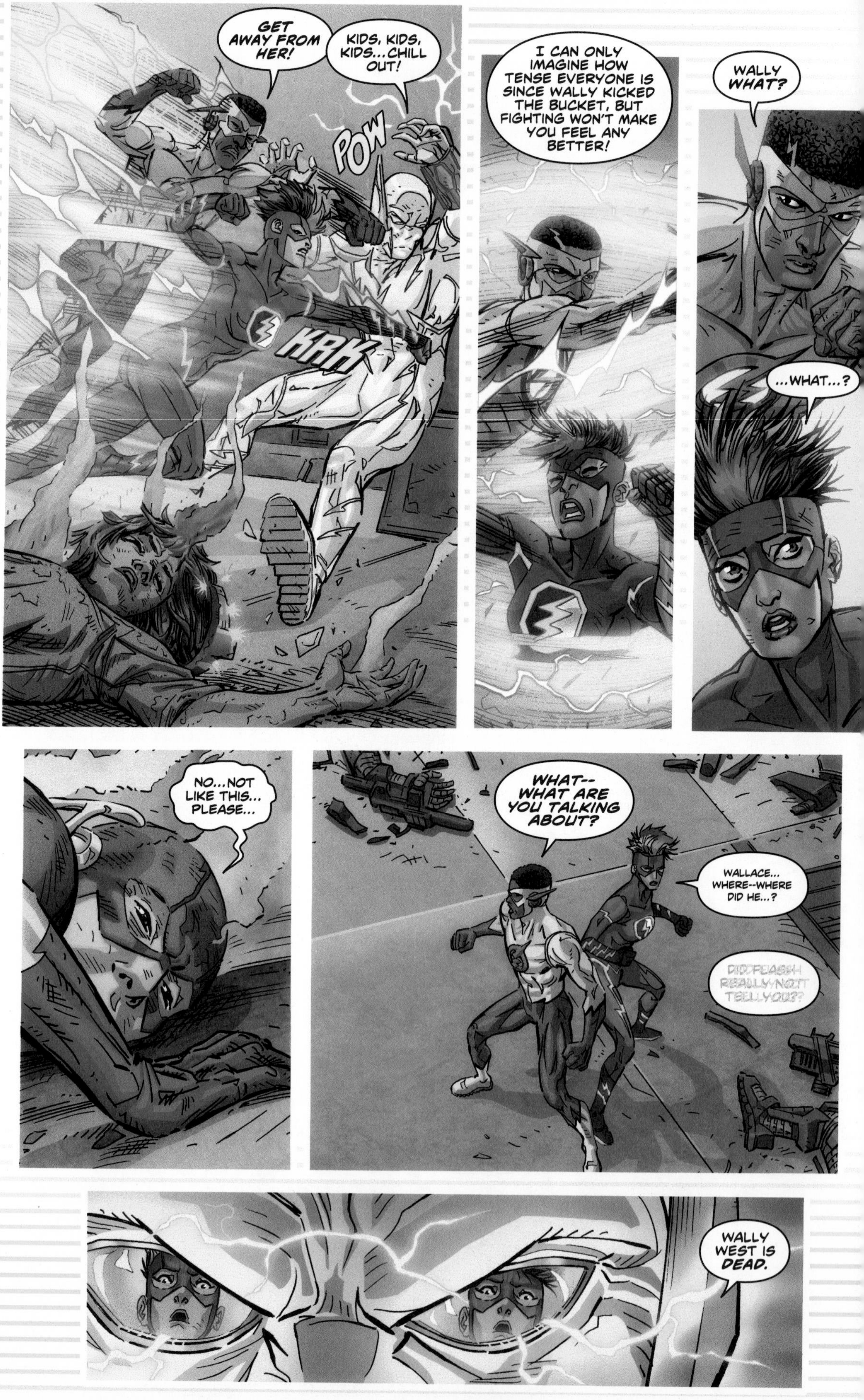
GET AWAY FROM HER!
KIDS, KIDS, KIDS... CHILL OUT!
POW
KRK
I CAN ONLY IMAGINE HOW TENSE EVERYONE IS SINCE WALLY KICKED THE BUCKET, BUT FIGHTING WON'T MAKE YOU FEEL ANY BETTER!
WALLY WHAT?
...WHAT...?
NO...NOT LIKE THIS... PLEASE...
WHAT-- WHAT ARE YOU TALKING ABOUT?
WALLACE... WHERE--WHERE DID HE...?
DID FLASH REALLY NOT TELL YOU??
WALLY WEST IS DEAD.

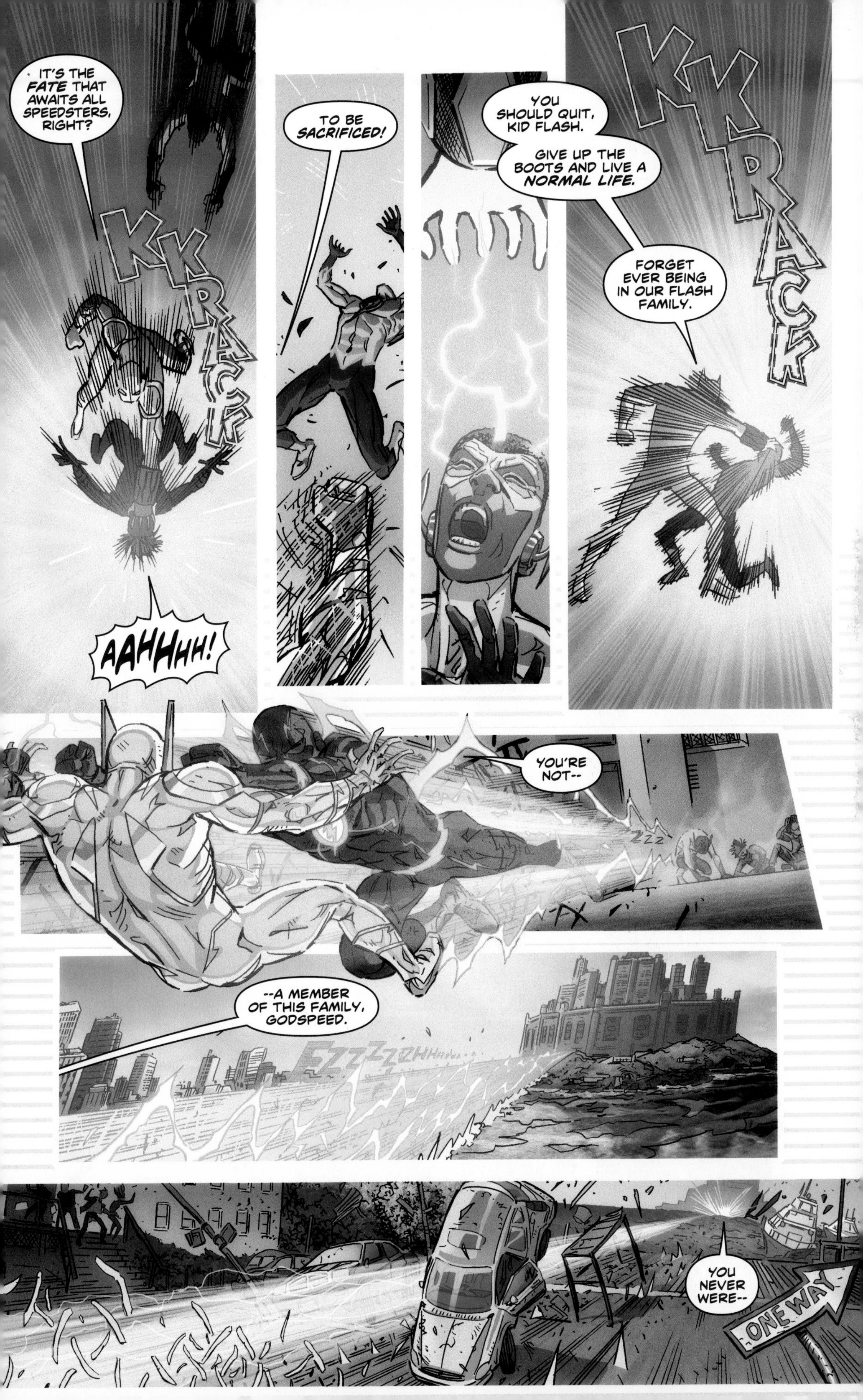
IT'S THE FATE THAT AWAITS ALL SPEEDSTERS, RIGHT?
KKRACK
AAHHHH!
TO BE SACRIFICED!
YOU SHOULD QUIT, KID FLASH.
GIVE UP THE BOOTS AND LIVE A NORMAL LIFE.
FORGET EVER BEING IN OUR FLASH FAMILY.
KKRACK
YOU'RE NOT--
ZZZ
--A MEMBER OF THIS FAMILY, GODSPEED.
EZZZZZHHH
YOU NEVER WERE--
ONE WAY

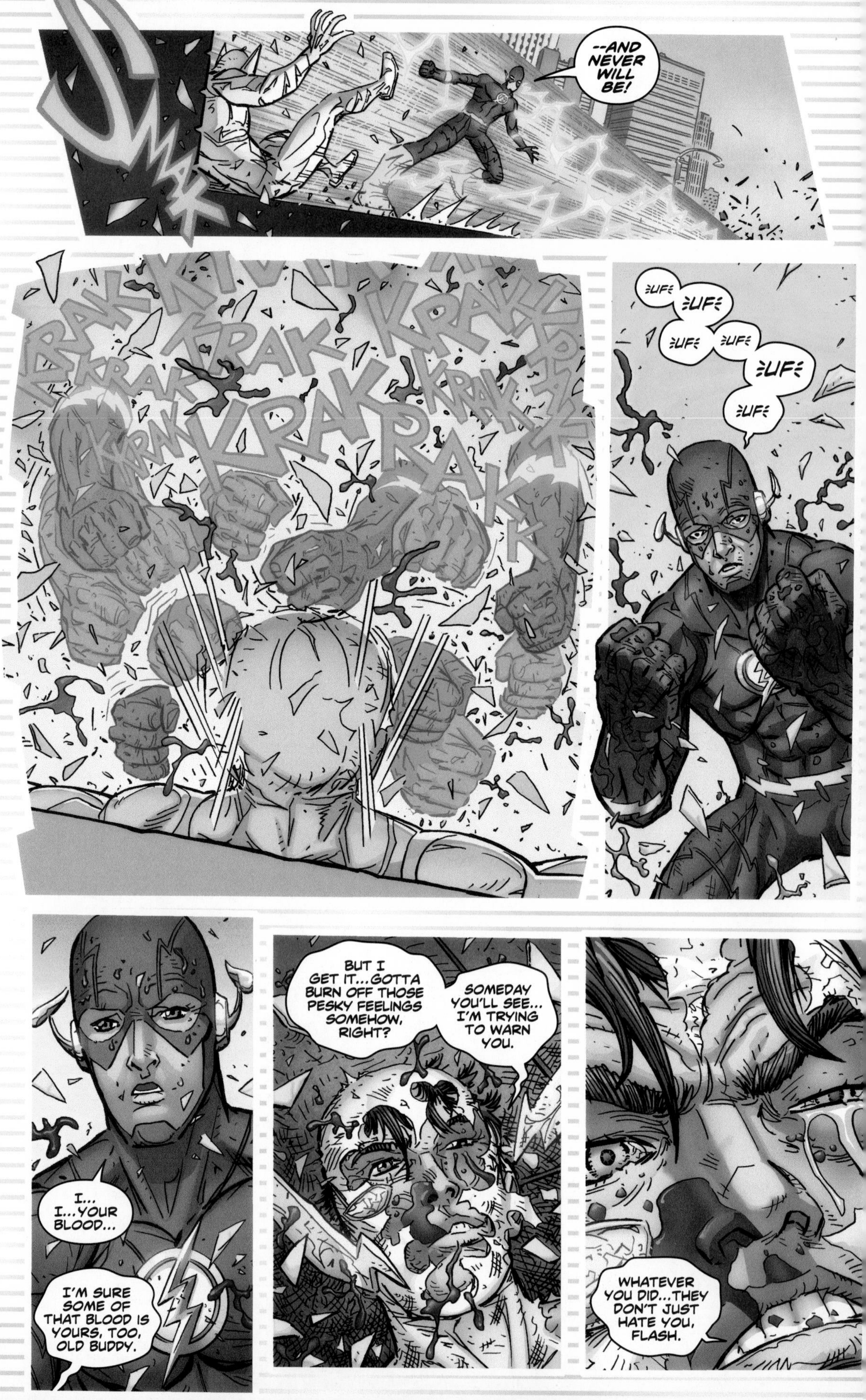
SMAK
--AND NEVER WILL BE!
KRAK KRAK KRAK KRAK KRAK KRAK KRAK
UF
UF
UF
UF
UF
UF
I... I...YOUR BLOOD...
I'M SURE SOME OF THAT BLOOD IS YOURS, TOO, OLD BUDDY.
BUT I GET IT...GOTTA BURN OFF THOSE PESKY FEELINGS SOMEHOW, RIGHT?
SOMEDAY YOU'LL SEE... I'M TRYING TO WARN YOU.
WHATEVER YOU DID...THEY DON'T JUST HATE YOU, FLASH.

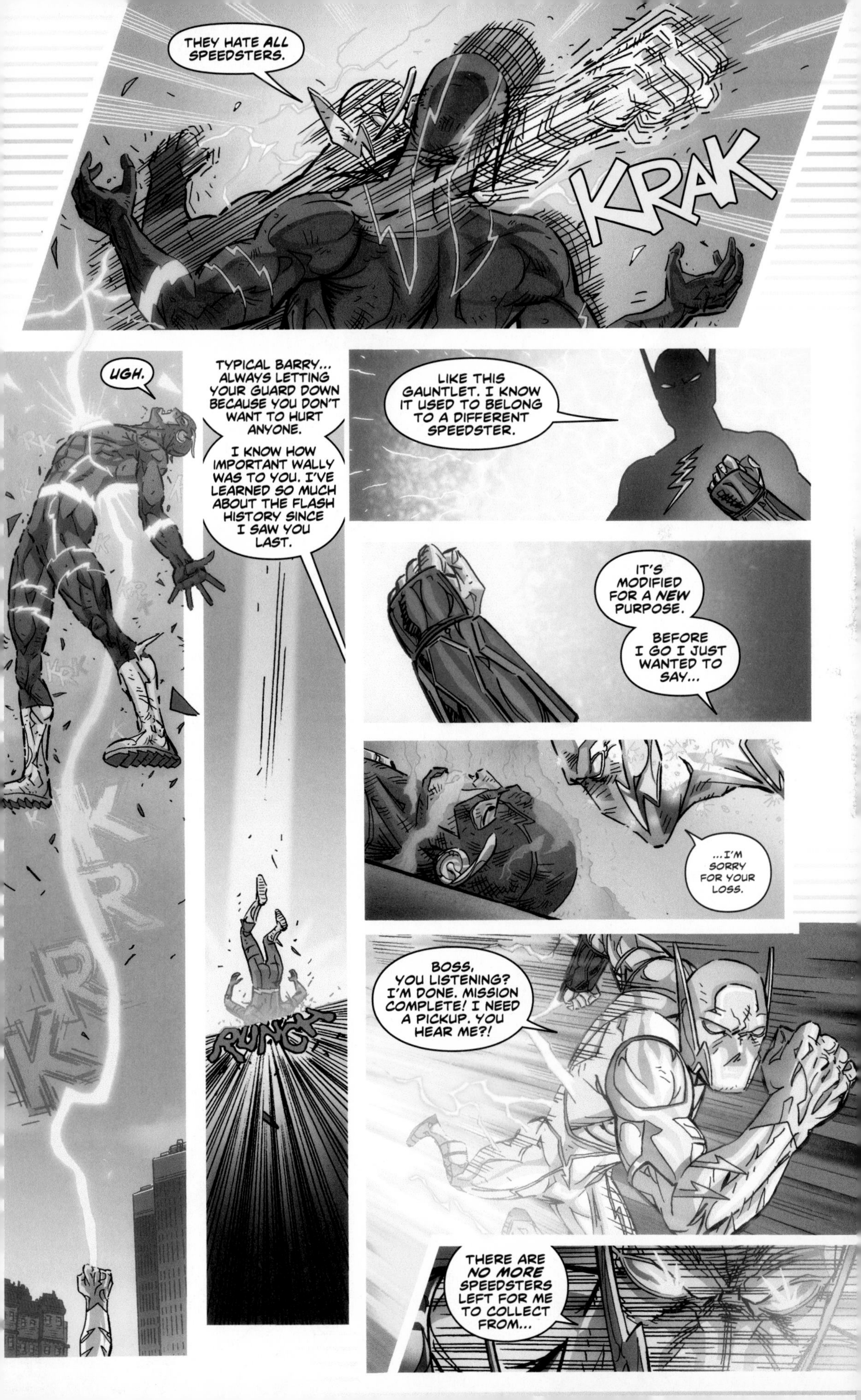
THEY HATE ALL SPEEDSTERS.
KRAK
UGH.
TYPICAL BARRY... ALWAYS LETTING YOUR GUARD DOWN BECAUSE YOU DON'T WANT TO HURT ANYONE.
I KNOW HOW IMPORTANT WALLY WAS TO YOU. I'VE LEARNED SO MUCH ABOUT THE FLASH HISTORY SINCE I SAW YOU LAST.
RUNCH
LIKE THIS GAUNTLET. I KNOW IT USED TO BELONG TO A DIFFERENT SPEEDSTER.
IT'S MODIFIED FOR A NEW PURPOSE.
BEFORE I GO I JUST WANTED TO SAY...
...I'M SORRY FOR YOUR LOSS.
BOSS, YOU LISTENING? I'M DONE. MISSION COMPLETE! I NEED A PICKUP. YOU HEAR ME?!
THERE ARE NO MORE SPEEDSTERS LEFT FOR ME TO COLLECT FROM...

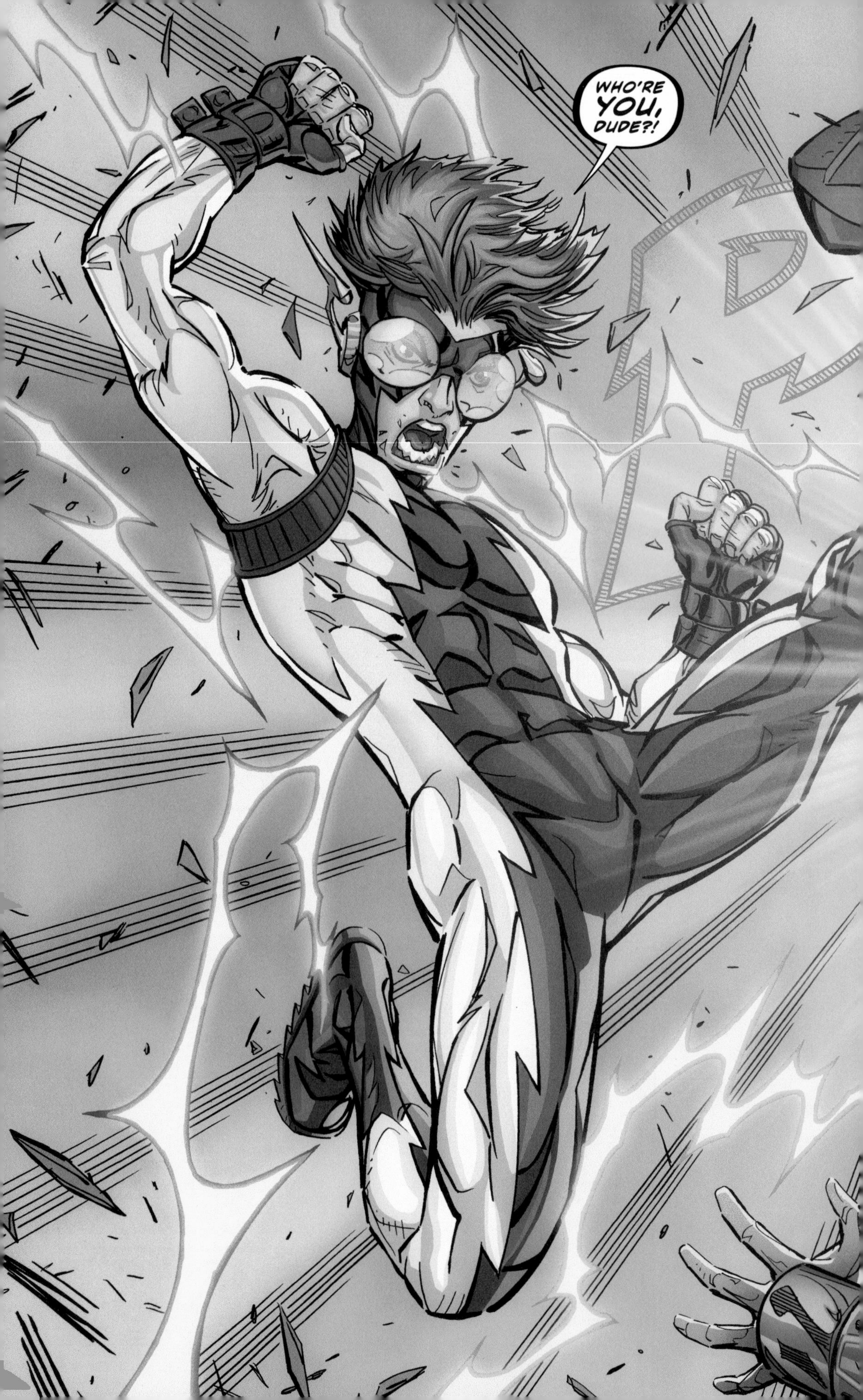
WHO'RE YOU, DUDE?!

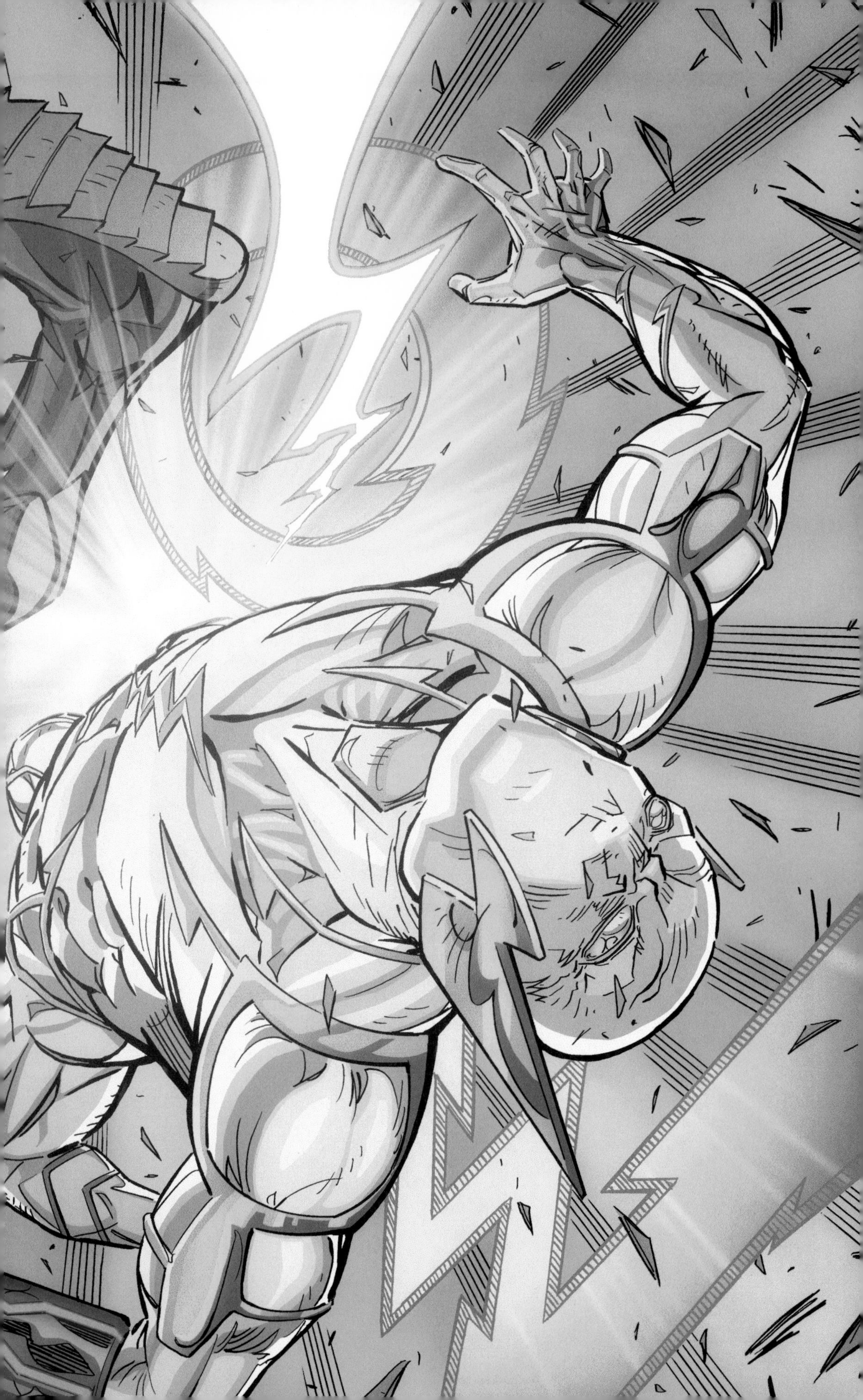

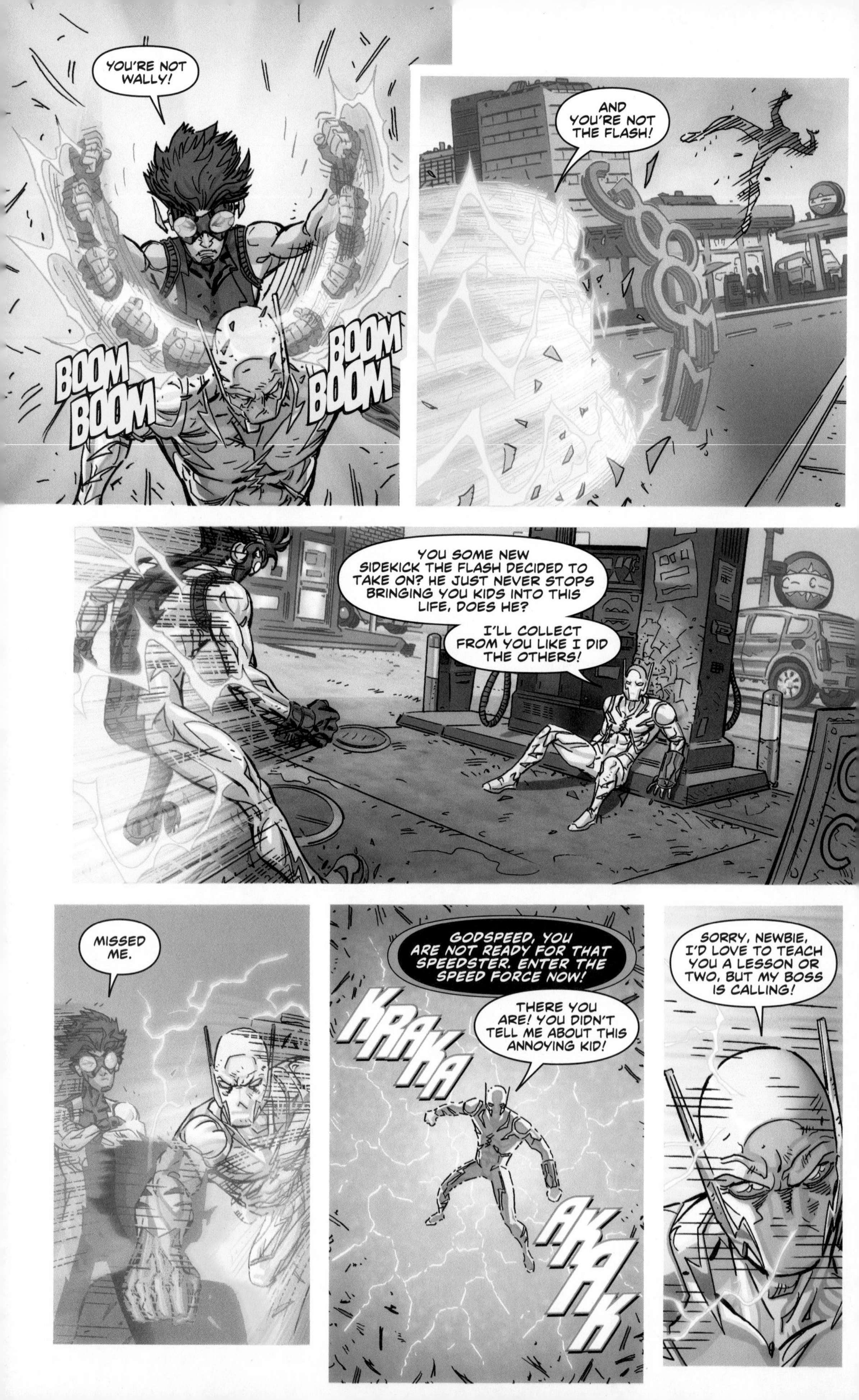
YOU'RE NOT WALLY!
BOOM BOOM
BOOM BOOM
AND YOU'RE NOT THE FLASH!
YOU SOME NEW SIDEKICK THE FLASH DECIDED TO TAKE ON? HE JUST NEVER STOPS BRINGING YOU KIDS INTO THIS LIFE, DOES HE?
I'LL COLLECT FROM YOU LIKE I DID THE OTHERS!
MISSED ME.
GODSPEED, YOU ARE NOT READY FOR THAT SPEEDSTER. ENTER THE SPEED FORCE NOW!
KRAKA
THERE YOU ARE! YOU DIDN'T TELL ME ABOUT THIS ANNOYING KID!
AKAK
SORRY, NEWBIE, I'D LOVE TO TEACH YOU A LESSON OR TWO, BUT MY BOSS IS CALLING!

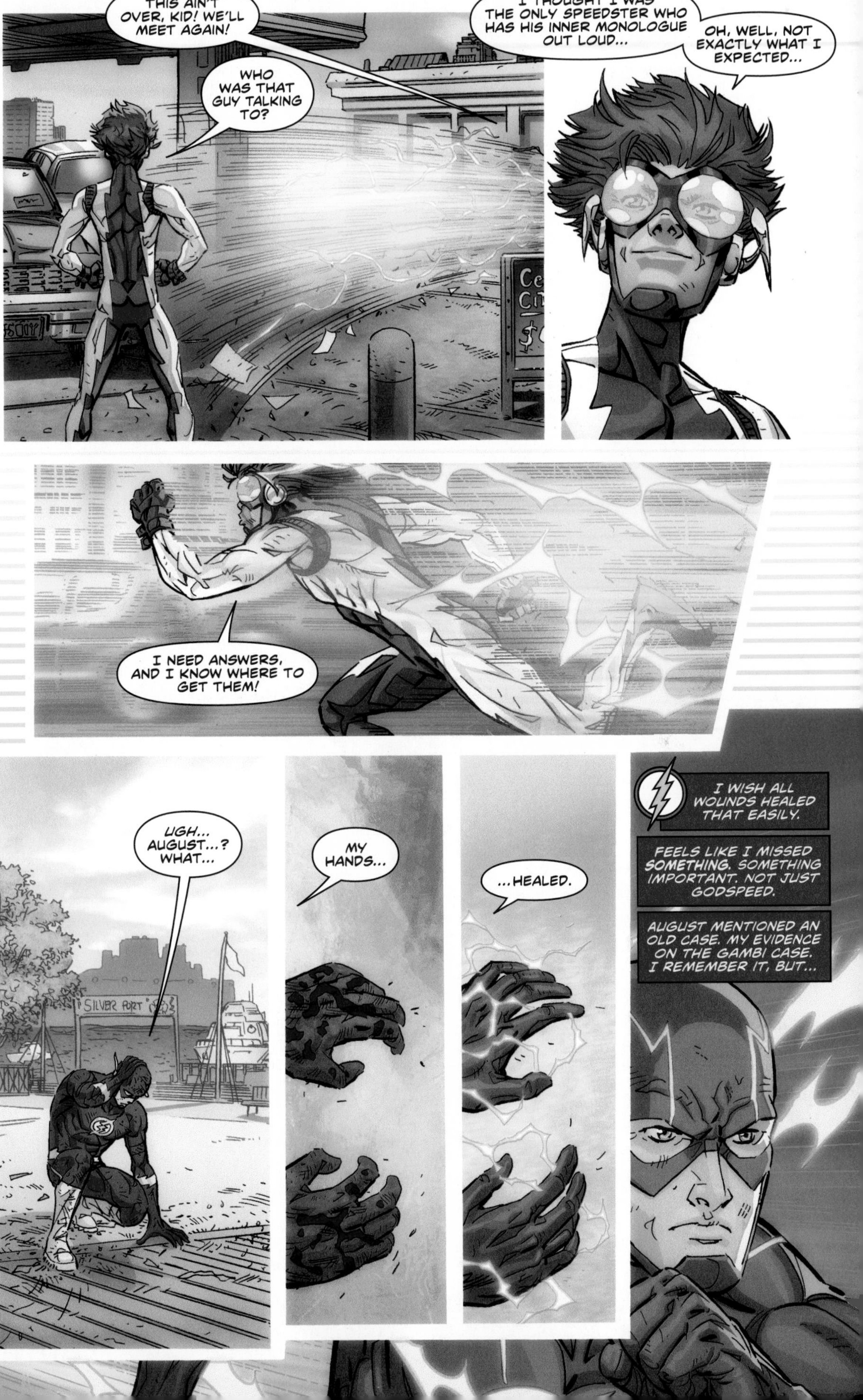
THIS AIN'T OVER, KID! WE'LL MEET AGAIN!
WHO WAS THAT GUY TALKING TO?
I THOUGHT I WAS THE ONLY SPEEDSTER WHO HAS HIS INNER MONOLOGUE OUT LOUD...
OH, WELL, NOT EXACTLY WHAT I EXPECTED...
I NEED ANSWERS, AND I KNOW WHERE TO GET THEM!
UGH... AUGUST...? WHAT...
SILVER PORT
MY HANDS...
...HEALED.
I WISH ALL WOUNDS HEALED THAT EASILY.
FEELS LIKE I MISSED SOMETHING. SOMETHING IMPORTANT. NOT JUST GODSPEED.
AUGUST MENTIONED AN OLD CASE. MY EVIDENCE ON THE GAMBI CASE. I REMEMBER IT, BUT...

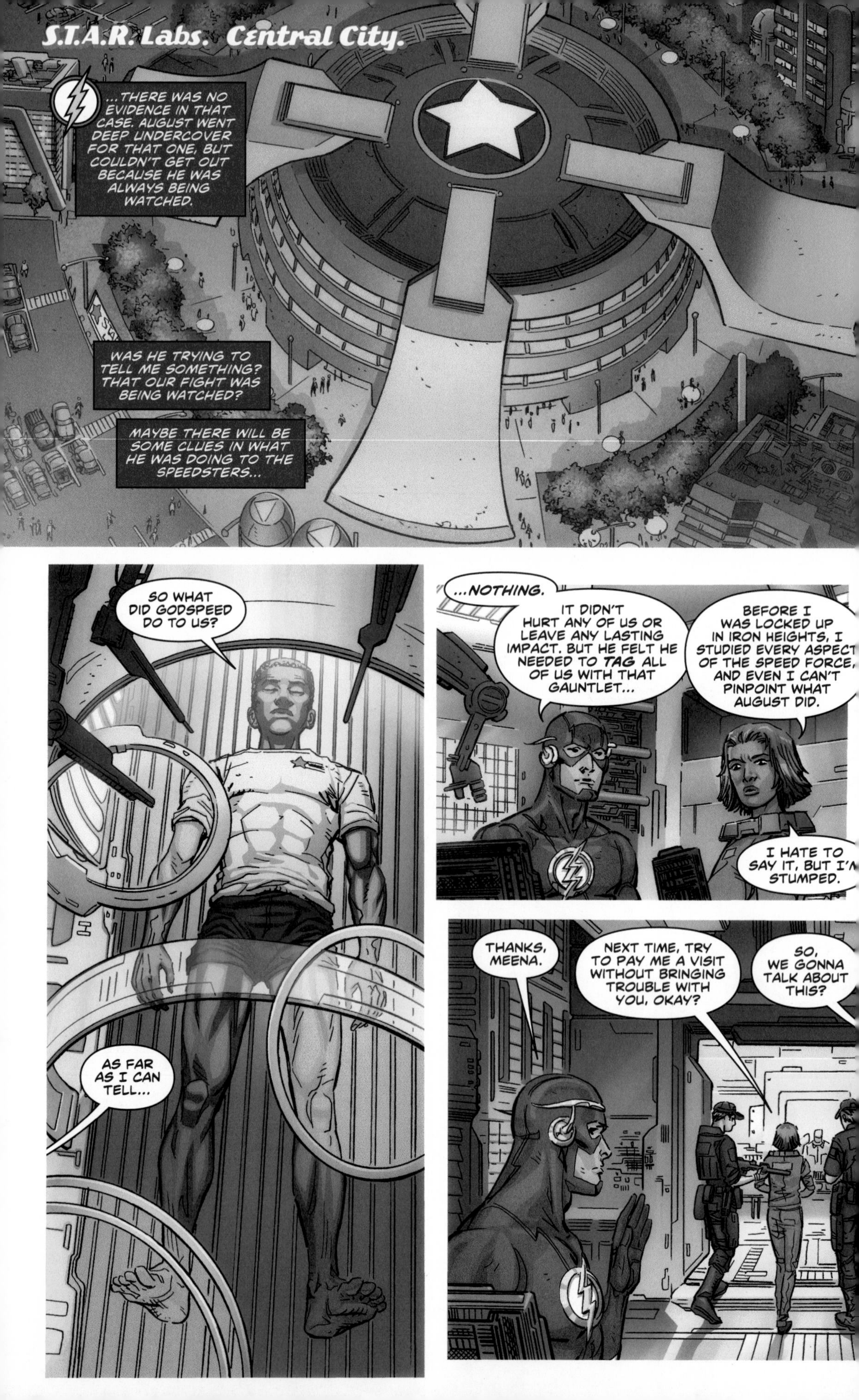
S.T.A.R. Labs. Central City.
...THERE WAS NO EVIDENCE IN THAT CASE. AUGUST WENT DEEP UNDERCOVER FOR THAT ONE, BUT COULDN'T GET OUT BECAUSE HE WAS ALWAYS BEING WATCHED.
WAS HE TRYING TO TELL ME SOMETHING? THAT OUR FIGHT WAS BEING WATCHED?
MAYBE THERE WILL BE SOME CLUES IN WHAT HE WAS DOING TO THE SPEEDSTERS...
SO WHAT DID GODSPEED DO TO US?
AS FAR AS I CAN TELL...
...NOTHING.
IT DIDN'T HURT ANY OF US OR LEAVE ANY LASTING IMPACT. BUT HE FELT HE NEEDED TO TAG ALL OF US WITH THAT GAUNTLET...
BEFORE I WAS LOCKED UP IN IRON HEIGHTS, I STUDIED EVERY ASPECT OF THE SPEED FORCE, AND EVEN I CAN'T PINPOINT WHAT AUGUST DID.
I HATE TO SAY IT, BUT I'M STUMPED.
THANKS, MEENA.
NEXT TIME, TRY TO PAY ME A VISIT WITHOUT BRINGING TROUBLE WITH YOU, OKAY?
SO, WE GONNA TALK ABOUT THIS?

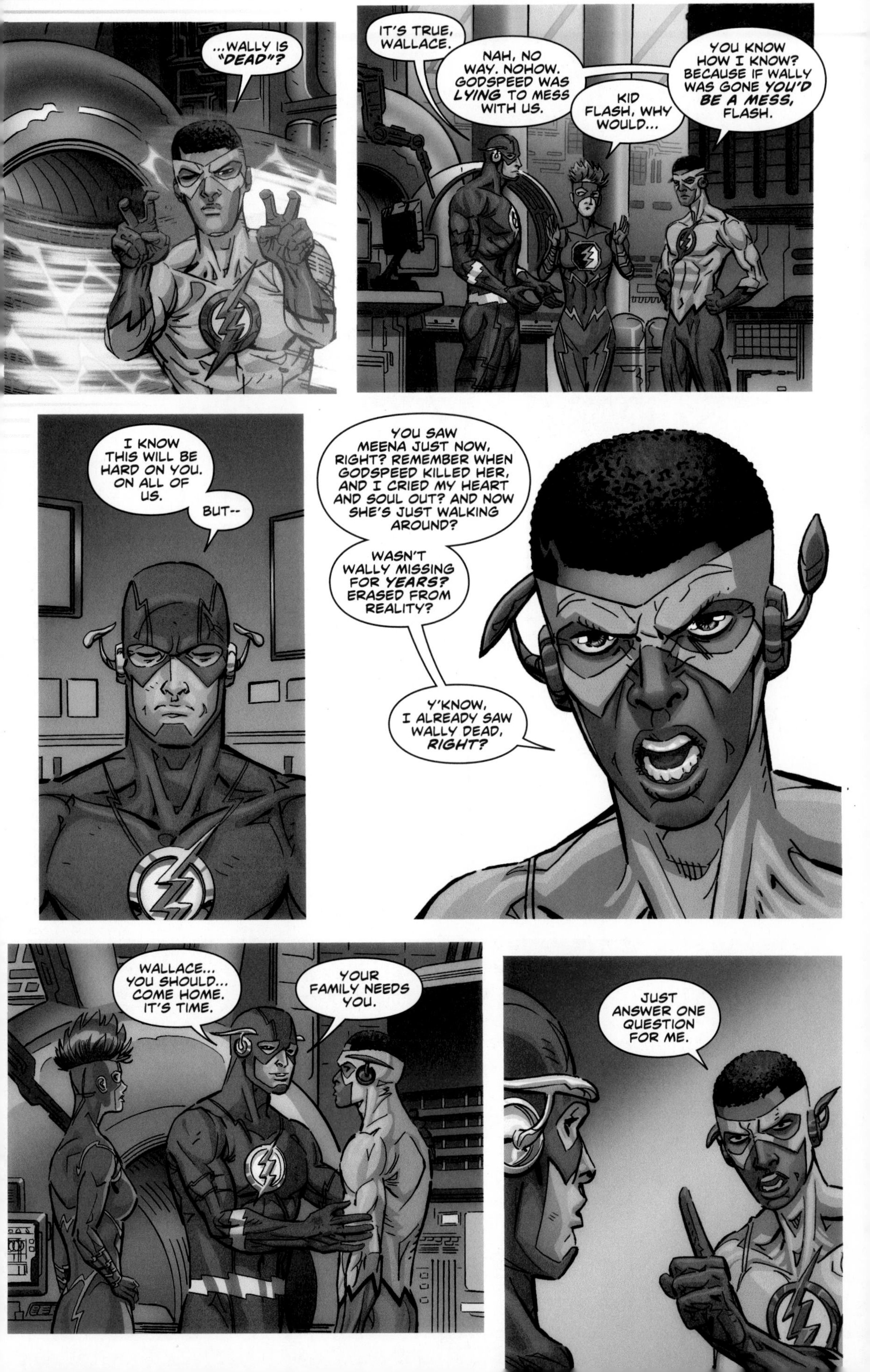
...WALLY IS "DEAD"?
IT'S TRUE, WALLACE.
NAH, NO WAY. NOHOW. GODSPEED WAS LYING TO MESS WITH US.
KID FLASH, WHY WOULD...
YOU KNOW HOW I KNOW? BECAUSE IF WALLY WAS GONE YOU'D BE A MESS, FLASH.
I KNOW THIS WILL BE HARD ON YOU. ON ALL OF US.
BUT--
YOU SAW MEENA JUST NOW, RIGHT? REMEMBER WHEN GODSPEED KILLED HER, AND I CRIED MY HEART AND SOUL OUT? AND NOW SHE'S JUST WALKING AROUND?
WASN'T WALLY MISSING FOR YEARS? ERASED FROM REALITY?
Y'KNOW, I ALREADY SAW WALLY DEAD, RIGHT?
WALLACE... YOU SHOULD... COME HOME. IT'S TIME.
YOUR FAMILY NEEDS YOU.
JUST ANSWER ONE QUESTION FOR ME.

DOES IRIS KNOW ABOUT WALLY YET?

I...

I KNEW IT. YOU CAN'T HELP YOURSELF. STILL KEEPING SECRETS NO MATTER WHO IT HURTS.

YOU NEVER CHANGE, BARRY. THAT'S A FLASH FACT.

EVERY TIME YOU'VE EVER DISAPPOINTED ME OR I GOT UPSET IN THE PAST, I WAS THE ONE WHO RAN AWAY. BUT THIS TIME...

...IT'S YOUR TURN TO RUN AWAY.

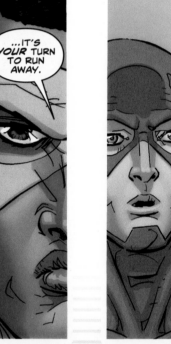

WALLACE IS RIGHT. I SHOULD HAVE TOLD IRIS THE MOMENT I FOUND OUT.

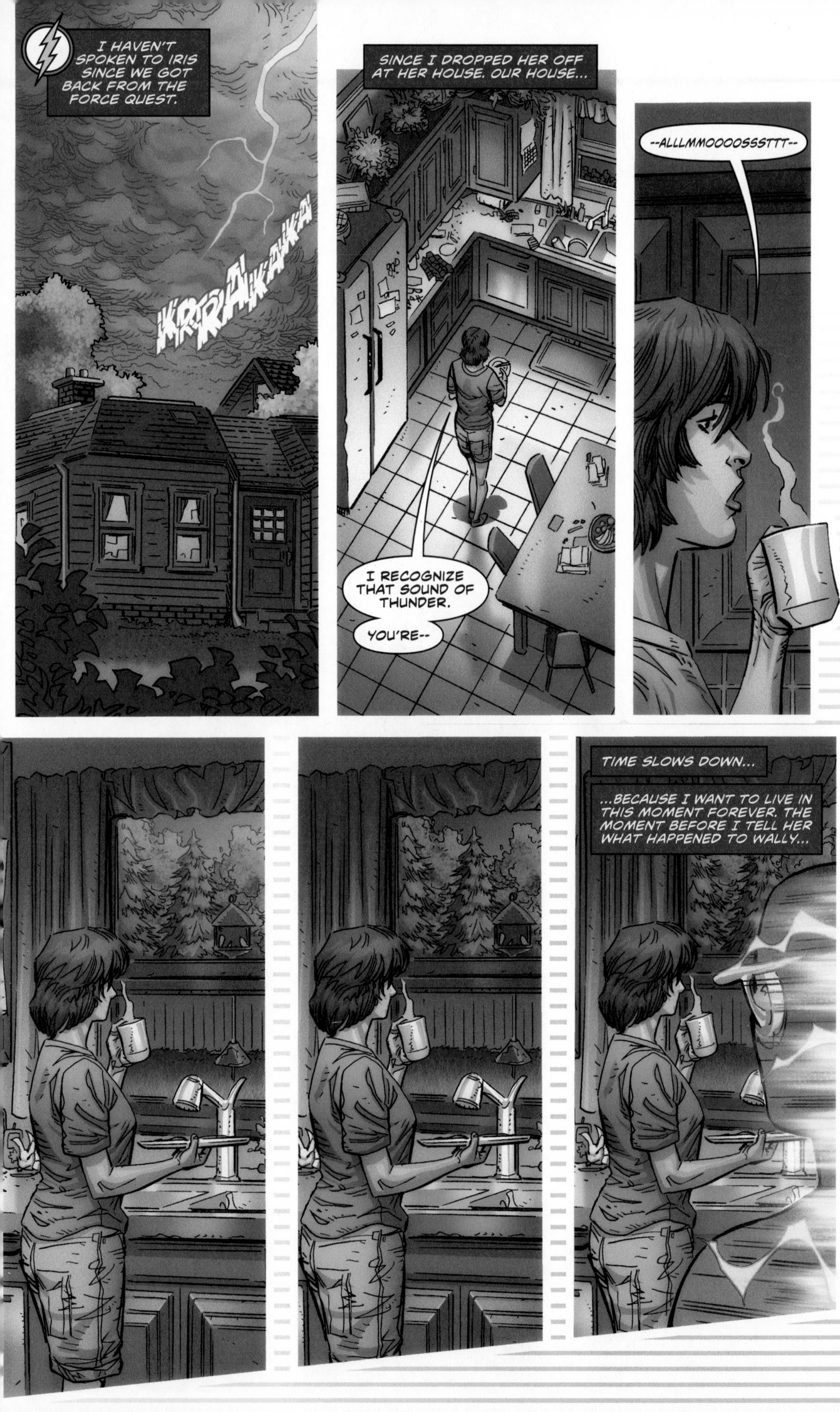
I HAVEN'T SPOKEN TO IRIS SINCE WE GOT BACK FROM THE FORCE QUEST.
KRAKAKA
SINCE I DROPPED HER OFF AT HER HOUSE. OUR HOUSE...
I RECOGNIZE THAT SOUND OF THUNDER.
YOU'RE--
--ALLLMMOOOOSSSTTT--
TIME SLOWS DOWN...
...BECAUSE I WANT TO LIVE IN THIS MOMENT FOREVER. THE MOMENT BEFORE I TELL HER WHAT HAPPENED TO WALLY...

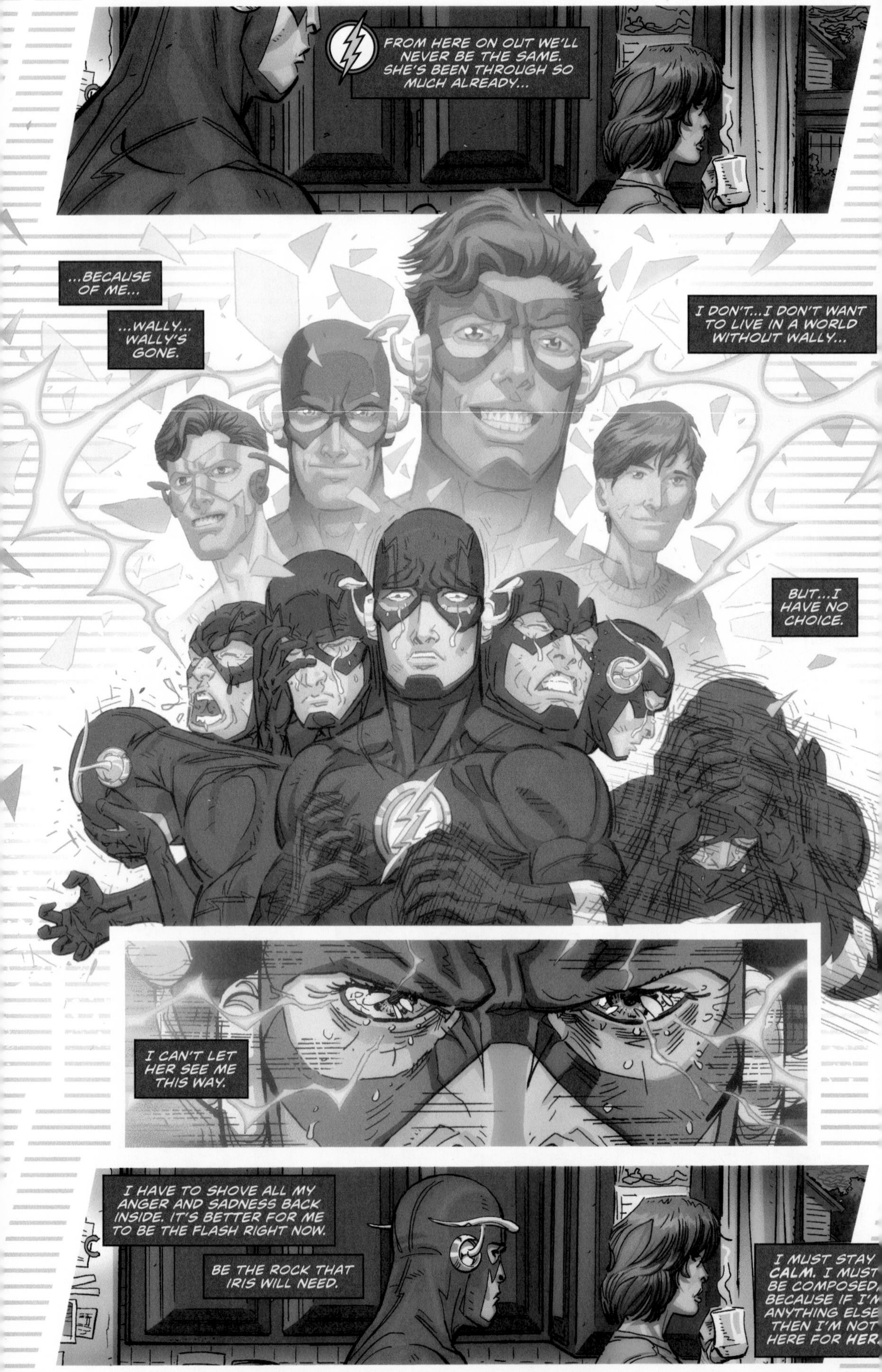
FROM HERE ON OUT WE'LL NEVER BE THE SAME. SHE'S BEEN THROUGH SO MUCH ALREADY...
...BECAUSE OF ME...
...WALLY... WALLY'S GONE.
I DON'T...I DON'T WANT TO LIVE IN A WORLD WITHOUT WALLY...
BUT...I HAVE NO CHOICE.
I CAN'T LET HER SEE ME THIS WAY.
I HAVE TO SHOVE ALL MY ANGER AND SADNESS BACK INSIDE. IT'S BETTER FOR ME TO BE THE FLASH RIGHT NOW.
BE THE ROCK THAT IRIS WILL NEED.
I MUST STAY **CALM.** I MUST BE COMPOSED BECAUSE IF I'M ANYTHING ELSE THEN I'M NOT HERE FOR **HER.**

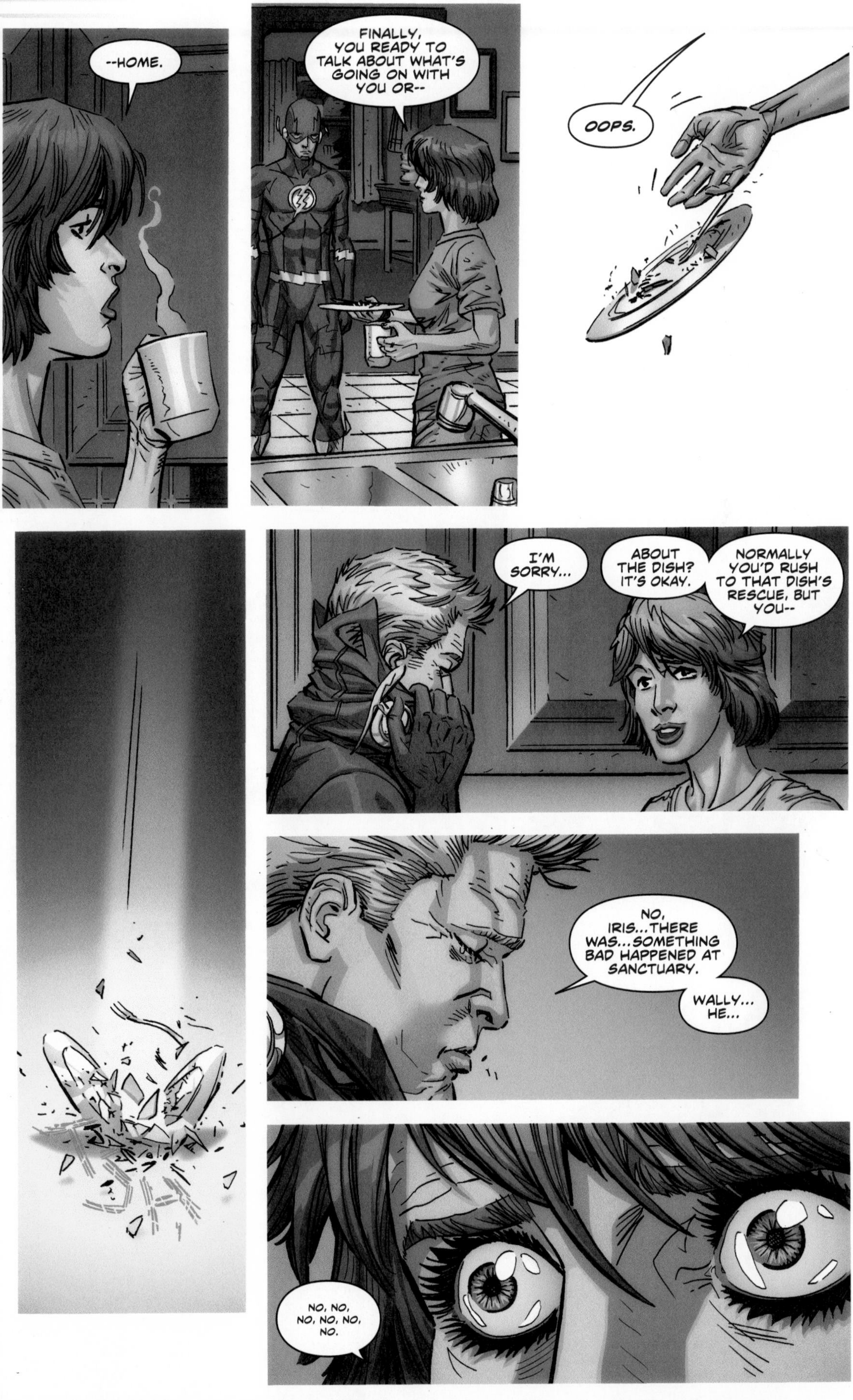

--HOME.
FINALLY, YOU READY TO TALK ABOUT WHAT'S GOING ON WITH YOU OR--
OOPS.
I'M SORRY...
ABOUT THE DISH? IT'S OKAY.
NORMALLY YOU'D RUSH TO THAT DISH'S RESCUE, BUT YOU--
NO, IRIS...THERE WAS...SOMETHING BAD HAPPENED AT SANCTUARY.
WALLY... HE...
NO, NO, NO, NO, NO, NO.

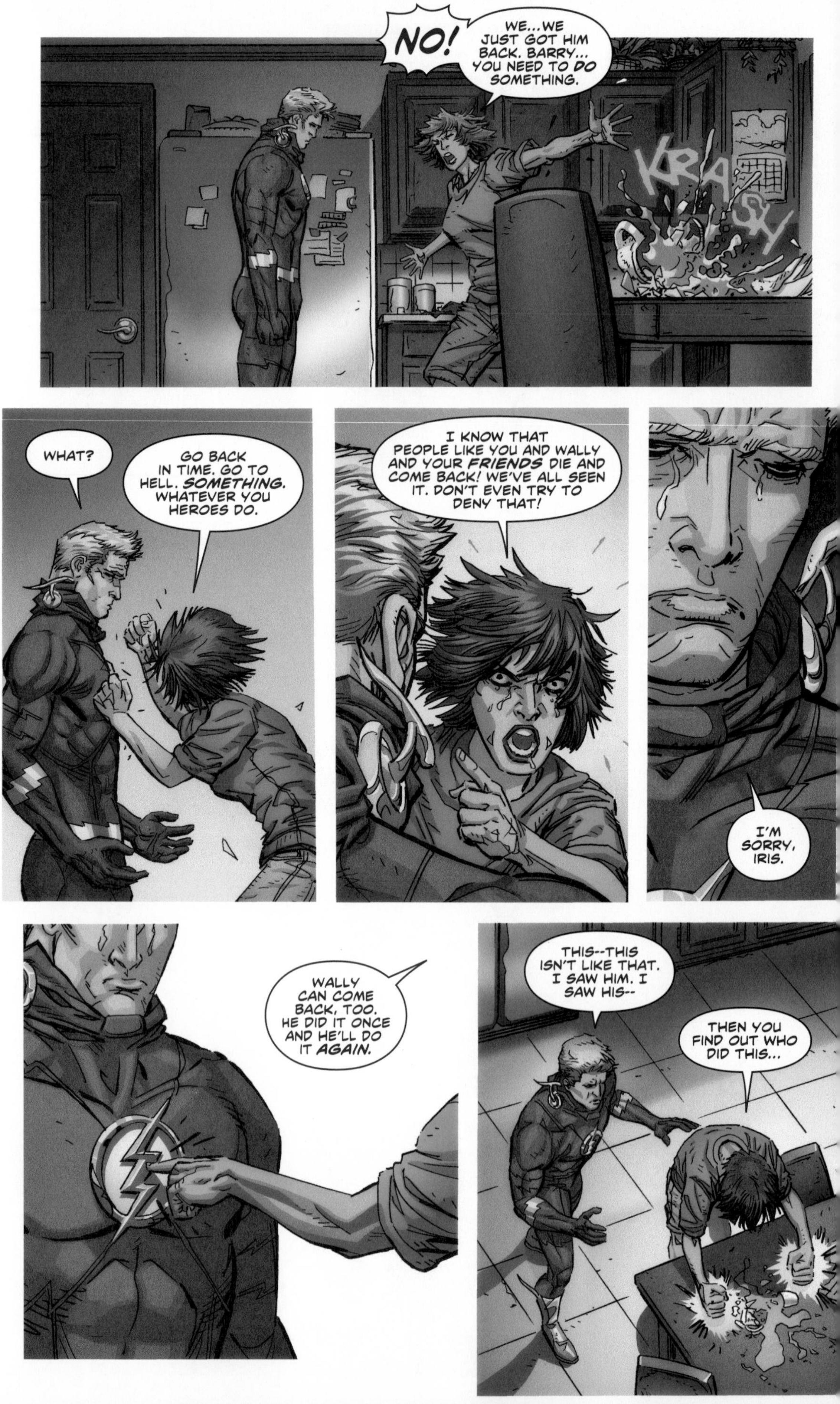
NO!
WE...WE JUST GOT HIM BACK. BARRY... YOU NEED TO DO SOMETHING.
KRASH
WHAT?
GO BACK IN TIME. GO TO HELL. SOMETHING. WHATEVER YOU HEROES DO.
I KNOW THAT PEOPLE LIKE YOU AND WALLY AND YOUR FRIENDS DIE AND COME BACK! WE'VE ALL SEEN IT. DON'T EVEN TRY TO DENY THAT!
I'M SORRY, IRIS.
WALLY CAN COME BACK, TOO. HE DID IT ONCE AND HE'LL DO IT AGAIN.
THIS--THIS ISN'T LIKE THAT. I SAW HIM. I SAW HIS--
THEN YOU FIND OUT WHO DID THIS...

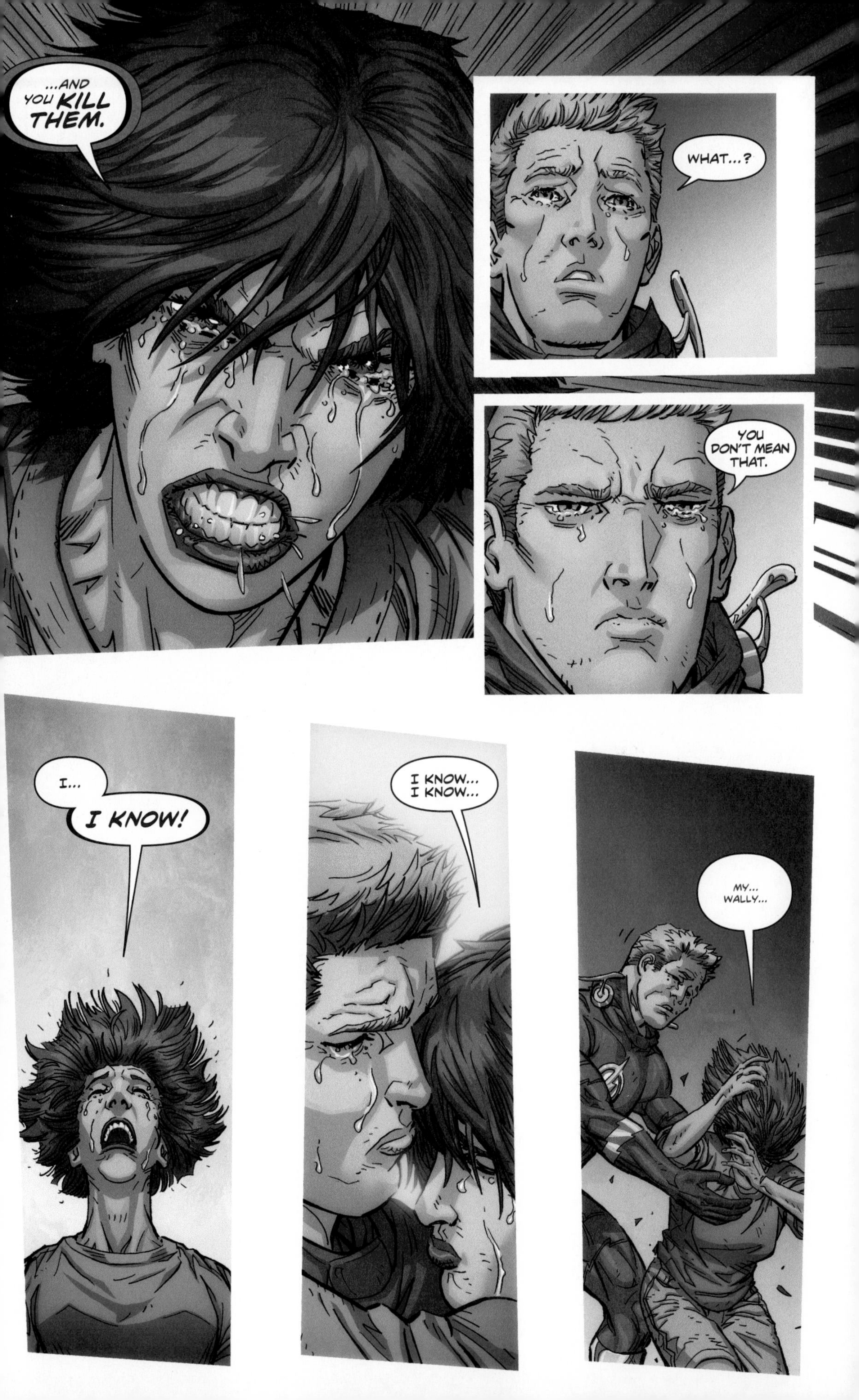
...AND YOU KILL THEM.
WHAT...?
YOU DON'T MEAN THAT.
I...
I KNOW!
I KNOW... I KNOW...
MY... WALLY...

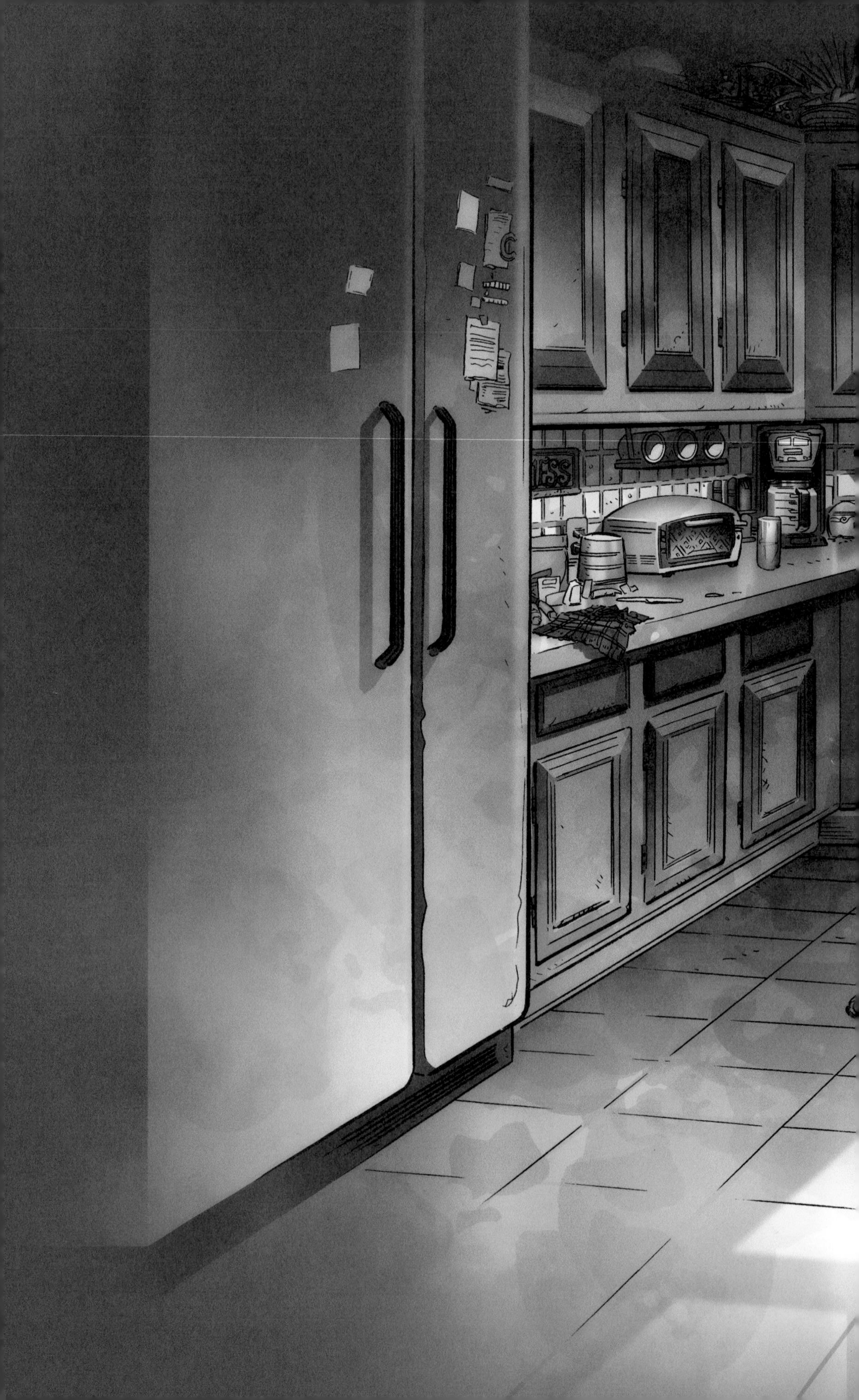

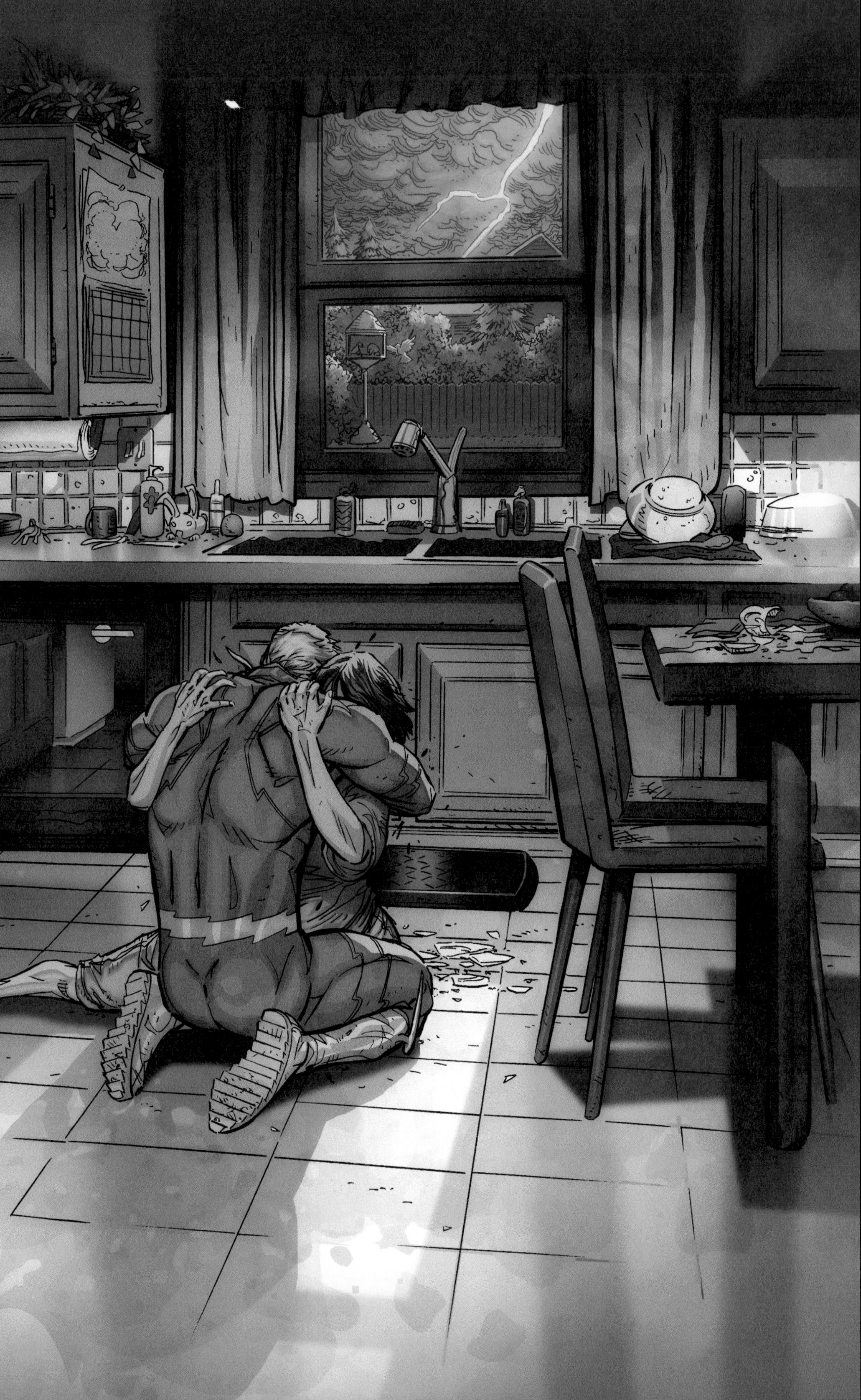

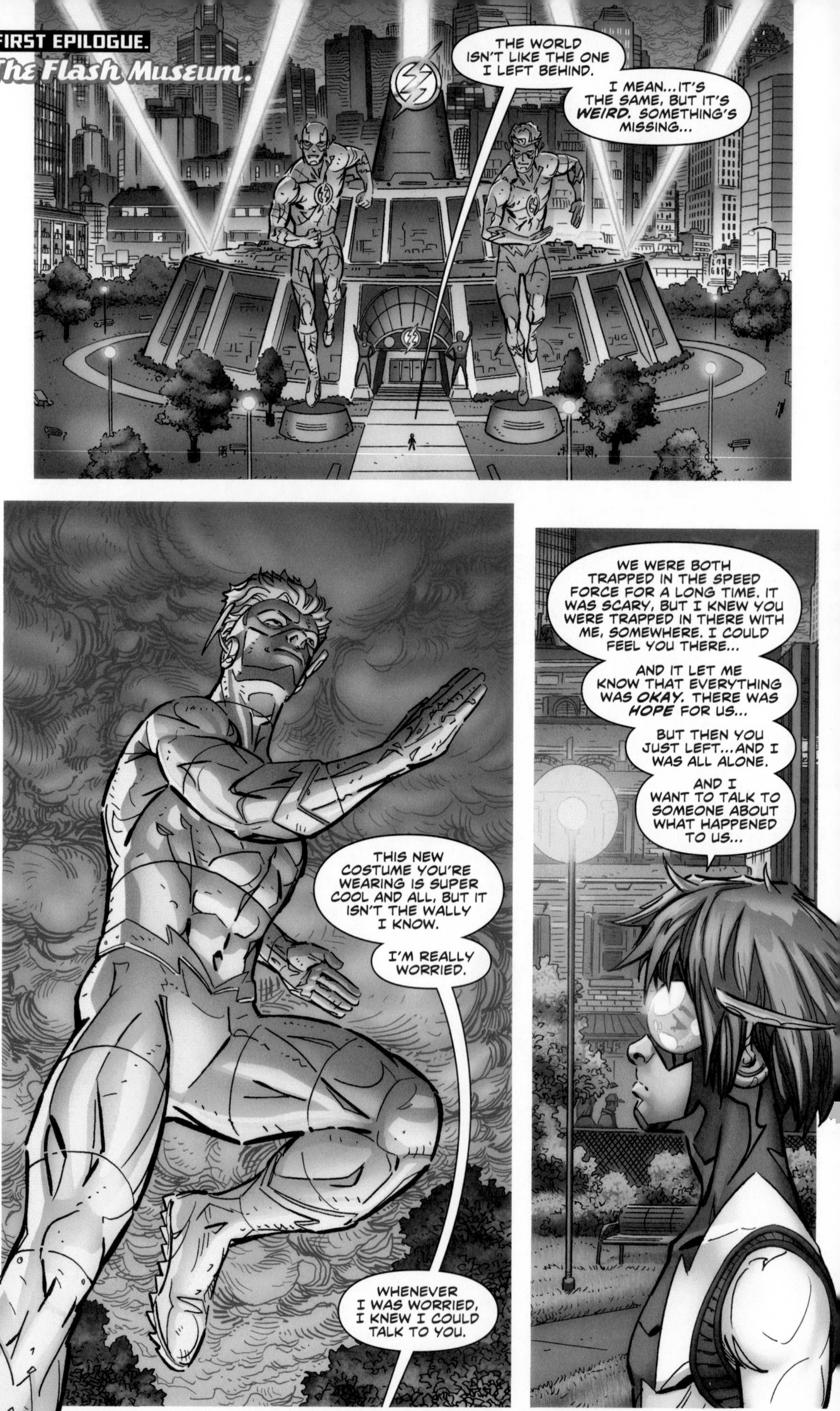
FIRST EPILOGUE.
The Flash Museum.
THE WORLD ISN'T LIKE THE ONE I LEFT BEHIND.
I MEAN...IT'S THE SAME, BUT IT'S WEIRD. SOMETHING'S MISSING...
THIS NEW COSTUME YOU'RE WEARING IS SUPER COOL AND ALL, BUT IT ISN'T THE WALLY I KNOW.
I'M REALLY WORRIED.
WHENEVER I WAS WORRIED, I KNEW I COULD TALK TO YOU.
WE WERE BOTH TRAPPED IN THE SPEED FORCE FOR A LONG TIME. IT WAS SCARY, BUT I KNEW YOU WERE TRAPPED IN THERE WITH ME, SOMEWHERE. I COULD FEEL YOU THERE...
AND IT LET ME KNOW THAT EVERYTHING WAS OKAY. THERE WAS HOPE FOR US...
BUT THEN YOU JUST LEFT...AND I WAS ALL ALONE.
AND I WANT TO TALK TO SOMEONE ABOUT WHAT HAPPENED TO US...

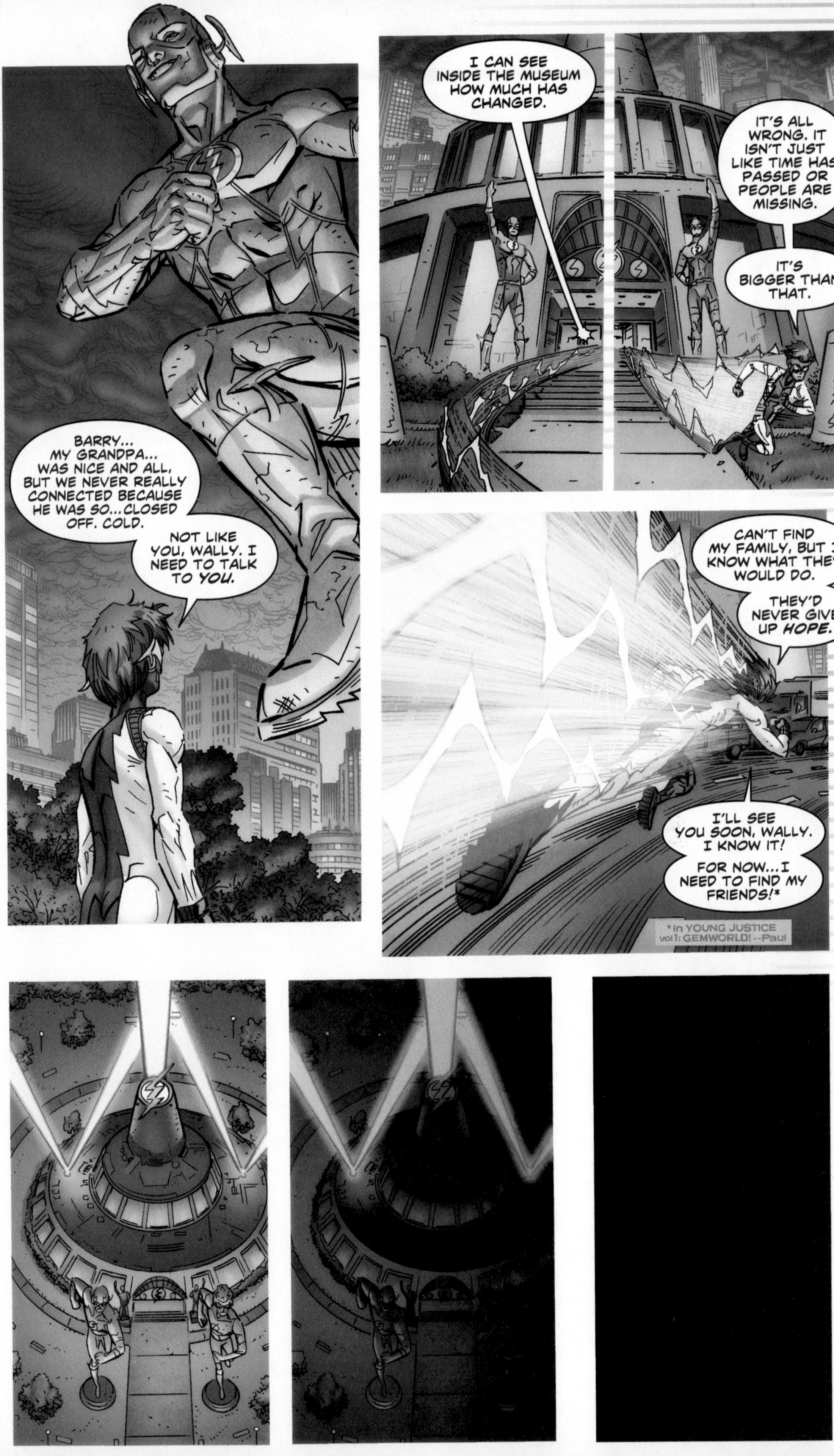
BARRY... MY GRANDPA... WAS NICE AND ALL, BUT WE NEVER REALLY CONNECTED BECAUSE HE WAS SO...CLOSED OFF. COLD.
NOT LIKE YOU, WALLY. I NEED TO TALK TO YOU.
I CAN SEE INSIDE THE MUSEUM HOW MUCH HAS CHANGED.
IT'S ALL WRONG. IT ISN'T JUST LIKE TIME HAS PASSED OR PEOPLE ARE MISSING.
IT'S BIGGER THAN THAT.
CAN'T FIND MY FAMILY, BUT I KNOW WHAT THEY WOULD DO.
THEY'D NEVER GIVE UP HOPE.
I'LL SEE YOU SOON, WALLY. I KNOW IT!
FOR NOW...I NEED TO FIND MY FRIENDS!*
*In YOUNG JUSTICE vol1: GEMWORLD! --Paul

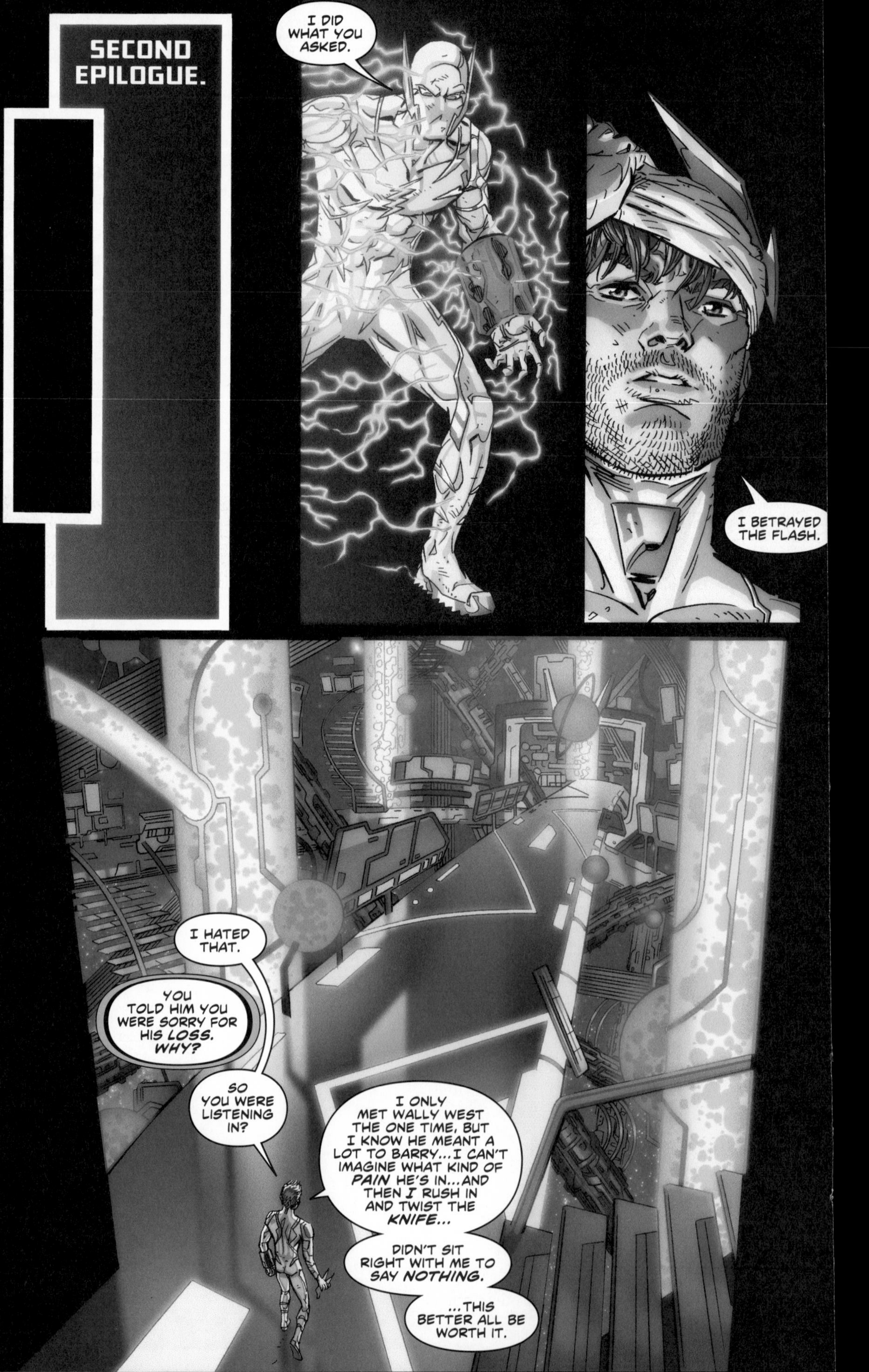
SECOND EPILOGUE.
I DID WHAT YOU ASKED.
I BETRAYED THE FLASH.
I HATED THAT.
YOU TOLD HIM YOU WERE SORRY FOR HIS LOSS. WHY?
SO YOU WERE LISTENING IN?
I ONLY MET WALLY WEST THE ONE TIME, BUT I KNOW HE MEANT A LOT TO BARRY...I CAN'T IMAGINE WHAT KIND OF PAIN HE'S IN...AND THEN I RUSH IN AND TWIST THE KNIFE...
DIDN'T SIT RIGHT WITH ME TO SAY NOTHING.
...THIS BETTER ALL BE WORTH IT.

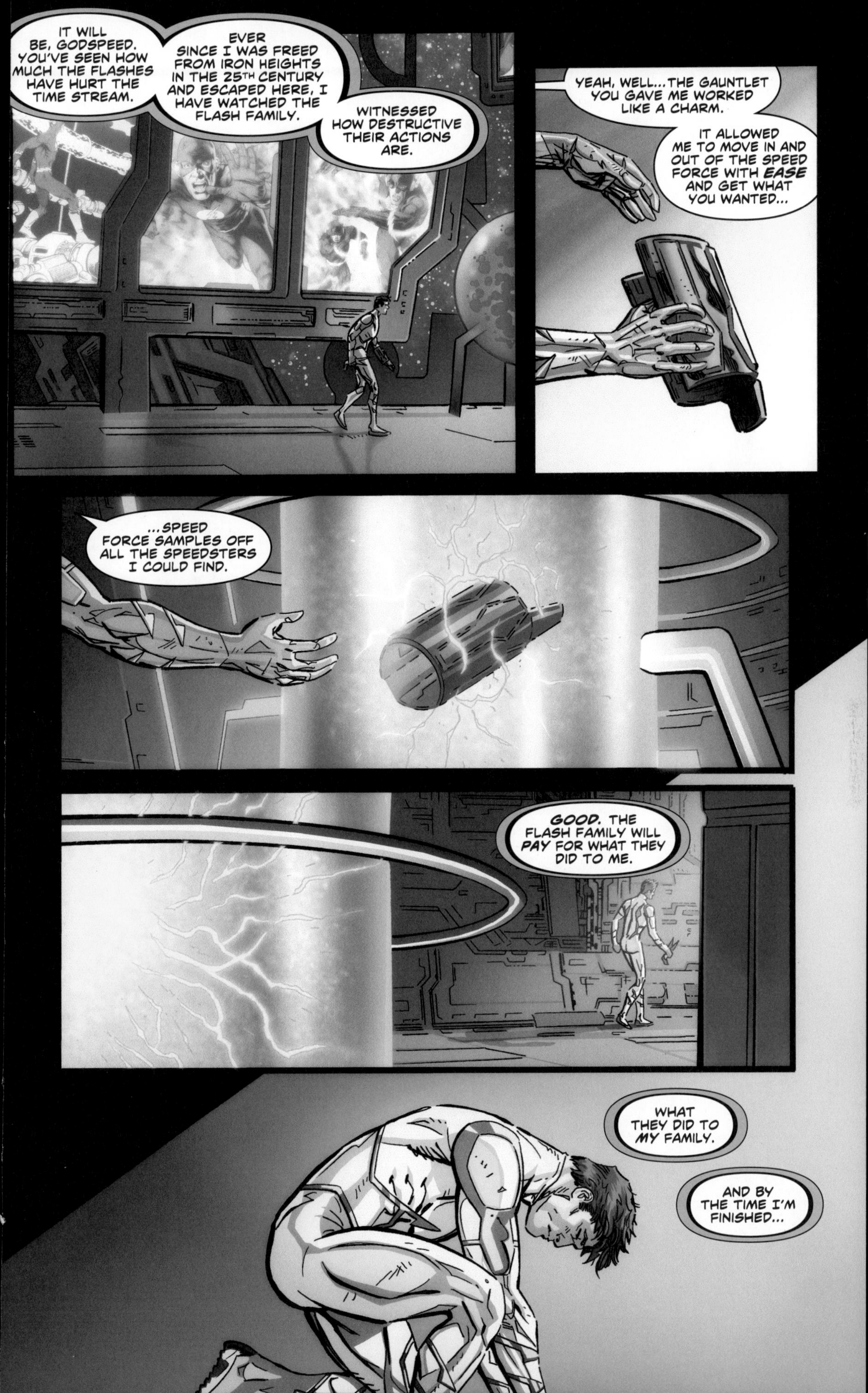
IT WILL BE, GODSPEED. YOU'VE SEEN HOW MUCH THE FLASHES HAVE HURT THE TIME STREAM.
EVER SINCE I WAS FREED FROM IRON HEIGHTS IN THE 25TH CENTURY AND ESCAPED HERE, I HAVE WATCHED THE FLASH FAMILY.
WITNESSED HOW DESTRUCTIVE THEIR ACTIONS ARE.
YEAH, WELL...THE GAUNTLET YOU GAVE ME WORKED LIKE A CHARM.
IT ALLOWED ME TO MOVE IN AND OUT OF THE SPEED FORCE WITH EASE AND GET WHAT YOU WANTED...
...SPEED FORCE SAMPLES OFF ALL THE SPEEDSTERS I COULD FIND.
GOOD. THE FLASH FAMILY WILL PAY FOR WHAT THEY DID TO ME.
WHAT THEY DID TO MY FAMILY.
AND BY THE TIME I'M FINISHED...

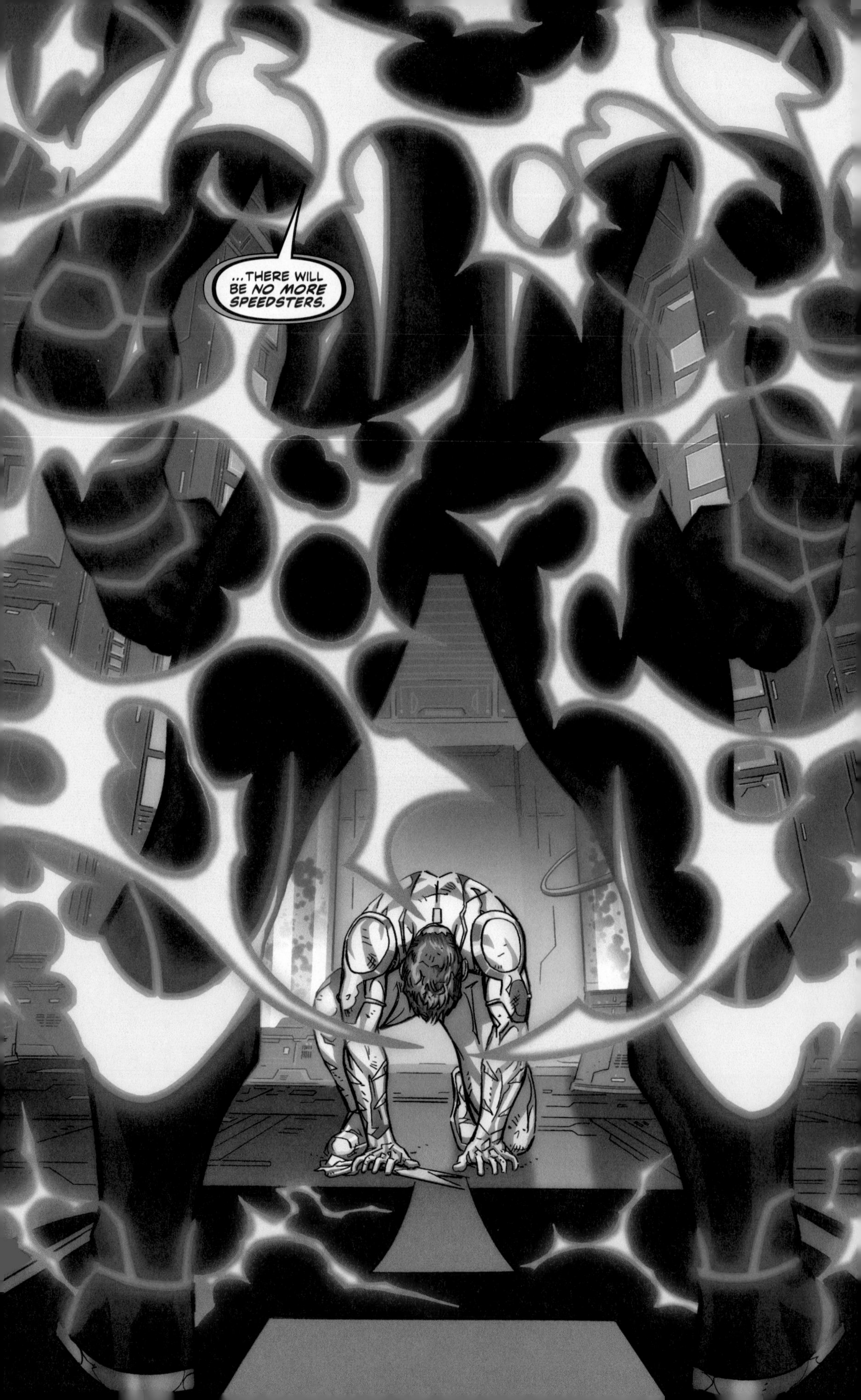
...THERE WILL BE NO MORE SPEEDSTERS.

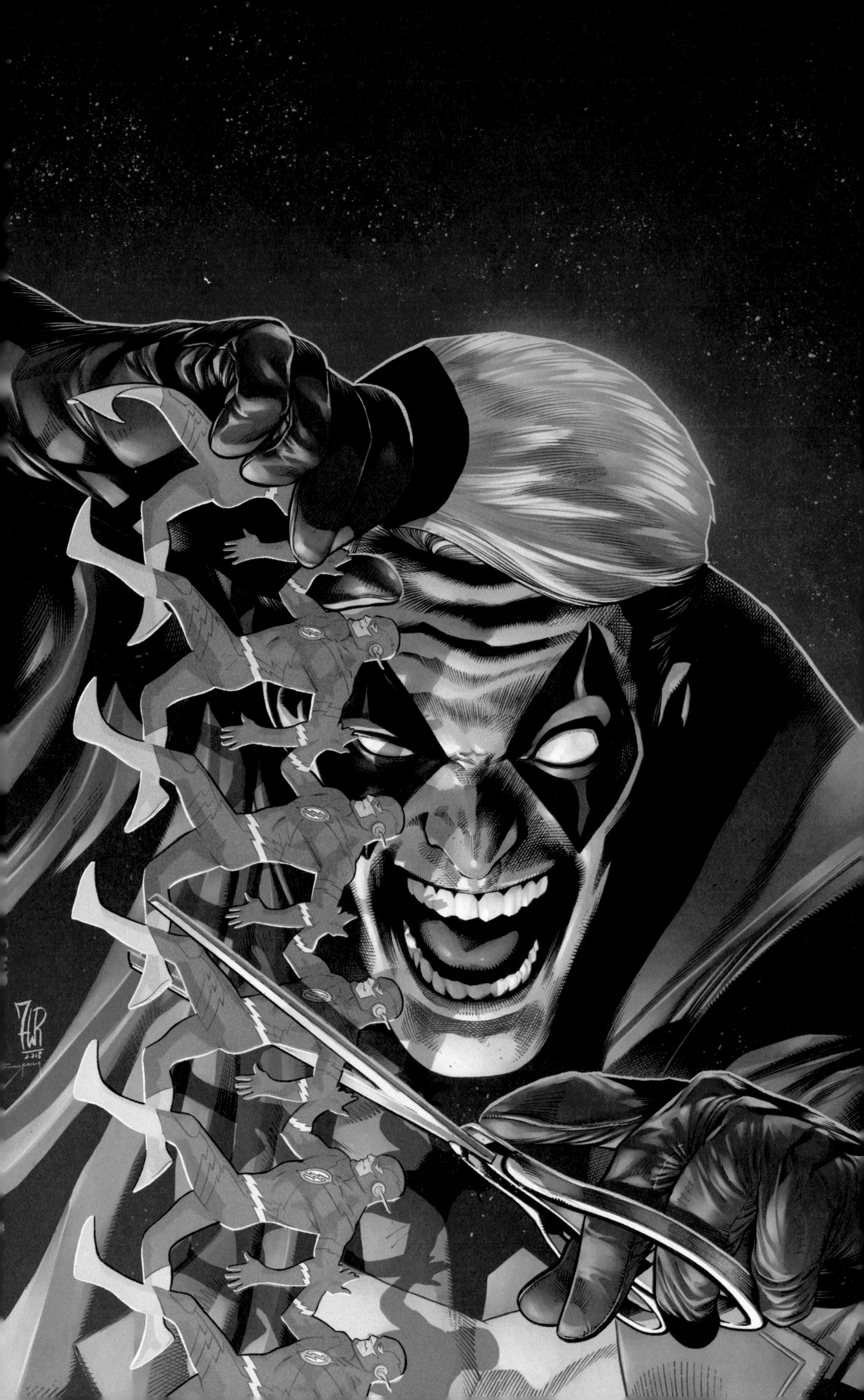

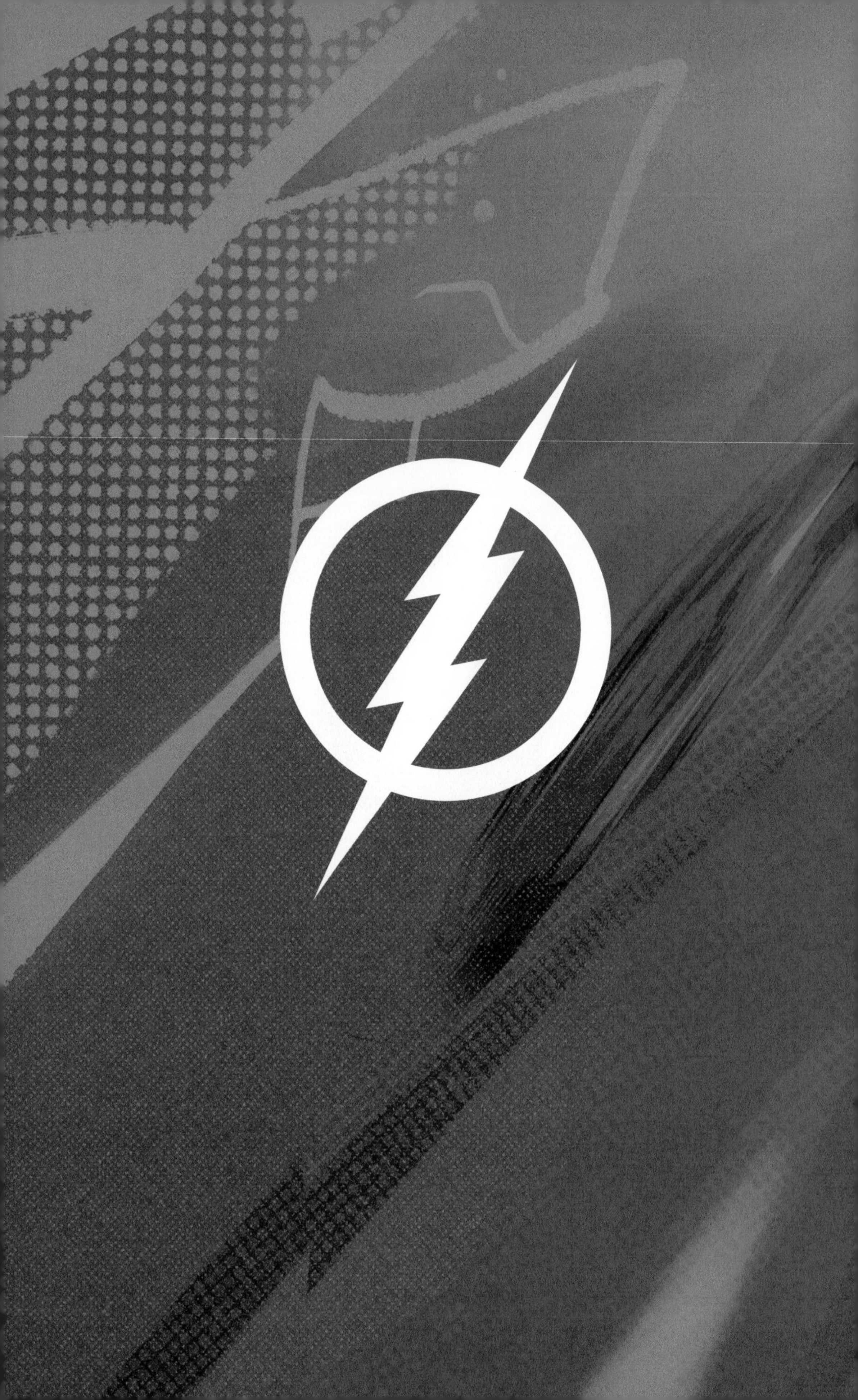

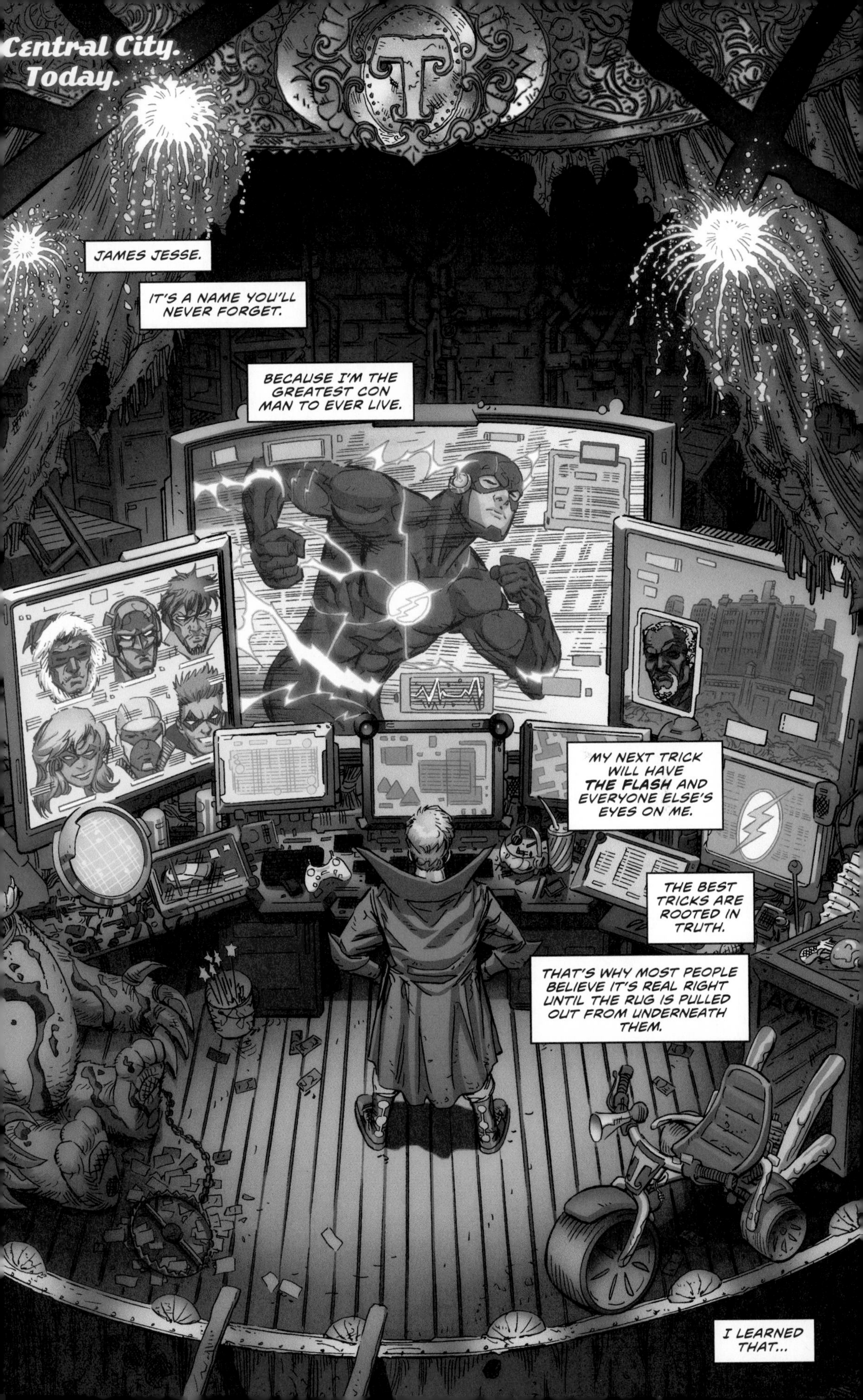
Central City.
Today.
JAMES JESSE.
IT'S A NAME YOU'LL NEVER FORGET.
BECAUSE I'M THE GREATEST CON MAN TO EVER LIVE.
MY NEXT TRICK WILL HAVE THE FLASH AND EVERYONE ELSE'S EYES ON ME.
THE BEST TRICKS ARE ROOTED IN TRUTH.
THAT'S WHY MOST PEOPLE BELIEVE IT'S REAL RIGHT UNTIL THE RUG IS PULLED OUT FROM UNDERNEATH THEM.
I LEARNED THAT...

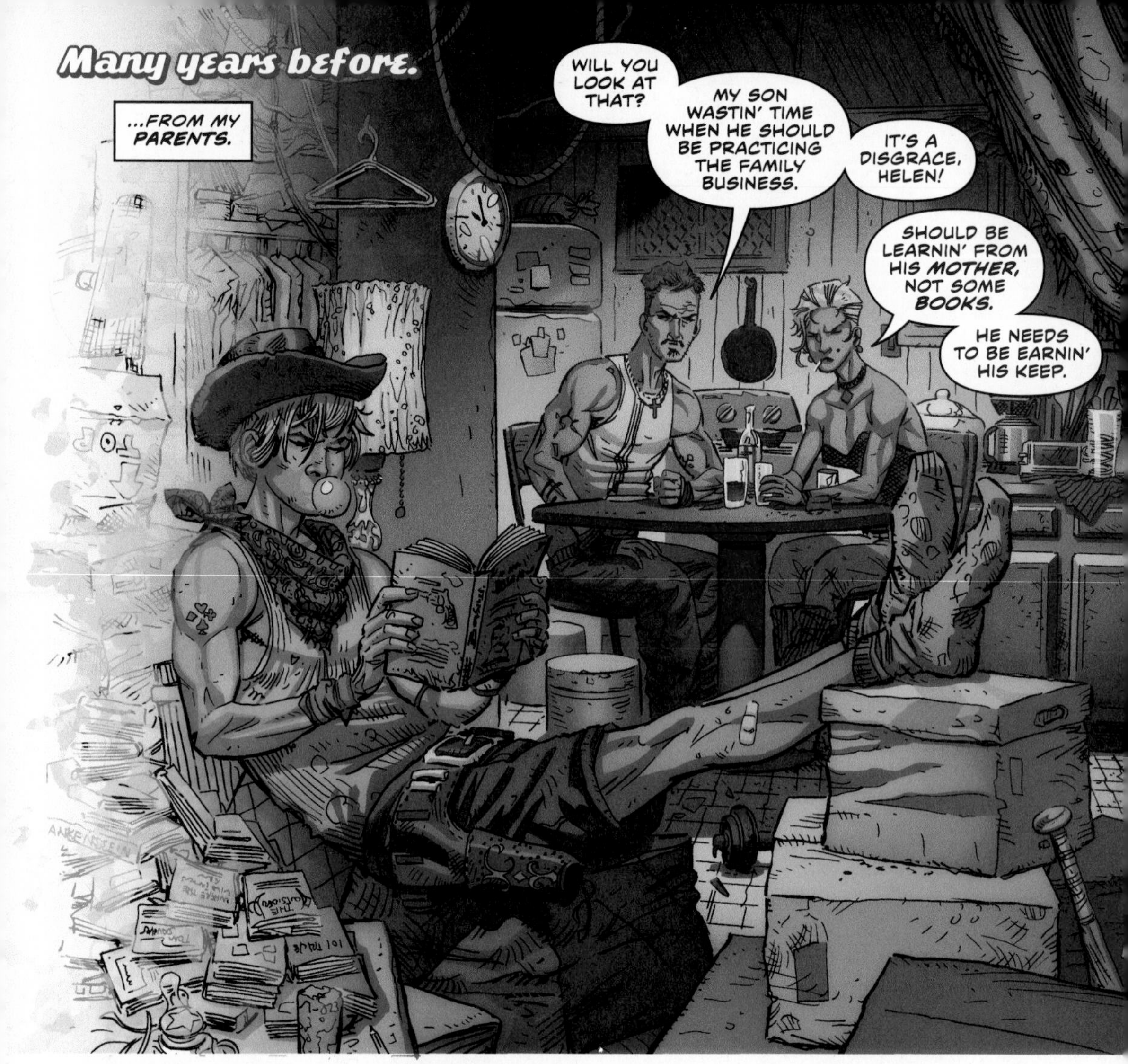
Many years before.
...FROM MY PARENTS.
WILL YOU LOOK AT THAT?
MY SON WASTIN' TIME WHEN HE SHOULD BE PRACTICING THE FAMILY BUSINESS.
IT'S A DISGRACE, HELEN!
SHOULD BE LEARNIN' FROM HIS MOTHER, NOT SOME BOOKS.
HE NEEDS TO BE EARNIN' HIS KEEP.

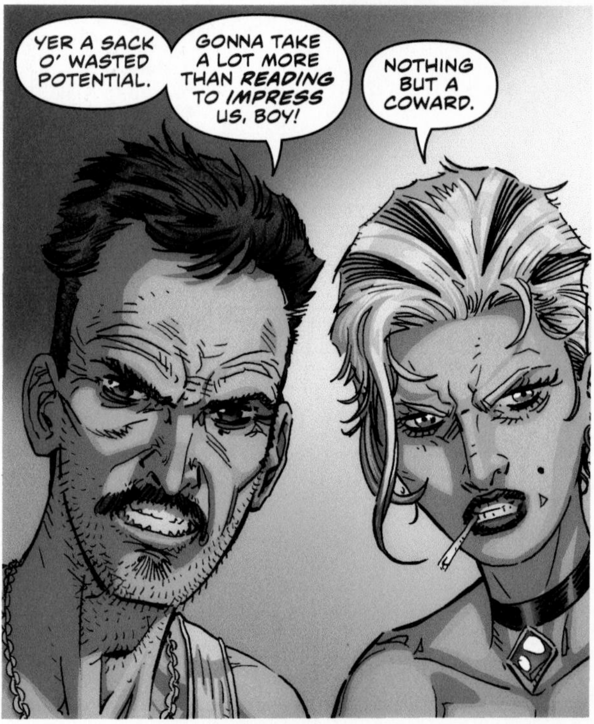
YER A SACK O' WASTED POTENTIAL.
GONNA TAKE A LOT MORE THAN READING TO IMPRESS US, BOY!
NOTHING BUT A COWARD.

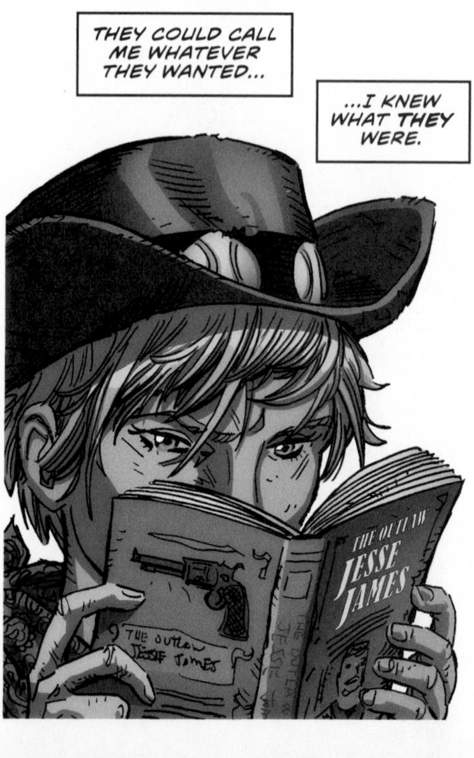
THEY COULD CALL ME WHATEVER THEY WANTED...
...I KNEW WHAT THEY WERE.
THE OUTLAW JESSE JAMES

LYING CHEATS.

WHEN THEY WEREN'T TRYING TO SCAM PEOPLE, THEY WERE TIGHTROPE WALKERS IN THE CENTRAL CITY CIRCUS.

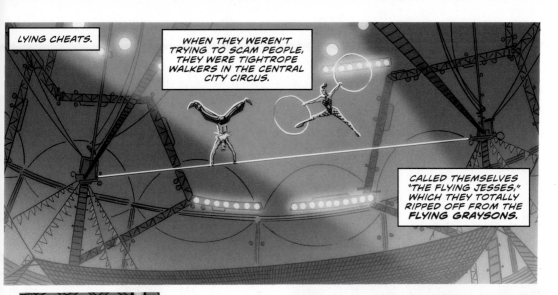

CALLED THEMSELVES "THE FLYING JESSES," WHICH THEY TOTALLY RIPPED OFF FROM THE FLYING GRAYSONS.

WORD AROUND THE CIRCUS WAS THAT THE GRAYSONS DIED DURING AN ACT IN GOTHAM.

MY PARENTS WANTED TO CAPITALIZE ON THEIR DEATHS AND CALLED THEIR ACT "THE NEW MOST DANGEROUS ACT IN THE WORLD!"

BUT I'VE ALWAYS BEEN TERRIFIED OF HEIGHTS.

YOU'RE GONNA GET UP ON THAT ROPE. YOU'RE NOT LETTING US DOWN AGAIN!

THERE'S GONNA BE A SAFETY NET, YOU BIG BABY!

I DIDN'T WANT TO BE A CIRCUS PERFORMER. SOMEONE WHO WORE A COSTUME.

I WANTED TO BE MORE THAN THAT.

BUT MY PARENTS THOUGHT I ONLY HAD ONE FUTURE.

NO MATTER HOW HARD IT WAS TO TUNE OUT THE CROWD IN THE STANDS, MY BOOKS KEPT MY FOCUS.

THE STORIES I READ WERE ABOUT MY HEROES. PEOPLE WITH HONOR. THEY GAVE ME HOPE.

MY BOOKS WERE MY ESCAPE.

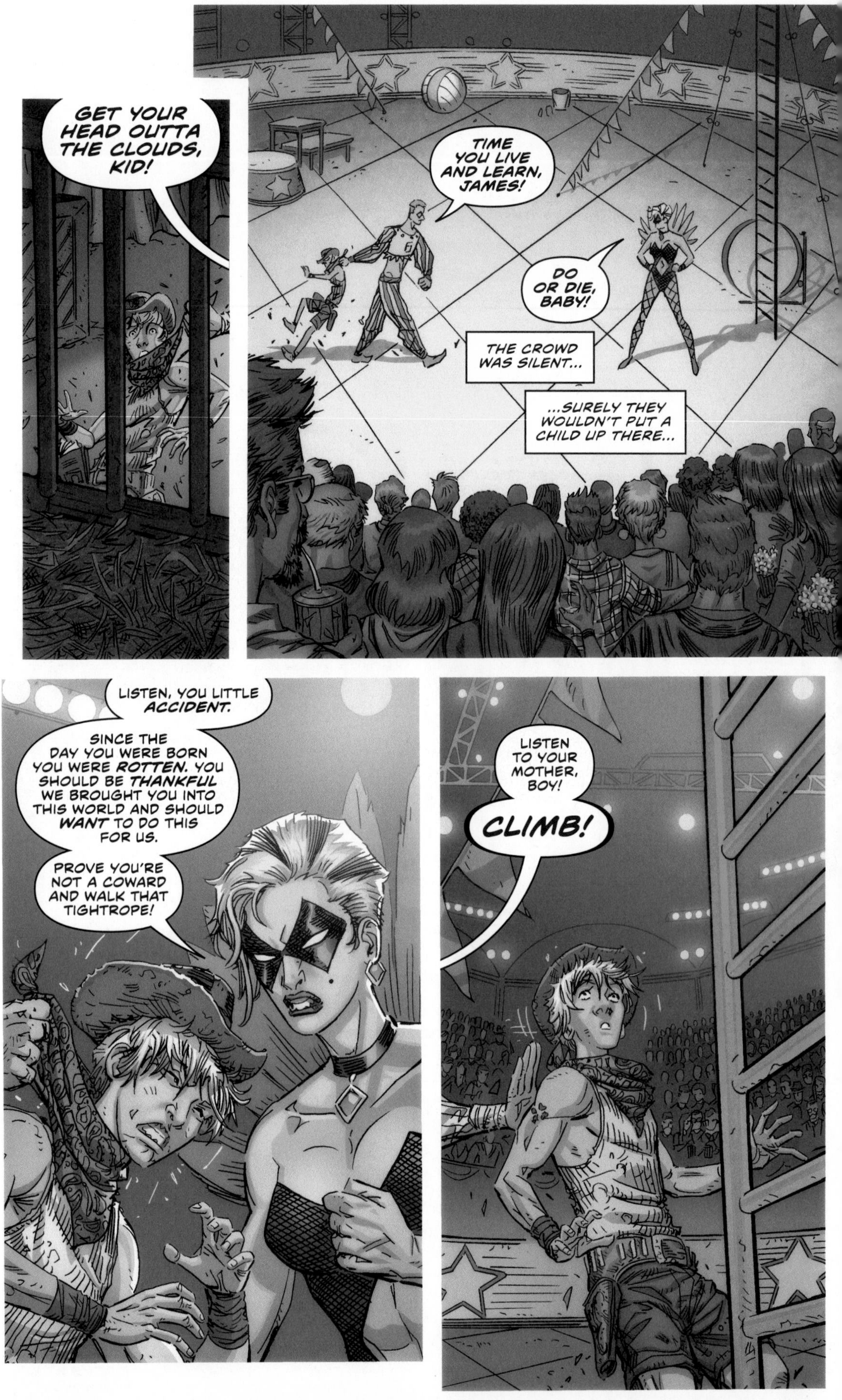
GET YOUR HEAD OUTTA THE CLOUDS, KID!
TIME YOU LIVE AND LEARN, JAMES!
DO OR DIE, BABY!
THE CROWD WAS SILENT...
...SURELY THEY WOULDN'T PUT A CHILD UP THERE...
LISTEN, YOU LITTLE ACCIDENT.
SINCE THE DAY YOU WERE BORN YOU WERE ROTTEN. YOU SHOULD BE THANKFUL WE BROUGHT YOU INTO THIS WORLD AND SHOULD WANT TO DO THIS FOR US.
PROVE YOU'RE NOT A COWARD AND WALK THAT TIGHTROPE!
LISTEN TO YOUR MOTHER, BOY!
CLIMB!

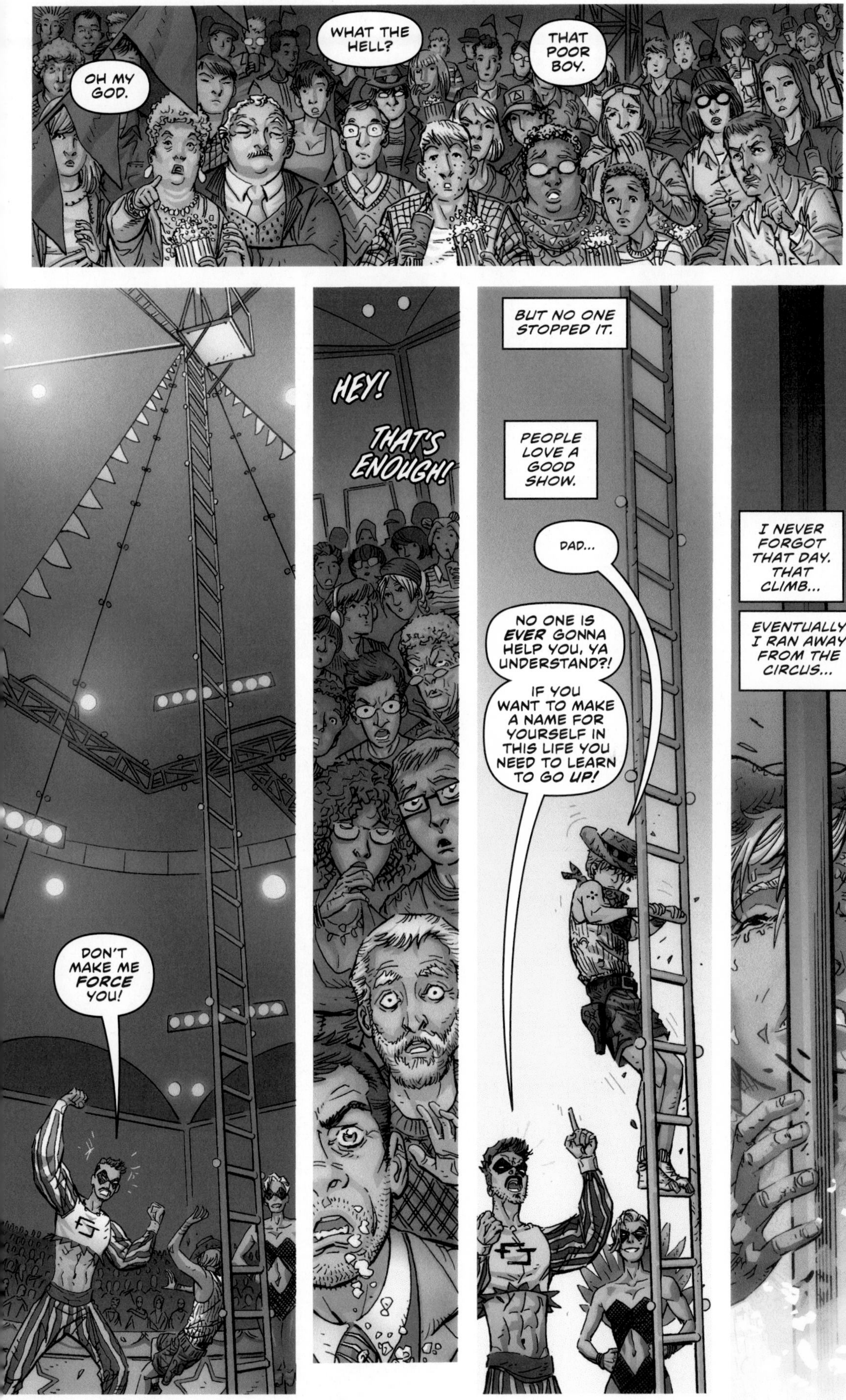
OH MY GOD.
WHAT THE HELL?
THAT POOR BOY.
DON'T MAKE ME FORCE YOU!
HEY!
THAT'S ENOUGH!
BUT NO ONE STOPPED IT.
PEOPLE LOVE A GOOD SHOW.
DAD...
NO ONE IS EVER GONNA HELP YOU, YA UNDERSTAND?!
IF YOU WANT TO MAKE A NAME FOR YOURSELF IN THIS LIFE YOU NEED TO LEARN TO GO UP!
I NEVER FORGOT THAT DAY. THAT CLIMB...
EVENTUALLY I RAN AWAY FROM THE CIRCUS...

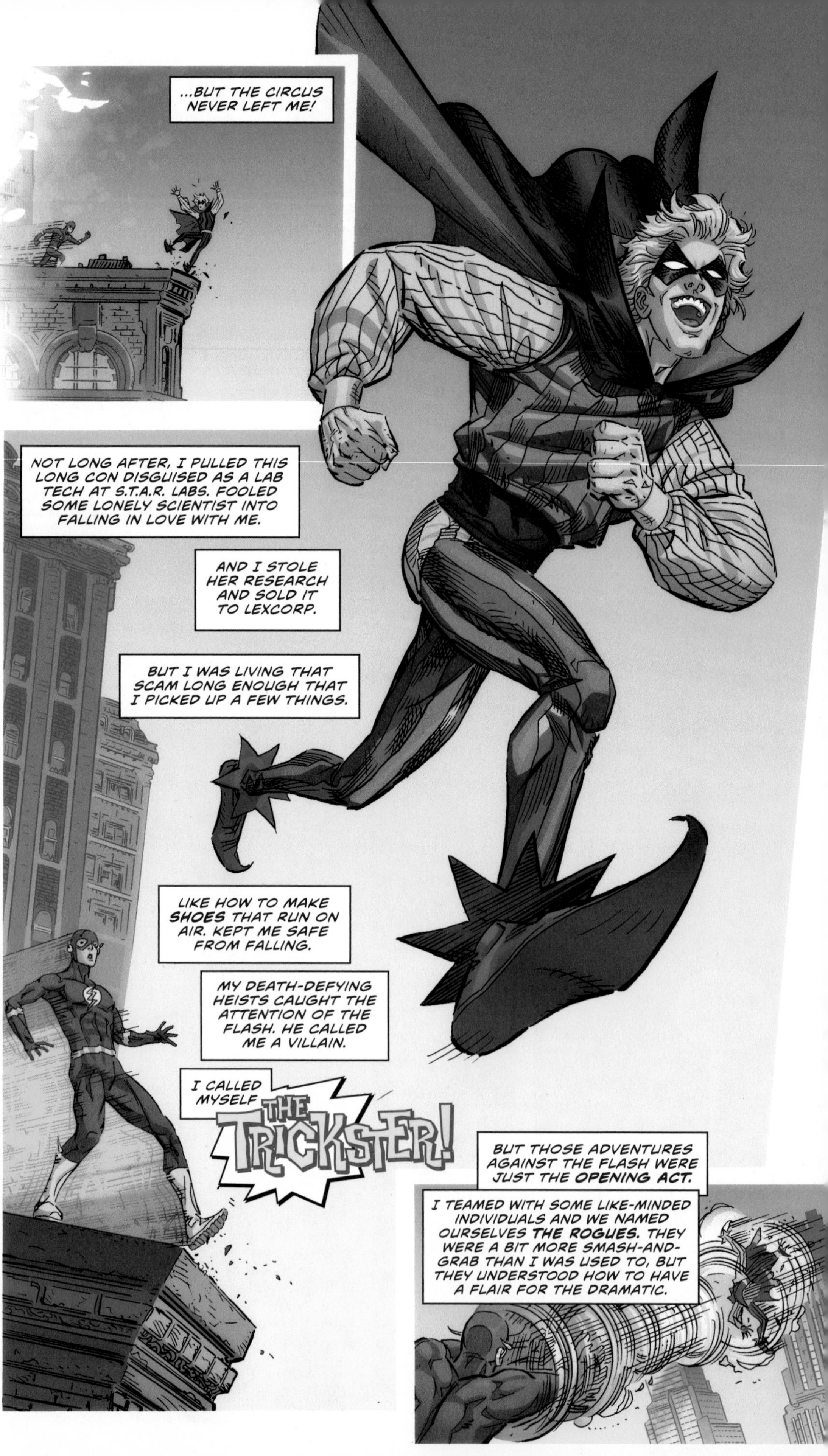
...BUT THE CIRCUS NEVER LEFT ME!
NOT LONG AFTER, I PULLED THIS LONG CON DISGUISED AS A LAB TECH AT S.T.A.R. LABS. FOOLED SOME LONELY SCIENTIST INTO FALLING IN LOVE WITH ME.
AND I STOLE HER RESEARCH AND SOLD IT TO LEXCORP.
BUT I WAS LIVING THAT SCAM LONG ENOUGH THAT I PICKED UP A FEW THINGS.
LIKE HOW TO MAKE SHOES THAT RUN ON AIR. KEPT ME SAFE FROM FALLING.
MY DEATH-DEFYING HEISTS CAUGHT THE ATTENTION OF THE FLASH. HE CALLED ME A VILLAIN.
I CALLED MYSELF
THE TRICKSTER!
BUT THOSE ADVENTURES AGAINST THE FLASH WERE JUST THE OPENING ACT.
I TEAMED WITH SOME LIKE-MINDED INDIVIDUALS AND WE NAMED OURSELVES THE ROGUES. THEY WERE A BIT MORE SMASH-AND-GRAB THAN I WAS USED TO, BUT THEY UNDERSTOOD HOW TO HAVE A FLAIR FOR THE DRAMATIC.

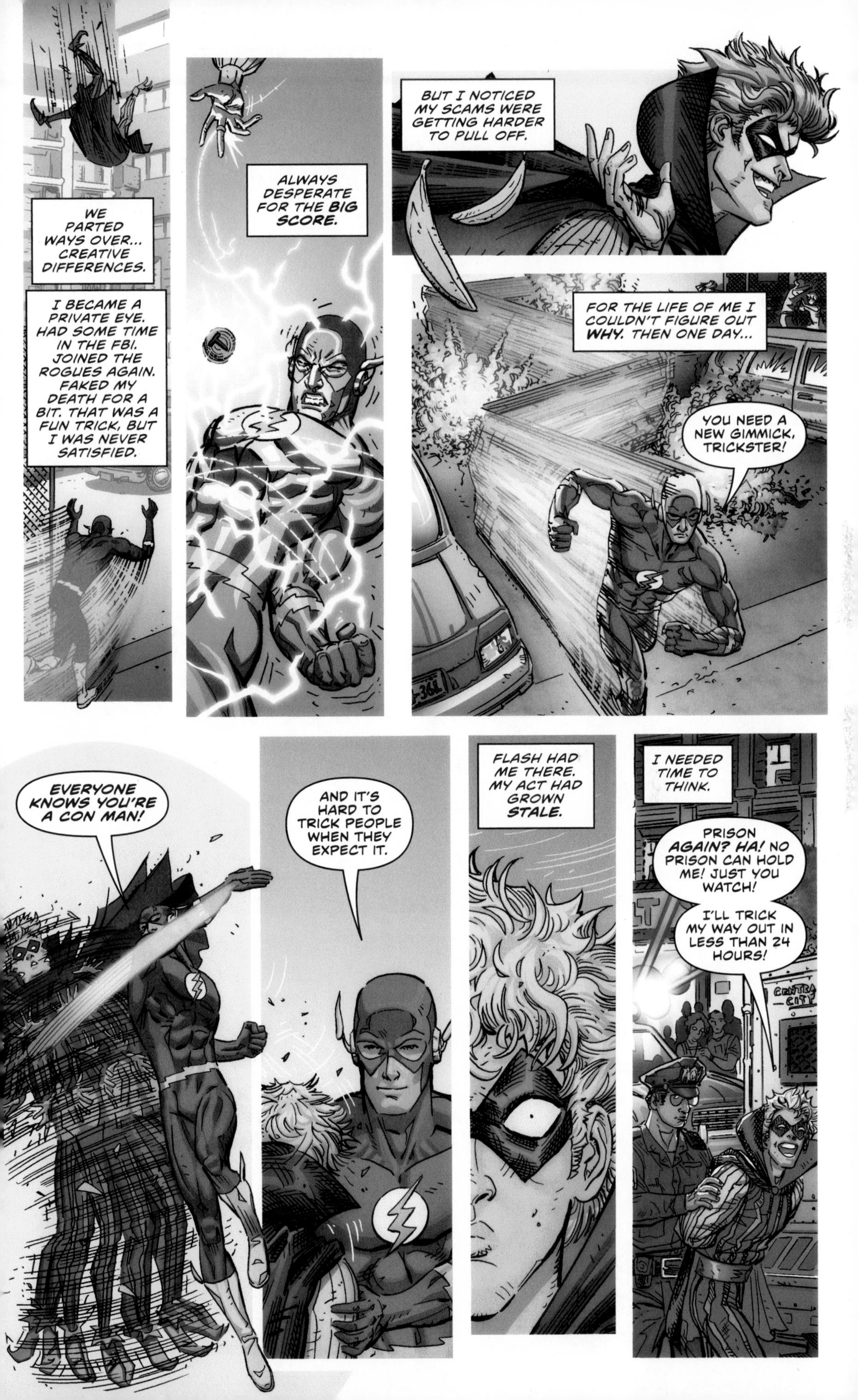

WE PARTED WAYS OVER... CREATIVE DIFFERENCES.
I BECAME A PRIVATE EYE. HAD SOME TIME IN THE FBI. JOINED THE ROGUES AGAIN. FAKED MY DEATH FOR A BIT. THAT WAS A FUN TRICK, BUT I WAS NEVER SATISFIED.
ALWAYS DESPERATE FOR THE BIG SCORE.
BUT I NOTICED MY SCAMS WERE GETTING HARDER TO PULL OFF.
FOR THE LIFE OF ME I COULDN'T FIGURE OUT WHY. THEN ONE DAY...
YOU NEED A NEW GIMMICK, TRICKSTER!
EVERYONE KNOWS YOU'RE A CON MAN!
AND IT'S HARD TO TRICK PEOPLE WHEN THEY EXPECT IT.
FLASH HAD ME THERE. MY ACT HAD GROWN STALE.
I NEEDED TIME TO THINK.
PRISON AGAIN? HA! NO PRISON CAN HOLD ME! JUST YOU WATCH!
I'LL TRICK MY WAY OUT IN LESS THAN 24 HOURS!

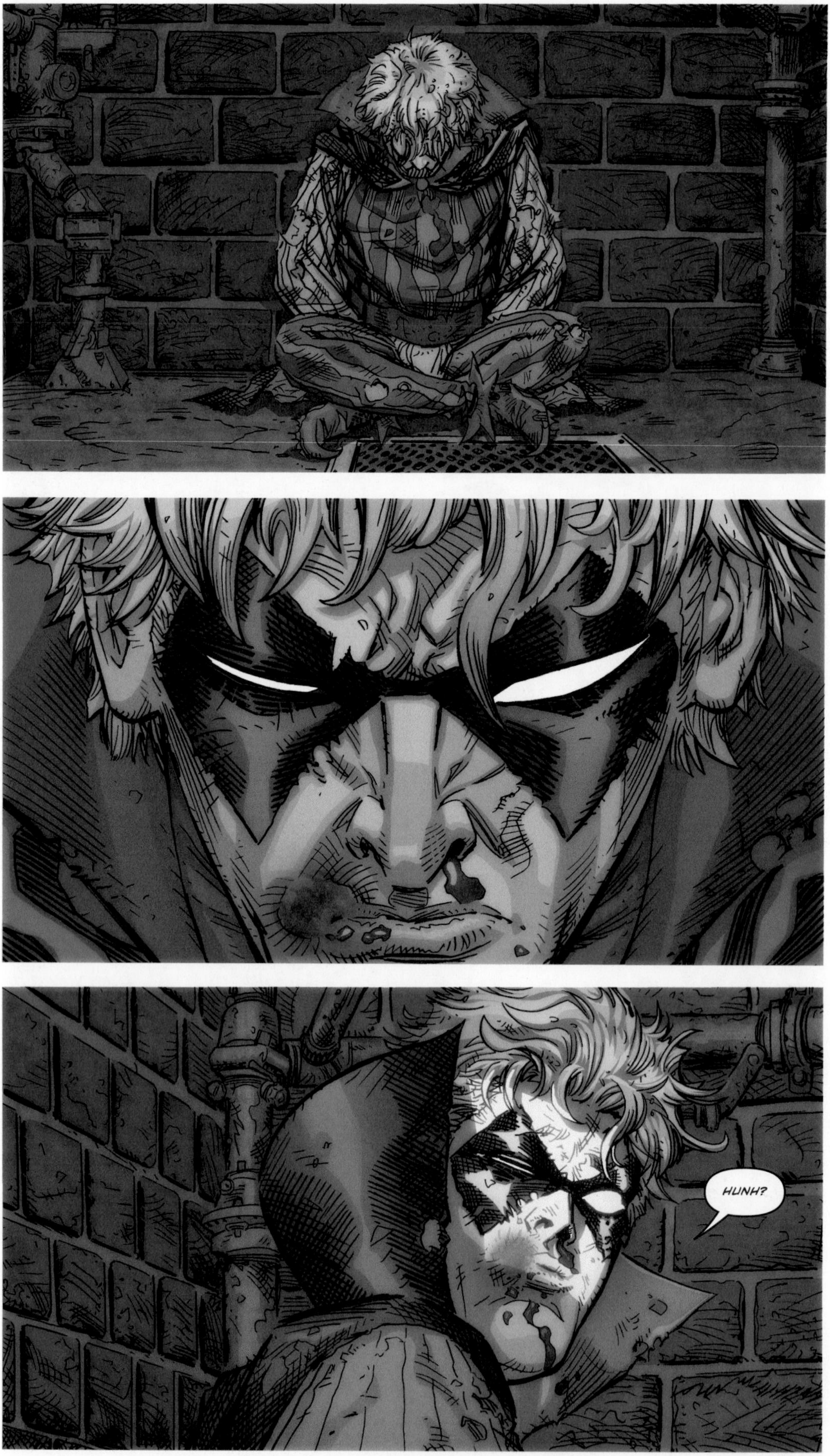
HUNH?

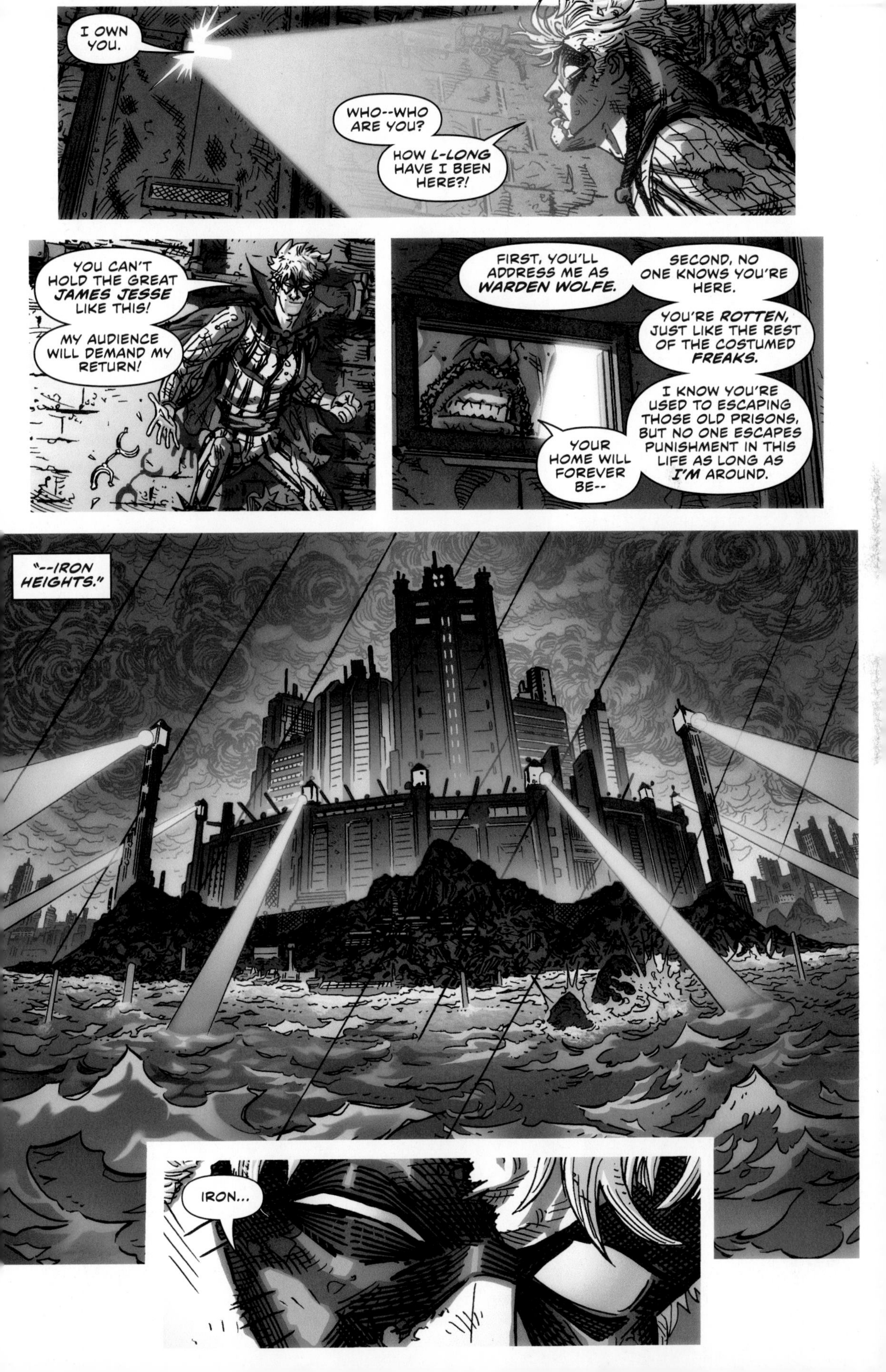
I OWN YOU.
WHO--WHO ARE YOU?
HOW L-LONG HAVE I BEEN HERE?!
YOU CAN'T HOLD THE GREAT JAMES JESSE LIKE THIS!
MY AUDIENCE WILL DEMAND MY RETURN!
FIRST, YOU'LL ADDRESS ME AS WARDEN WOLFE.
SECOND, NO ONE KNOWS YOU'RE HERE.
YOU'RE ROTTEN, JUST LIKE THE REST OF THE COSTUMED FREAKS.
I KNOW YOU'RE USED TO ESCAPING THOSE OLD PRISONS, BUT NO ONE ESCAPES PUNISHMENT IN THIS LIFE AS LONG AS I'M AROUND.
YOUR HOME WILL FOREVER BE--
"--IRON HEIGHTS."
IRON...

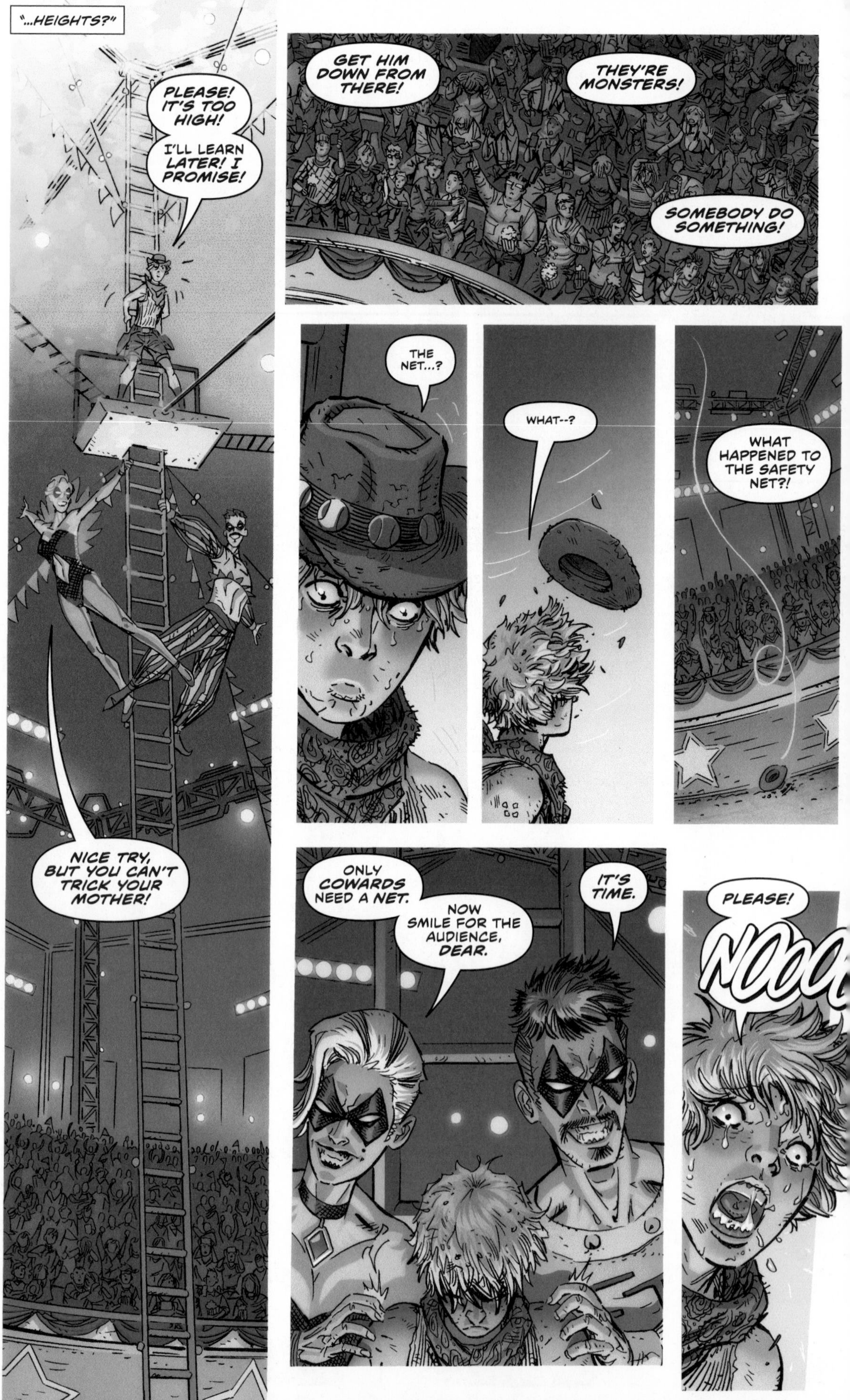
"...HEIGHTS?"
PLEASE! IT'S TOO HIGH!
I'LL LEARN LATER! I PROMISE!
NICE TRY, BUT YOU CAN'T TRICK YOUR MOTHER!
GET HIM DOWN FROM THERE!
THEY'RE MONSTERS!
SOMEBODY DO SOMETHING!
THE NET...?
WHAT--?
WHAT HAPPENED TO THE SAFETY NET?!
ONLY COWARDS NEED A NET.
NOW SMILE FOR THE AUDIENCE, DEAR.
IT'S TIME.
PLEASE!

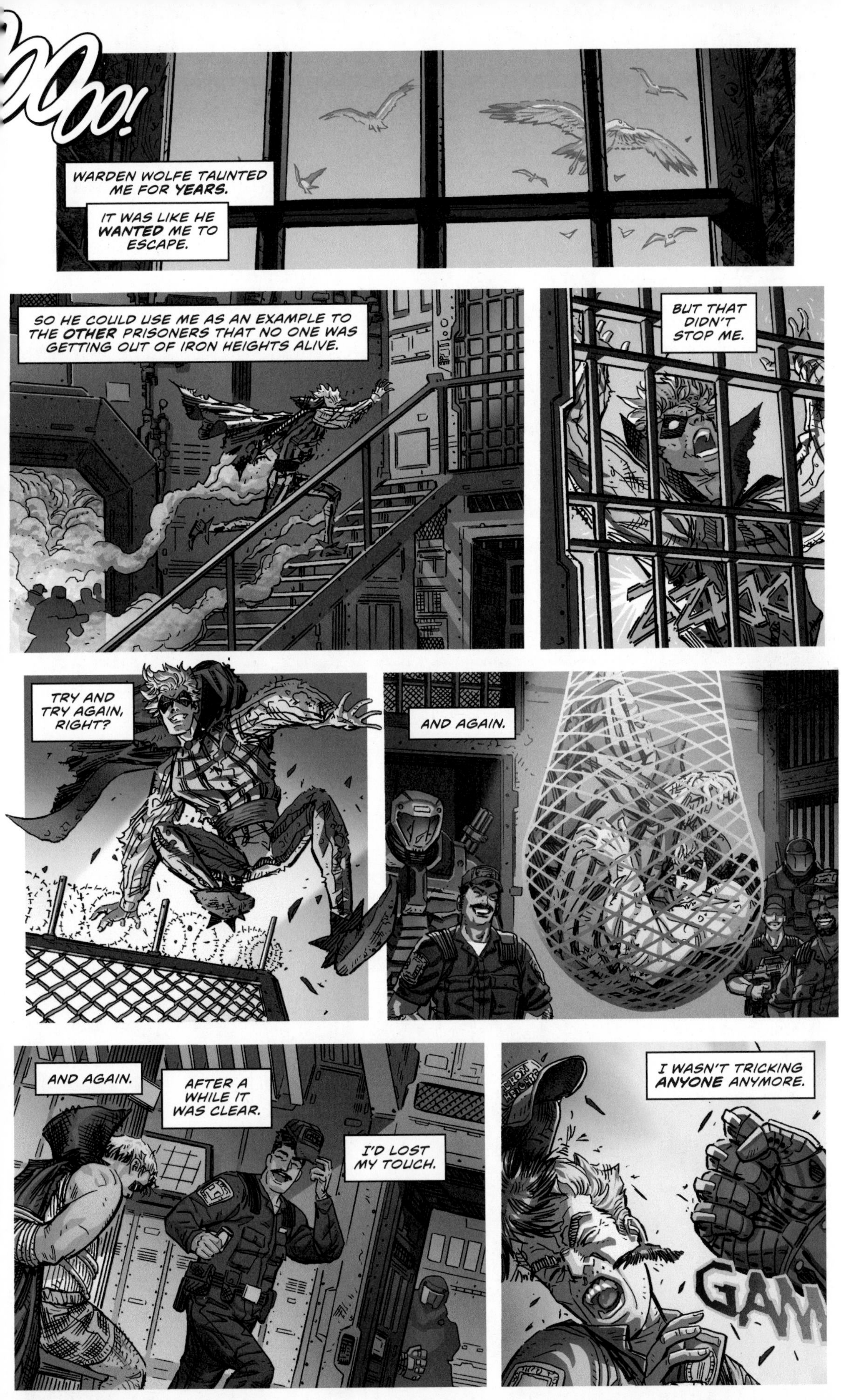
OOOO!
WARDEN WOLFE TAUNTED ME FOR YEARS.
IT WAS LIKE HE WANTED ME TO ESCAPE.
SO HE COULD USE ME AS AN EXAMPLE TO THE OTHER PRISONERS THAT NO ONE WAS GETTING OUT OF IRON HEIGHTS ALIVE.
BUT THAT DIDN'T STOP ME.
ZZAKK
TRY AND TRY AGAIN, RIGHT?
AND AGAIN.
AND AGAIN.
AFTER A WHILE IT WAS CLEAR.
I'D LOST MY TOUCH.
I WASN'T TRICKING ANYONE ANYMORE.
IRON HEIGHTS
GAM

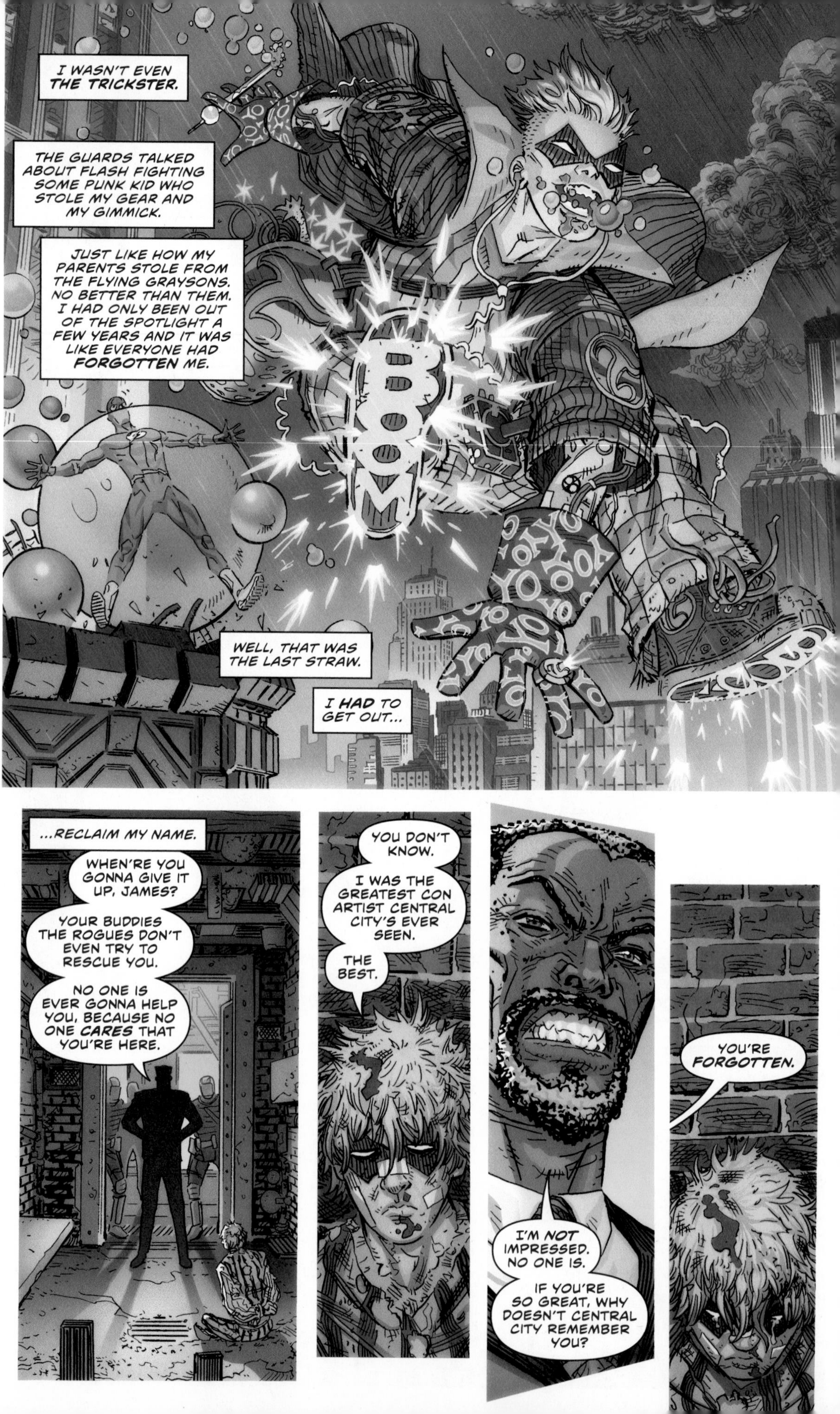
I WASN'T EVEN THE TRICKSTER.
THE GUARDS TALKED ABOUT FLASH FIGHTING SOME PUNK KID WHO STOLE MY GEAR AND MY GIMMICK.
JUST LIKE HOW MY PARENTS STOLE FROM THE FLYING GRAYSONS. NO BETTER THAN THEM. I HAD ONLY BEEN OUT OF THE SPOTLIGHT A FEW YEARS AND IT WAS LIKE EVERYONE HAD FORGOTTEN ME.
BOOM
WELL, THAT WAS THE LAST STRAW.
I HAD TO GET OUT...
...RECLAIM MY NAME.
WHEN'RE YOU GONNA GIVE IT UP, JAMES?
YOUR BUDDIES THE ROGUES DON'T EVEN TRY TO RESCUE YOU.
NO ONE IS EVER GONNA HELP YOU, BECAUSE NO ONE CARES THAT YOU'RE HERE.
YOU DON'T KNOW.
I WAS THE GREATEST CON ARTIST CENTRAL CITY'S EVER SEEN.
THE BEST.
I'M NOT IMPRESSED. NO ONE IS.
IF YOU'RE SO GREAT, WHY DOESN'T CENTRAL CITY REMEMBER YOU?
YOU'RE FORGOTTEN.

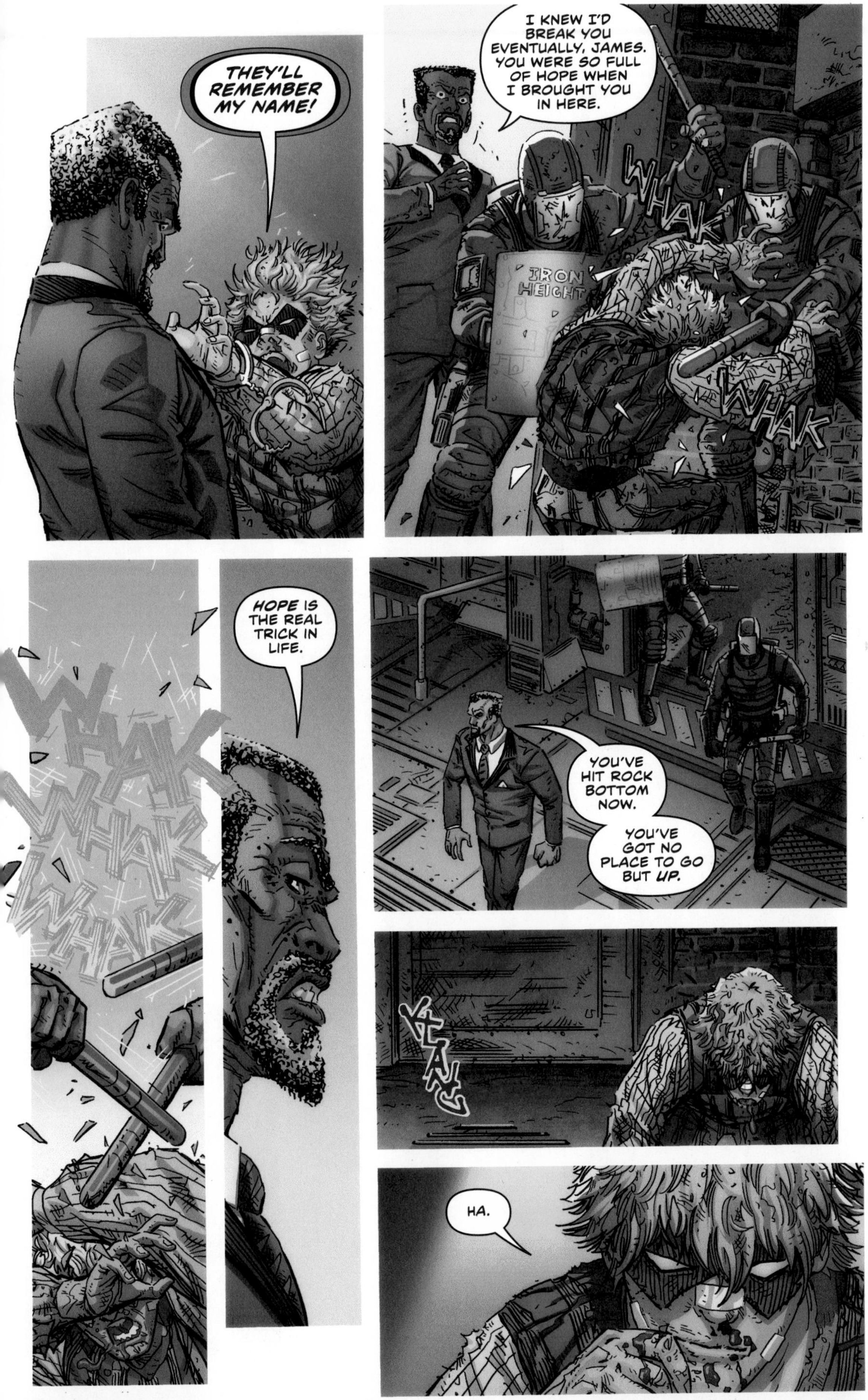
THEY'LL REMEMBER MY NAME!
I KNEW I'D BREAK YOU EVENTUALLY, JAMES. YOU WERE SO FULL OF HOPE WHEN I BROUGHT YOU IN HERE.
WHAK
WHAK
IRON HEIGHT
WHAK
WHAK
WHAK
HOPE IS THE REAL TRICK IN LIFE.
YOU'VE HIT ROCK BOTTOM NOW.
YOU'VE GOT NO PLACE TO GO BUT UP.
HA.

I'D SPENT SO MANY YEARS TRAPPED IN IRON HEIGHTS.

I TRIED EVERY SINGLE WAY I COULD TO ESCAPE.

EXCEPT ONE.

STOP BEING SUCH A DAMN COWARD AND GET OUT THERE!

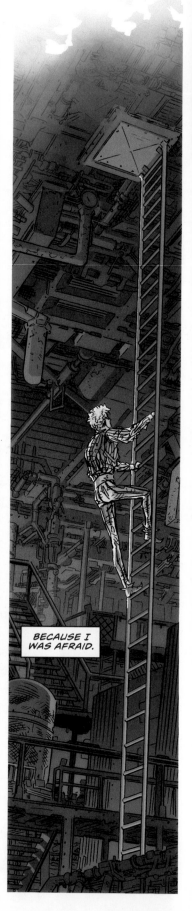

BECAUSE I WAS AFRAID.

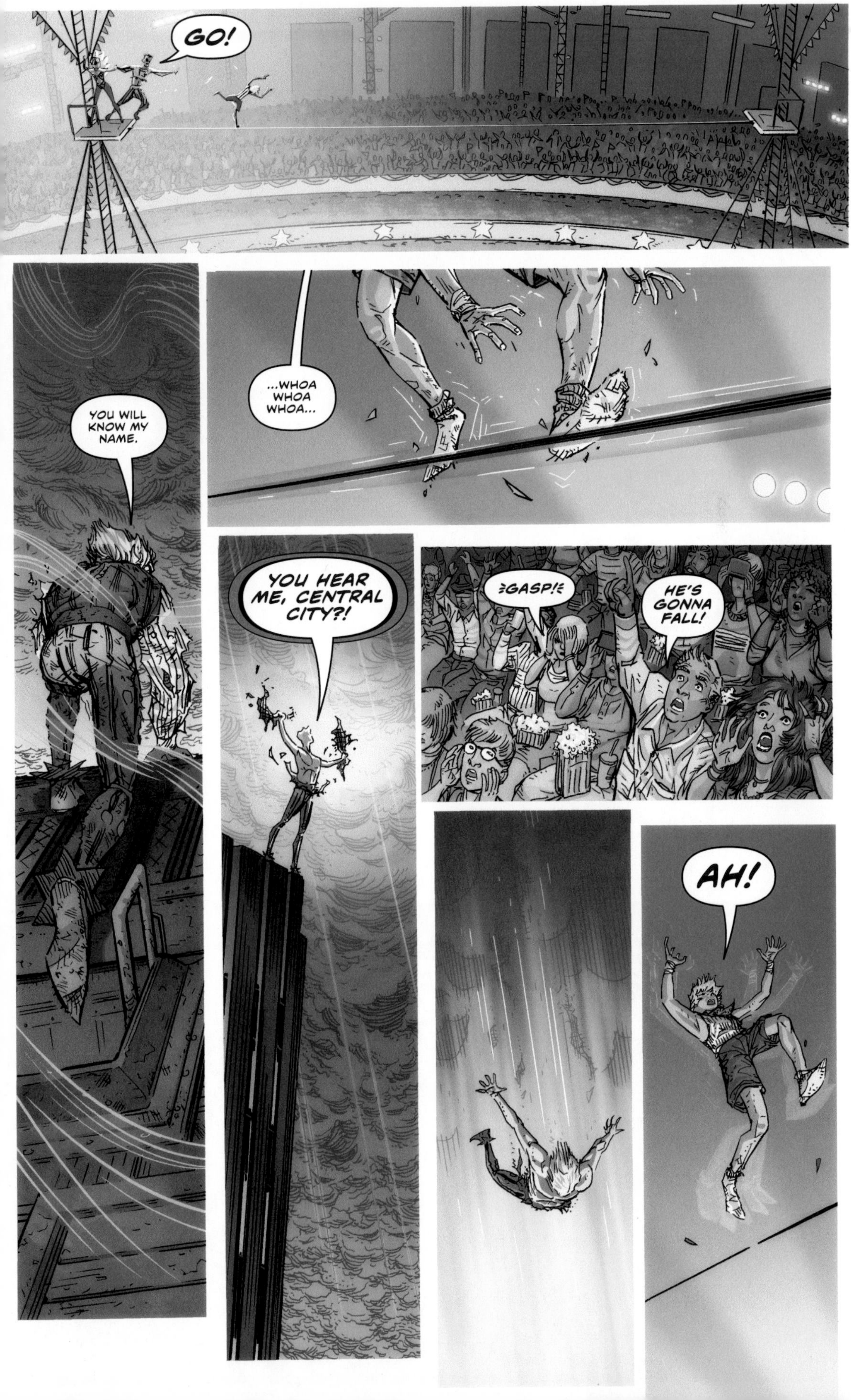
GO!
YOU WILL KNOW MY NAME.
...WHOA WHOA WHOA...
YOU HEAR ME, CENTRAL CITY?!
GASP!
HE'S GONNA FALL!
AH!

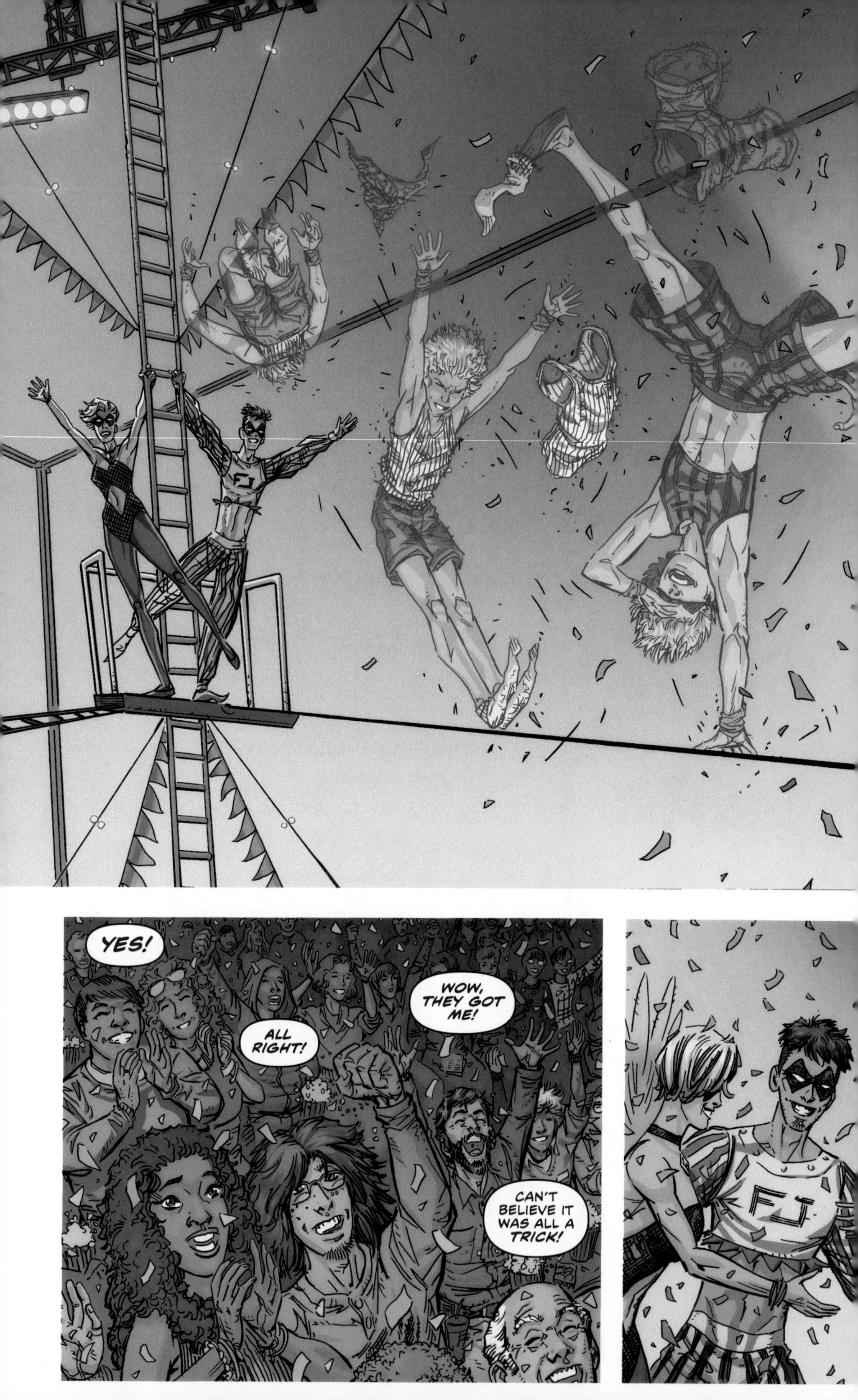
YES!
ALL RIGHT!
WOW, THEY GOT ME!
CAN'T BELIEVE IT WAS ALL A TRICK!

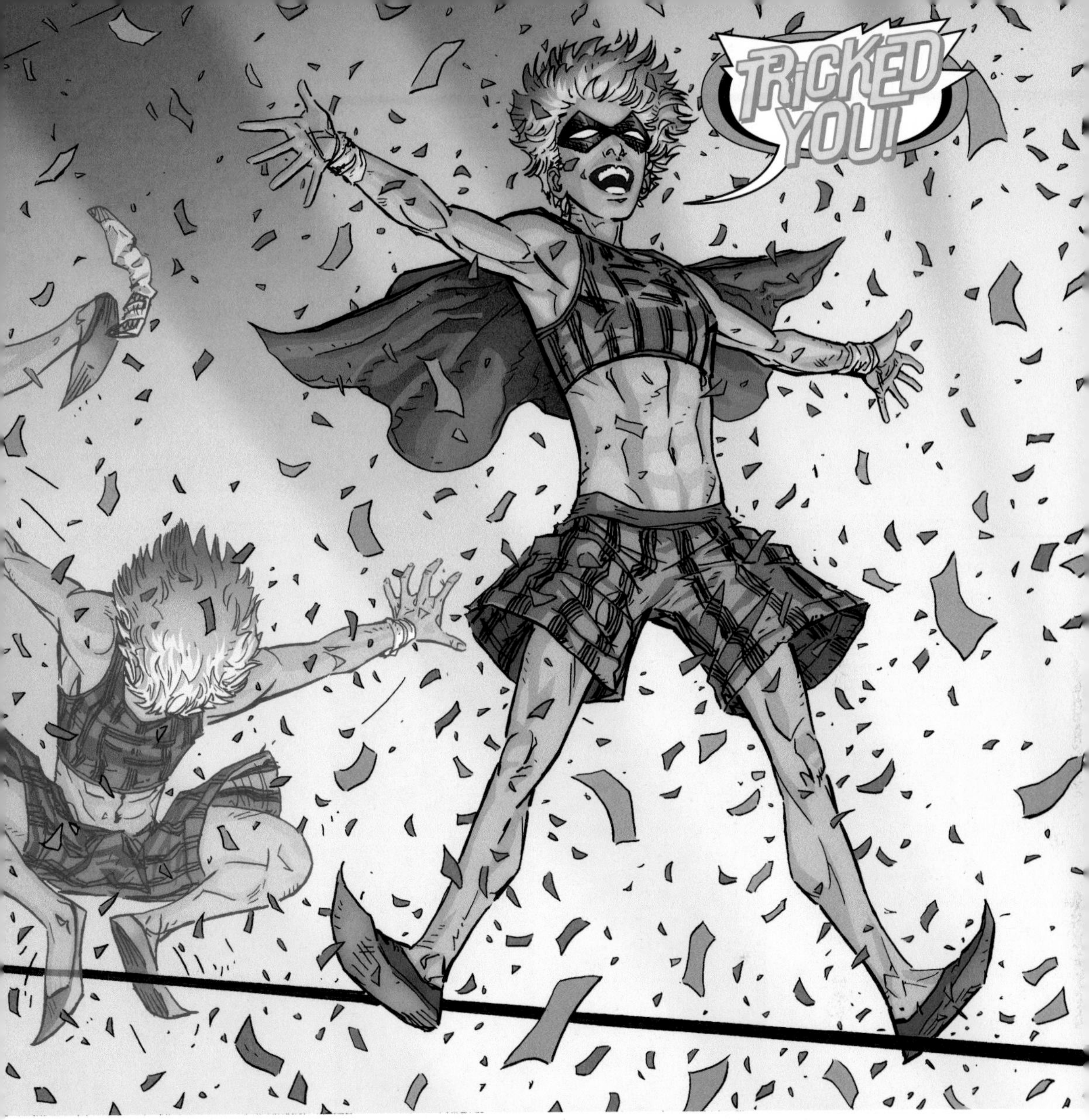
TRICKED YOU!

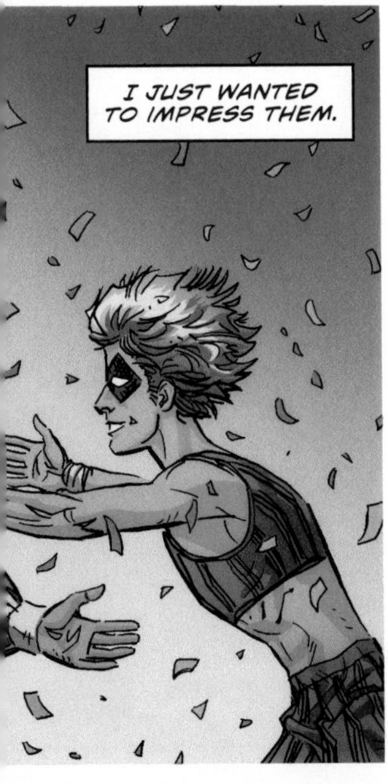
I JUST WANTED TO IMPRESS THEM.

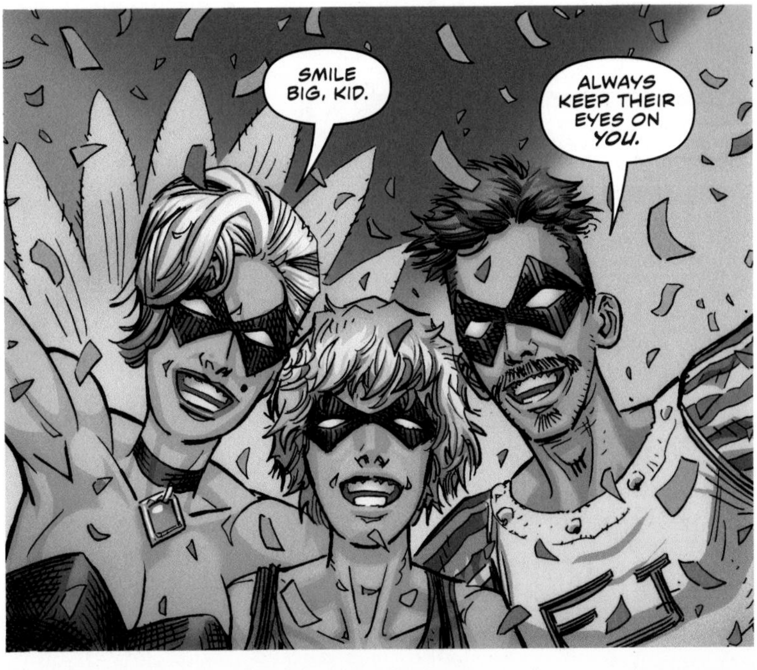
SMILE BIG, KID.
ALWAYS KEEP THEIR EYES ON YOU.

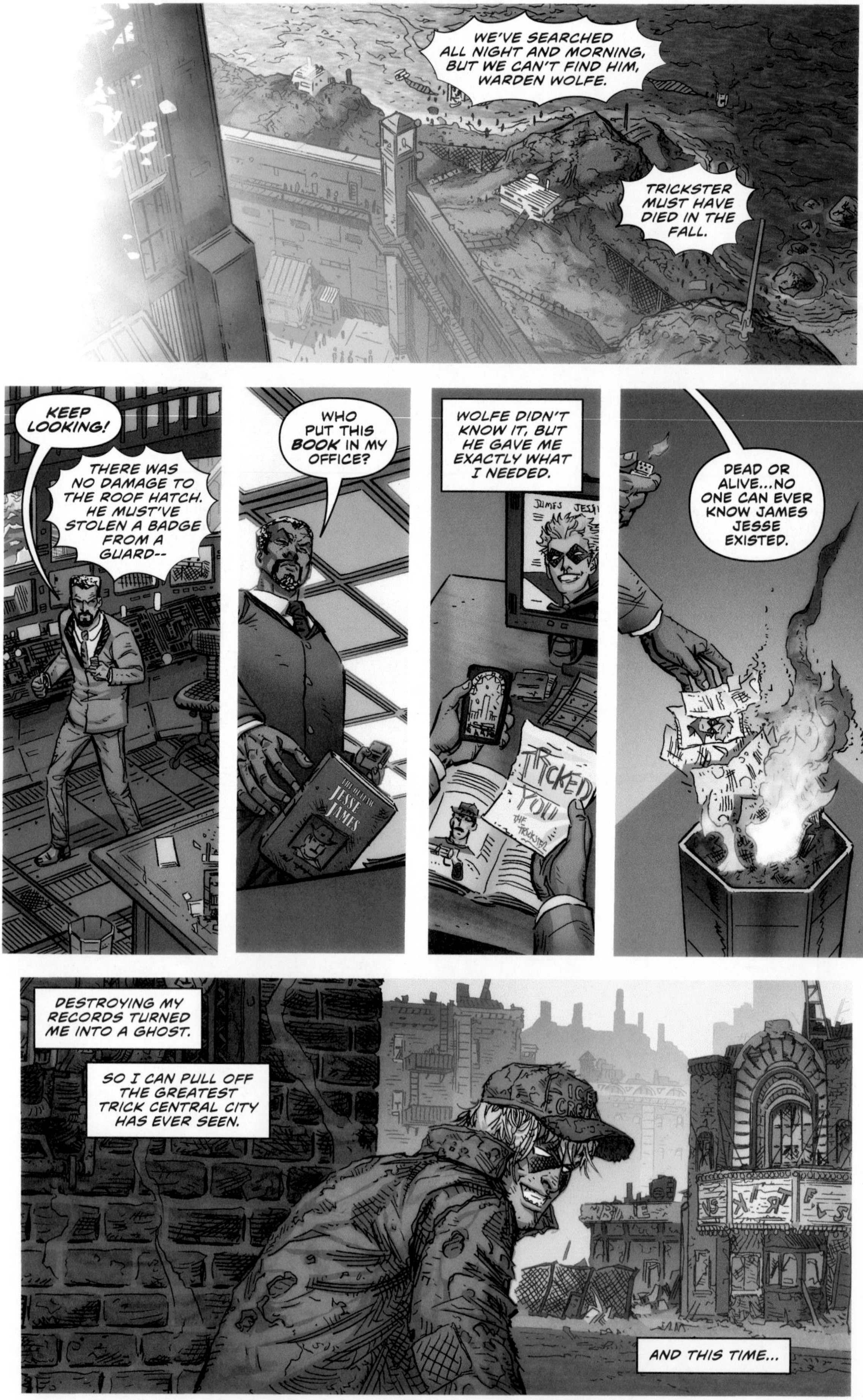
WE'VE SEARCHED ALL NIGHT AND MORNING, BUT WE CAN'T FIND HIM, WARDEN WOLFE.
TRICKSTER MUST HAVE DIED IN THE FALL.
KEEP LOOKING!
THERE WAS NO DAMAGE TO THE ROOF HATCH. HE MUST'VE STOLEN A BADGE FROM A GUARD--
WHO PUT THIS BOOK IN MY OFFICE?
THE OUTLAW JESSE JAMES
WOLFE DIDN'T KNOW IT, BUT HE GAVE ME EXACTLY WHAT I NEEDED.
TRICKED YOU
THE TRICKSTER
DEAD OR ALIVE...NO ONE CAN EVER KNOW JAMES JESSE EXISTED.
DESTROYING MY RECORDS TURNED ME INTO A GHOST.
SO I CAN PULL OFF THE GREATEST TRICK CENTRAL CITY HAS EVER SEEN.
AND THIS TIME...

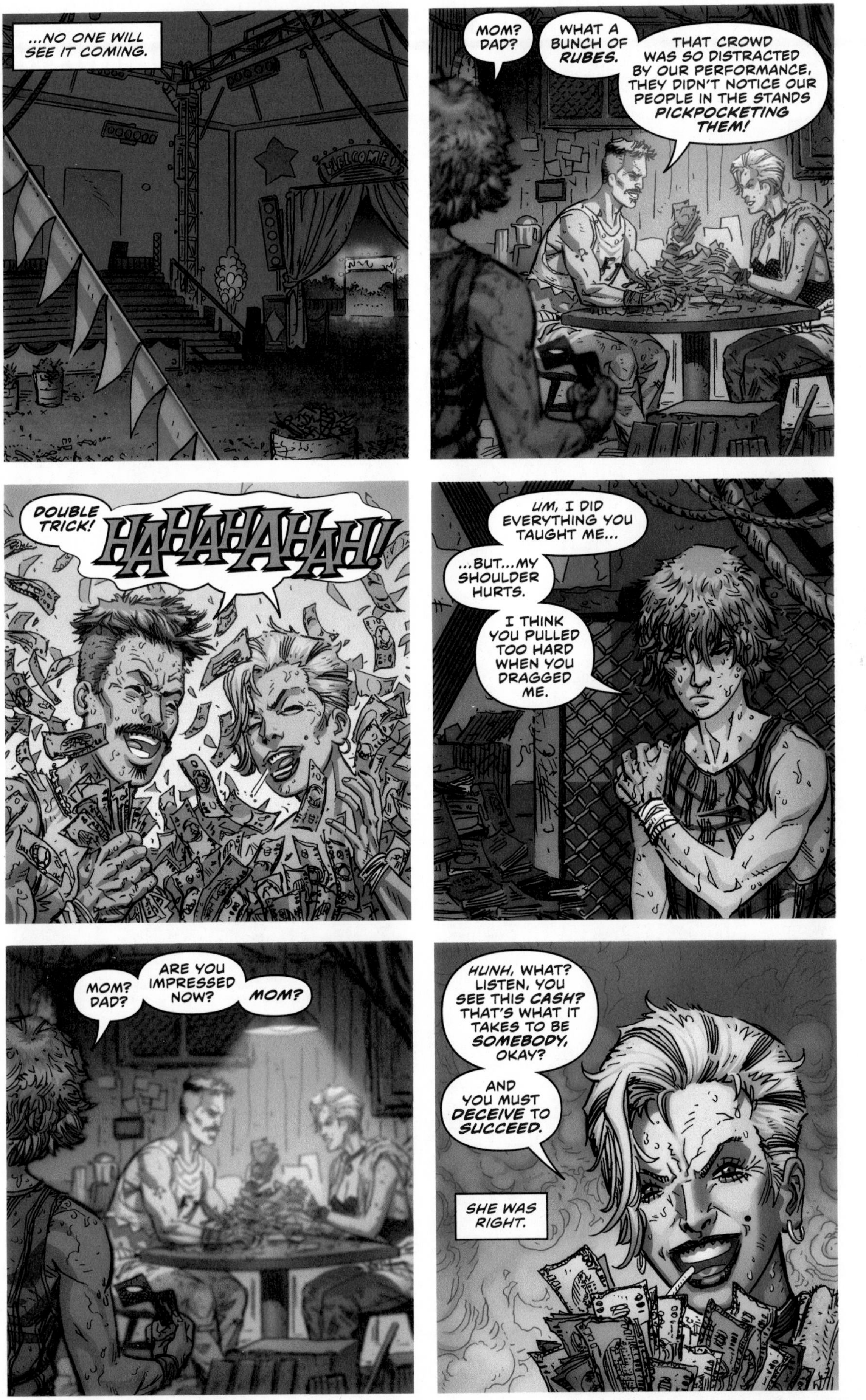
...NO ONE WILL SEE IT COMING.
MOM? DAD?
WHAT A BUNCH OF RUBES.
THAT CROWD WAS SO DISTRACTED BY OUR PERFORMANCE, THEY DIDN'T NOTICE OUR PEOPLE IN THE STANDS PICKPOCKETING THEM!
DOUBLE TRICK!
HAHAHAHAH!
UM, I DID EVERYTHING YOU TAUGHT ME...
...BUT...MY SHOULDER HURTS.
I THINK YOU PULLED TOO HARD WHEN YOU DRAGGED ME.
MOM? DAD?
ARE YOU IMPRESSED NOW?
MOM?
HUNH, WHAT? LISTEN, YOU SEE THIS CASH? THAT'S WHAT IT TAKES TO BE SOMEBODY, OKAY?
AND YOU MUST DECEIVE TO SUCCEED.
SHE WAS RIGHT.

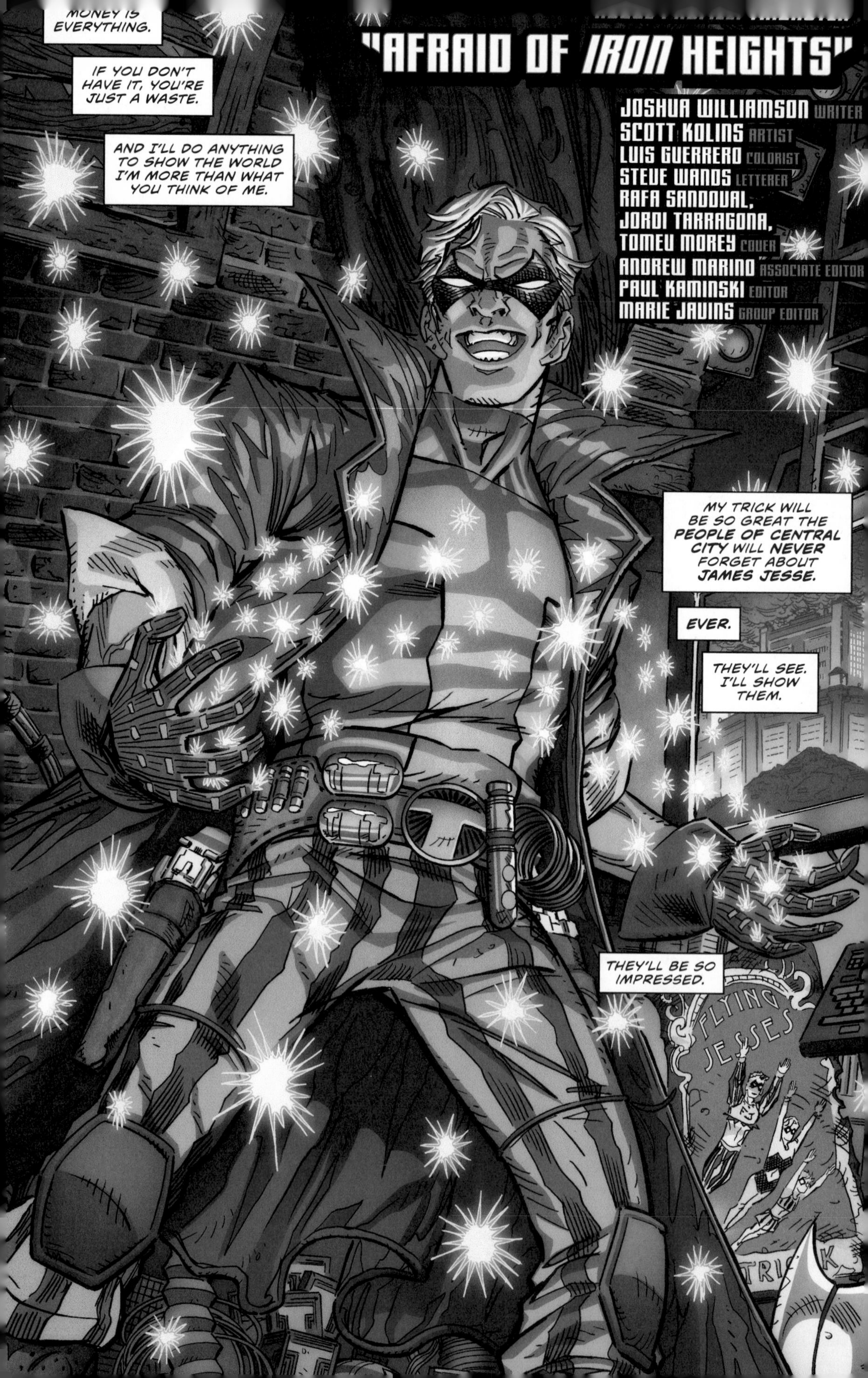
MONEY IS EVERYTHING.
IF YOU DON'T HAVE IT, YOU'RE JUST A WASTE.
AND I'LL DO ANYTHING TO SHOW THE WORLD I'M MORE THAN WHAT YOU THINK OF ME.
"AFRAID OF IRON HEIGHTS"
JOSHUA WILLIAMSON WRITER
SCOTT KOLINS ARTIST
LUIS GUERRERO COLORIST
STEVE WANDS LETTERER
RAFA SANDOVAL, JORDI TARRAGONA, TOMEU MOREY COVER
ANDREW MARINO ASSOCIATE EDITOR
PAUL KAMINSKI EDITOR
MARIE JAVINS GROUP EDITOR
MY TRICK WILL BE SO GREAT THE PEOPLE OF CENTRAL CITY WILL NEVER FORGET ABOUT JAMES JESSE.
EVER.
THEY'LL SEE. I'LL SHOW THEM.
THEY'LL BE SO IMPRESSED.
FLYING JESSES

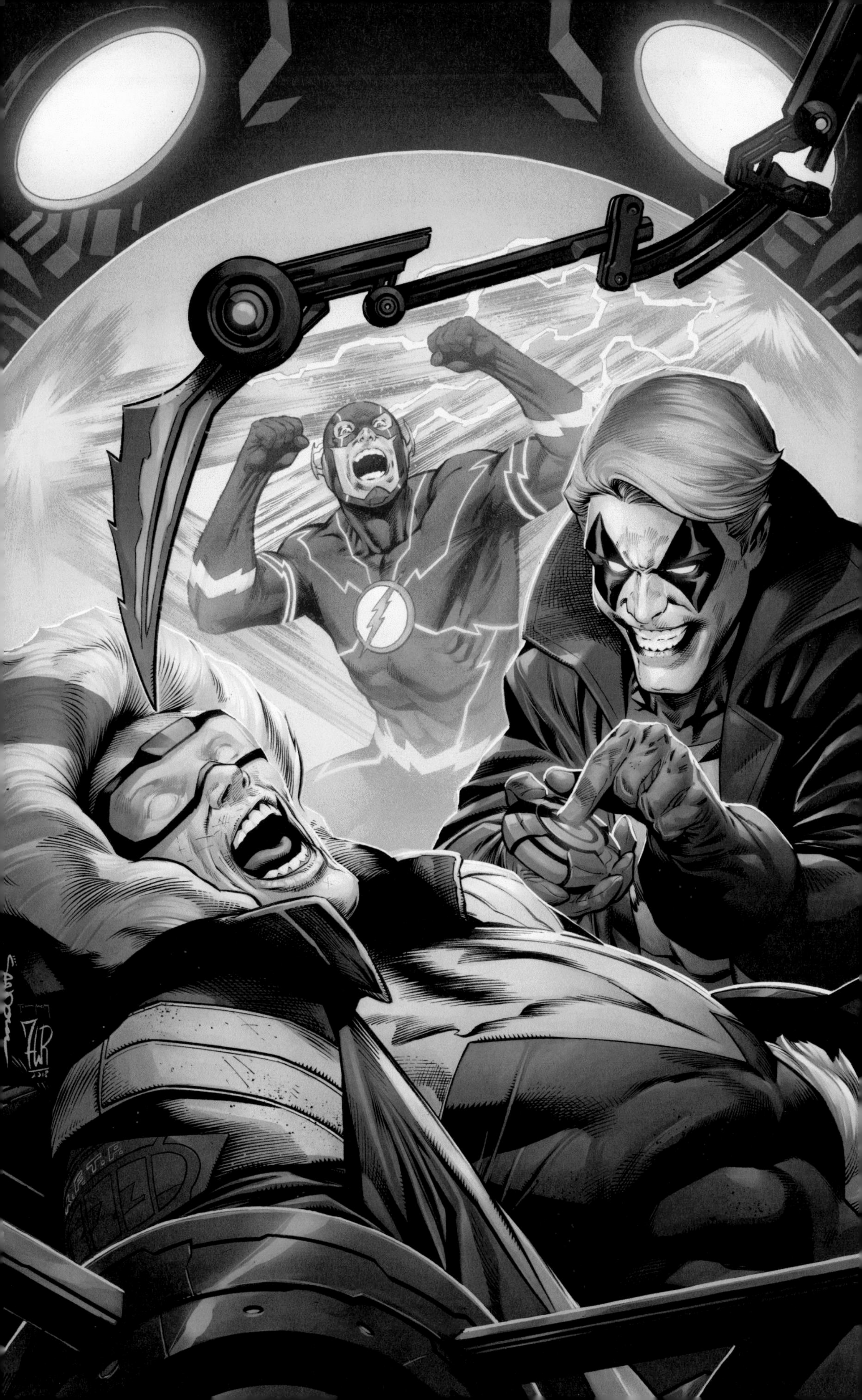

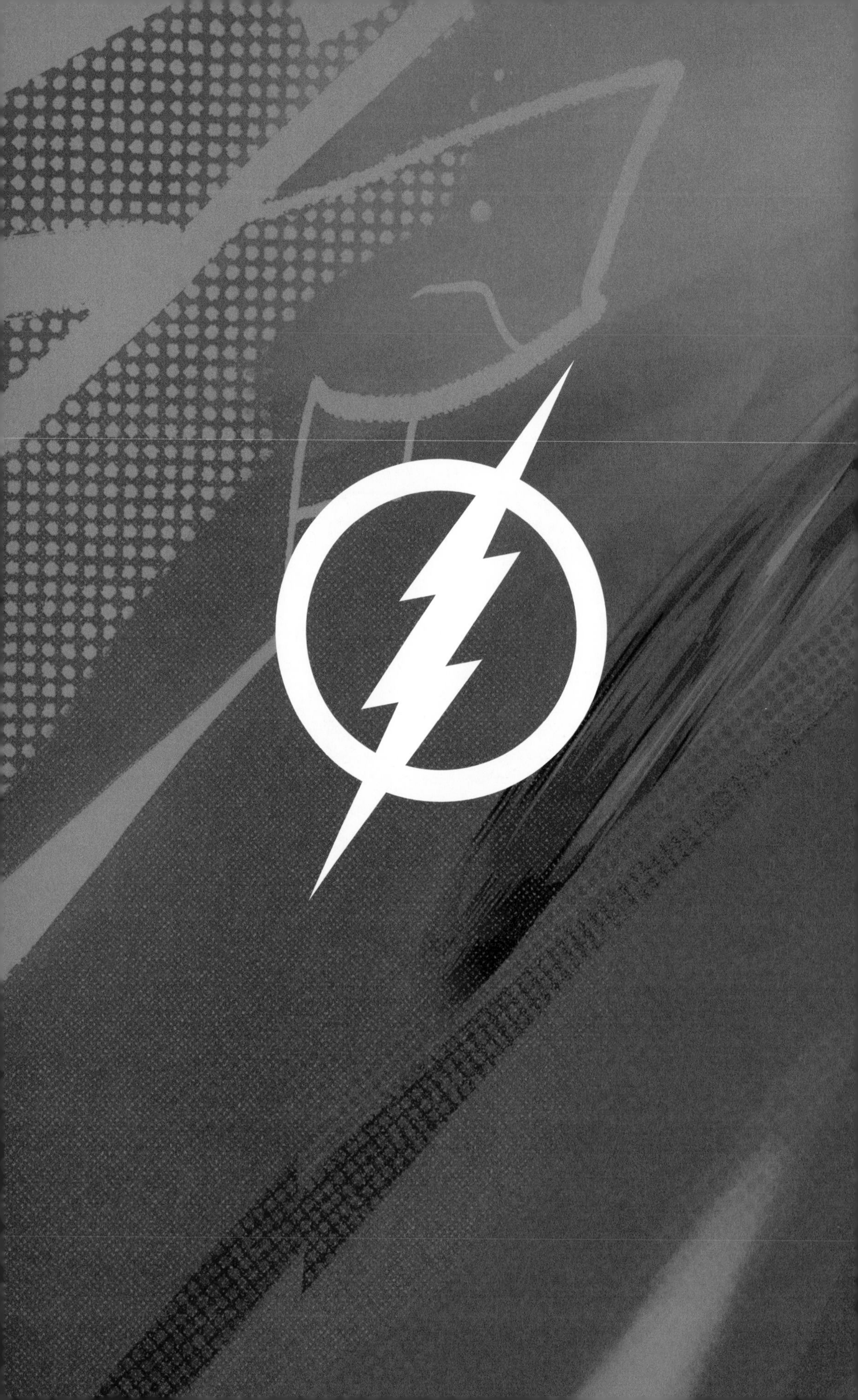

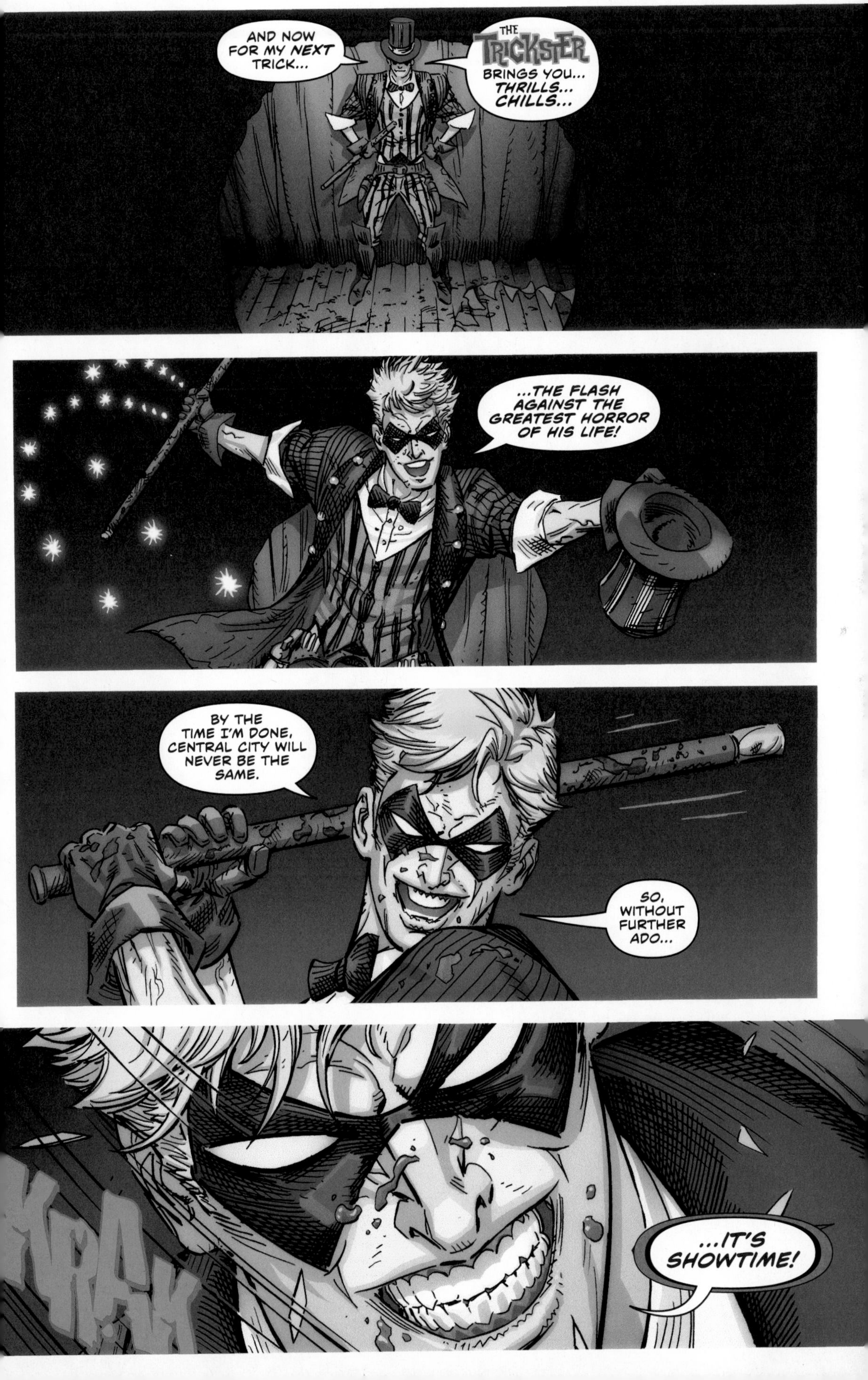
AND NOW FOR MY NEXT TRICK...
THE TRICKSTER BRINGS YOU... THRILLS... CHILLS...
...THE FLASH AGAINST THE GREATEST HORROR OF HIS LIFE!
BY THE TIME I'M DONE, CENTRAL CITY WILL NEVER BE THE SAME.
SO, WITHOUT FURTHER ADO...
KRAK
...IT'S SHOWTIME!

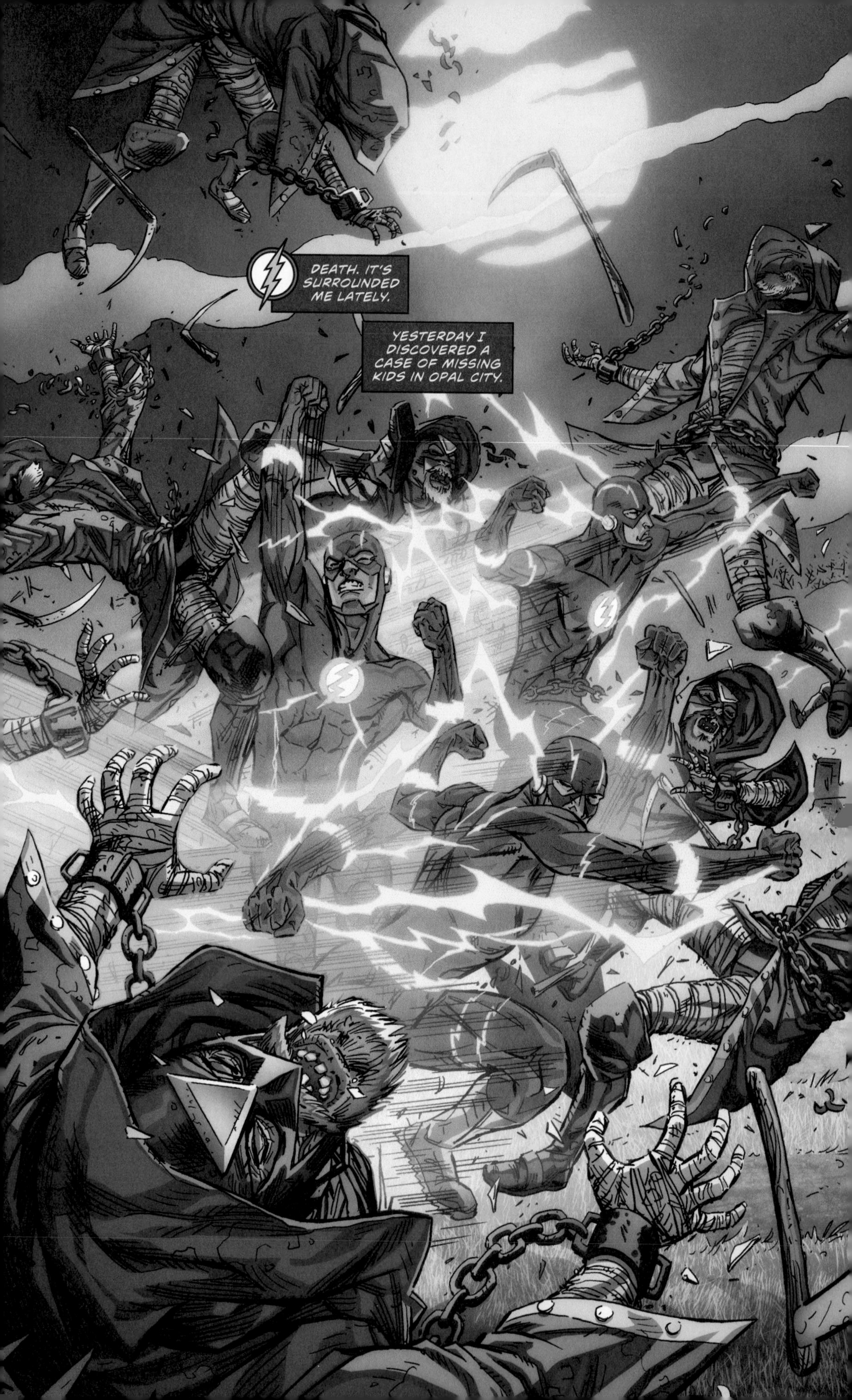
DEATH. IT'S SURROUNDED ME LATELY.
YESTERDAY I DISCOVERED A CASE OF MISSING KIDS IN OPAL CITY.

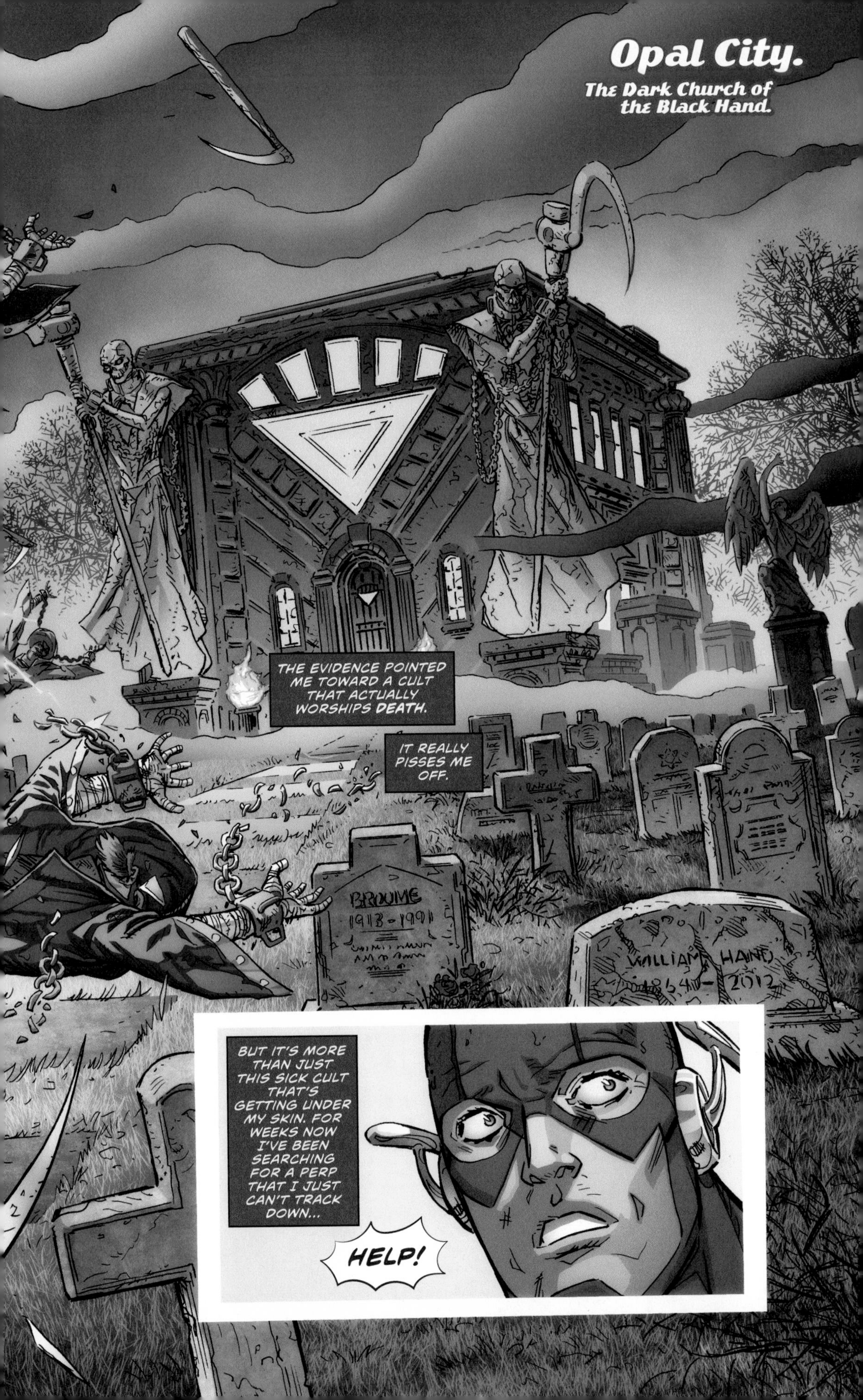
Opal City.
The Dark Church of the Black Hand.
THE EVIDENCE POINTED ME TOWARD A CULT THAT ACTUALLY WORSHIPS DEATH.
IT REALLY PISSES ME OFF.
BROOME 1913-1991
WILLIAM HAND 1864-2012
BUT IT'S MORE THAN JUST THIS SICK CULT THAT'S GETTING UNDER MY SKIN. FOR WEEKS NOW I'VE BEEN SEARCHING FOR A PERP THAT I JUST CAN'T TRACK DOWN...
HELP!

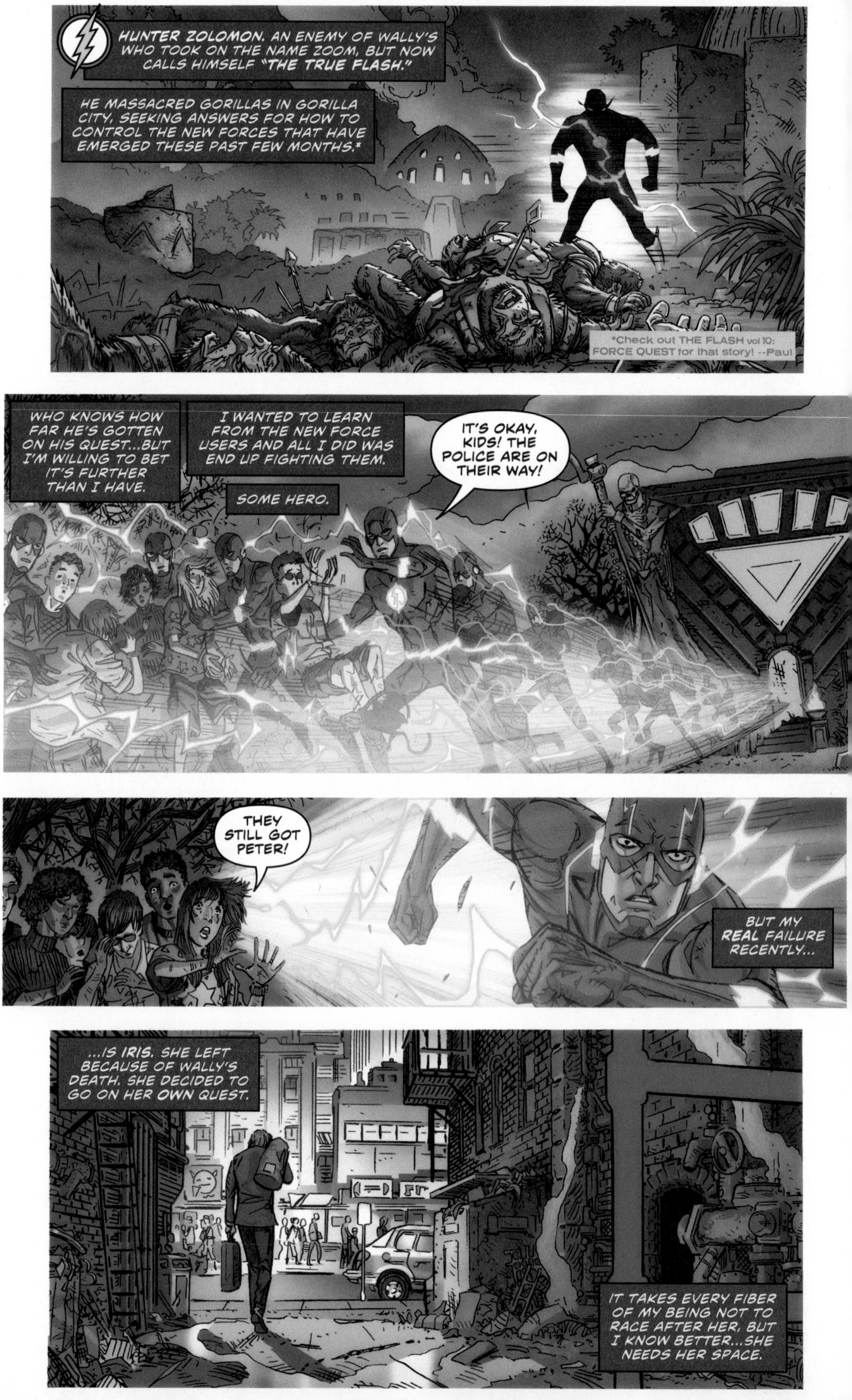
HUNTER ZOLOMON. AN ENEMY OF WALLY'S WHO TOOK ON THE NAME ZOOM, BUT NOW CALLS HIMSELF "THE TRUE FLASH."
HE MASSACRED GORILLAS IN GORILLA CITY, SEEKING ANSWERS FOR HOW TO CONTROL THE NEW FORCES THAT HAVE EMERGED THESE PAST FEW MONTHS.*
*Check out THE FLASH vol 10: FORCE QUEST for that story! --Paul
WHO KNOWS HOW FAR HE'S GOTTEN ON HIS QUEST...BUT I'M WILLING TO BET IT'S FURTHER THAN I HAVE.
I WANTED TO LEARN FROM THE NEW FORCE USERS AND ALL I DID WAS END UP FIGHTING THEM.
SOME HERO.
IT'S OKAY, KIDS! THE POLICE ARE ON THEIR WAY!
THEY STILL GOT PETER!
BUT MY REAL FAILURE RECENTLY...
...IS IRIS. SHE LEFT BECAUSE OF WALLY'S DEATH. SHE DECIDED TO GO ON HER OWN QUEST.
IT TAKES EVERY FIBER OF MY BEING NOT TO RACE AFTER HER, BUT I KNOW BETTER...SHE NEEDS HER SPACE.

THE UNIVERSE IS BROKEN!

THE TIME IS NEAR! THE END IS UPON US, AND WE WILL NEED NEKRON!

EVER SINCE THESE NEW FORCES WERE UNLEASHED I FEEL LIKE I KEEP FAILING...

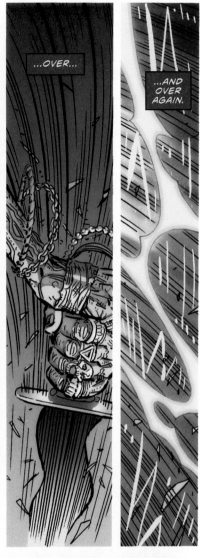

...OVER...

...AND OVER AGAIN.

WHA--?

BUT I'VE NOTICED SOMETHING ELSE...

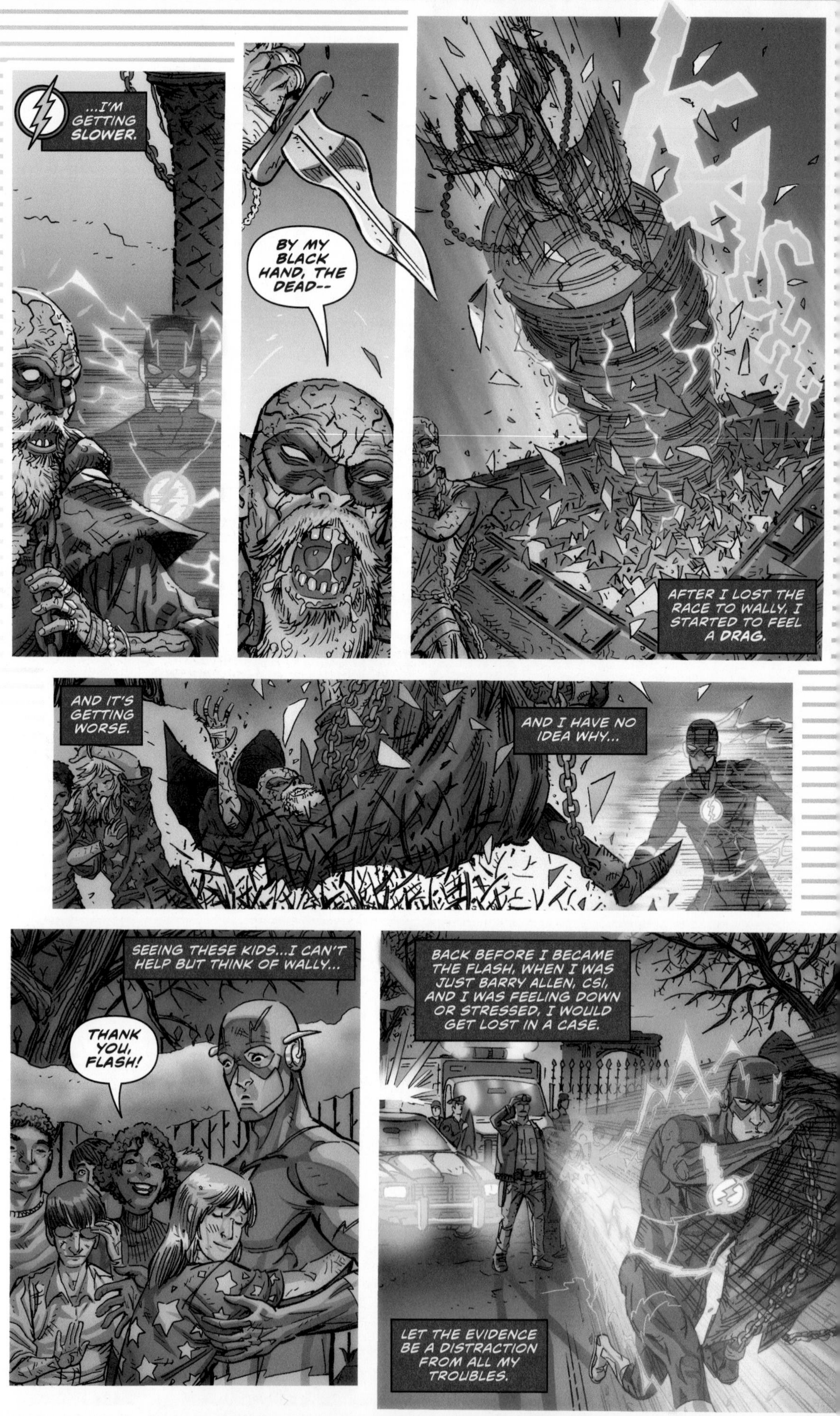
...I'M GETTING SLOWER.
BY MY BLACK HAND, THE DEAD--
KRASSHH
AFTER I LOST THE RACE TO WALLY, I STARTED TO FEEL A DRAG.
AND IT'S GETTING WORSE.
AND I HAVE NO IDEA WHY...
SEEING THESE KIDS...I CAN'T HELP BUT THINK OF WALLY...
THANK YOU, FLASH!
BACK BEFORE I BECAME THE FLASH, WHEN I WAS JUST BARRY ALLEN, CSI, AND I WAS FEELING DOWN OR STRESSED, I WOULD GET LOST IN A CASE.
LET THE EVIDENCE BE A DISTRACTION FROM ALL MY TROUBLES.

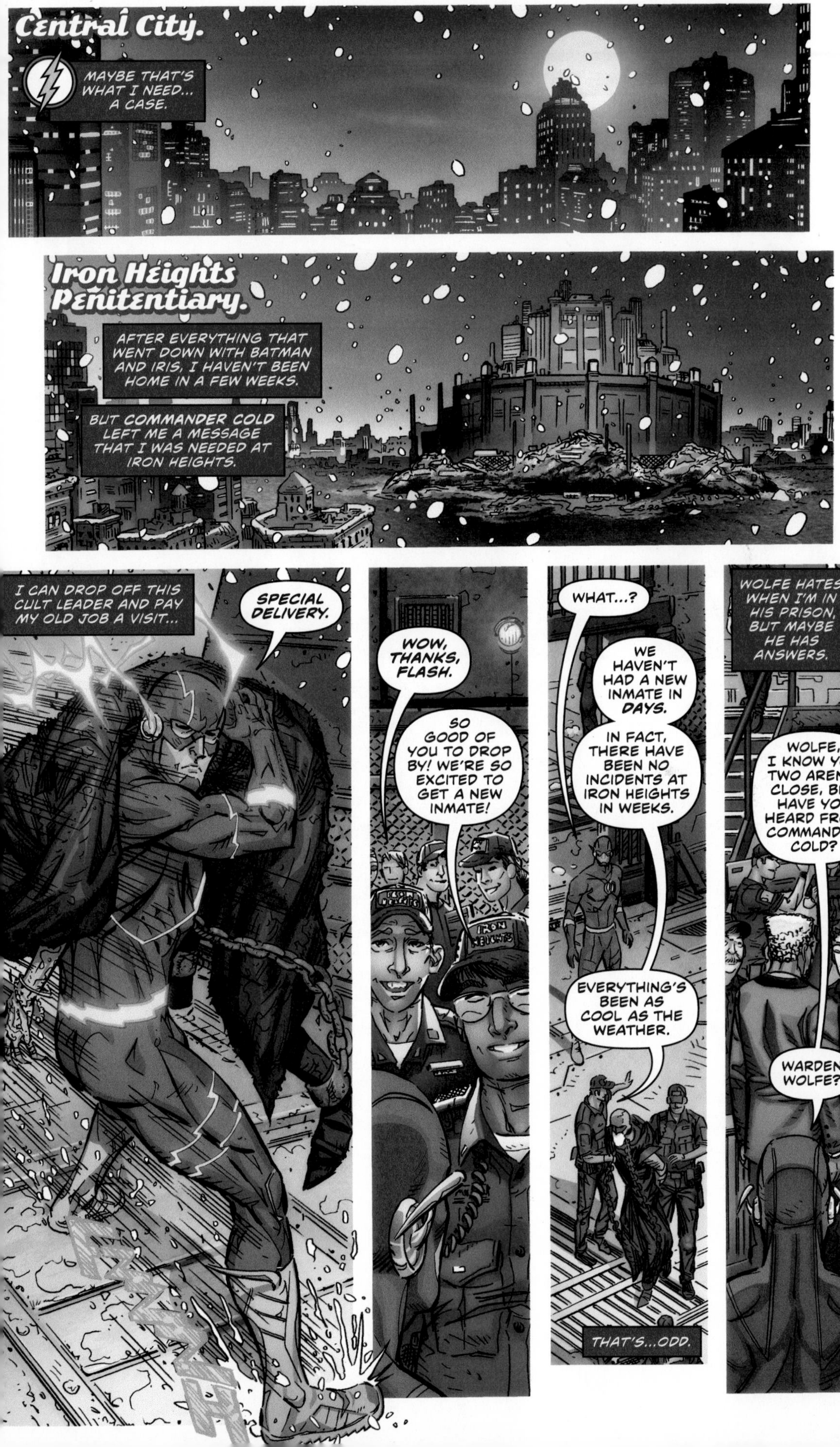
Central City.
MAYBE THAT'S WHAT I NEED... A CASE.
Iron Heights Penitentiary.
AFTER EVERYTHING THAT WENT DOWN WITH BATMAN AND IRIS, I HAVEN'T BEEN HOME IN A FEW WEEKS.
BUT COMMANDER COLD LEFT ME A MESSAGE THAT I WAS NEEDED AT IRON HEIGHTS.
I CAN DROP OFF THIS CULT LEADER AND PAY MY OLD JOB A VISIT...
SPECIAL DELIVERY.
WOW, THANKS, FLASH.
SO GOOD OF YOU TO DROP BY! WE'RE SO EXCITED TO GET A NEW INMATE!
WHAT...?
WE HAVEN'T HAD A NEW INMATE IN DAYS.
IN FACT, THERE HAVE BEEN NO INCIDENTS AT IRON HEIGHTS IN WEEKS.
EVERYTHING'S BEEN AS COOL AS THE WEATHER.
THAT'S...ODD.
WOLFE HATES WHEN I'M IN HIS PRISON, BUT MAYBE HE HAS ANSWERS.
WOLFE, I KNOW YOU TWO AREN'T CLOSE, BUT HAVE YOU HEARD FROM COMMANDER COLD?
WARDEN WOLFE?

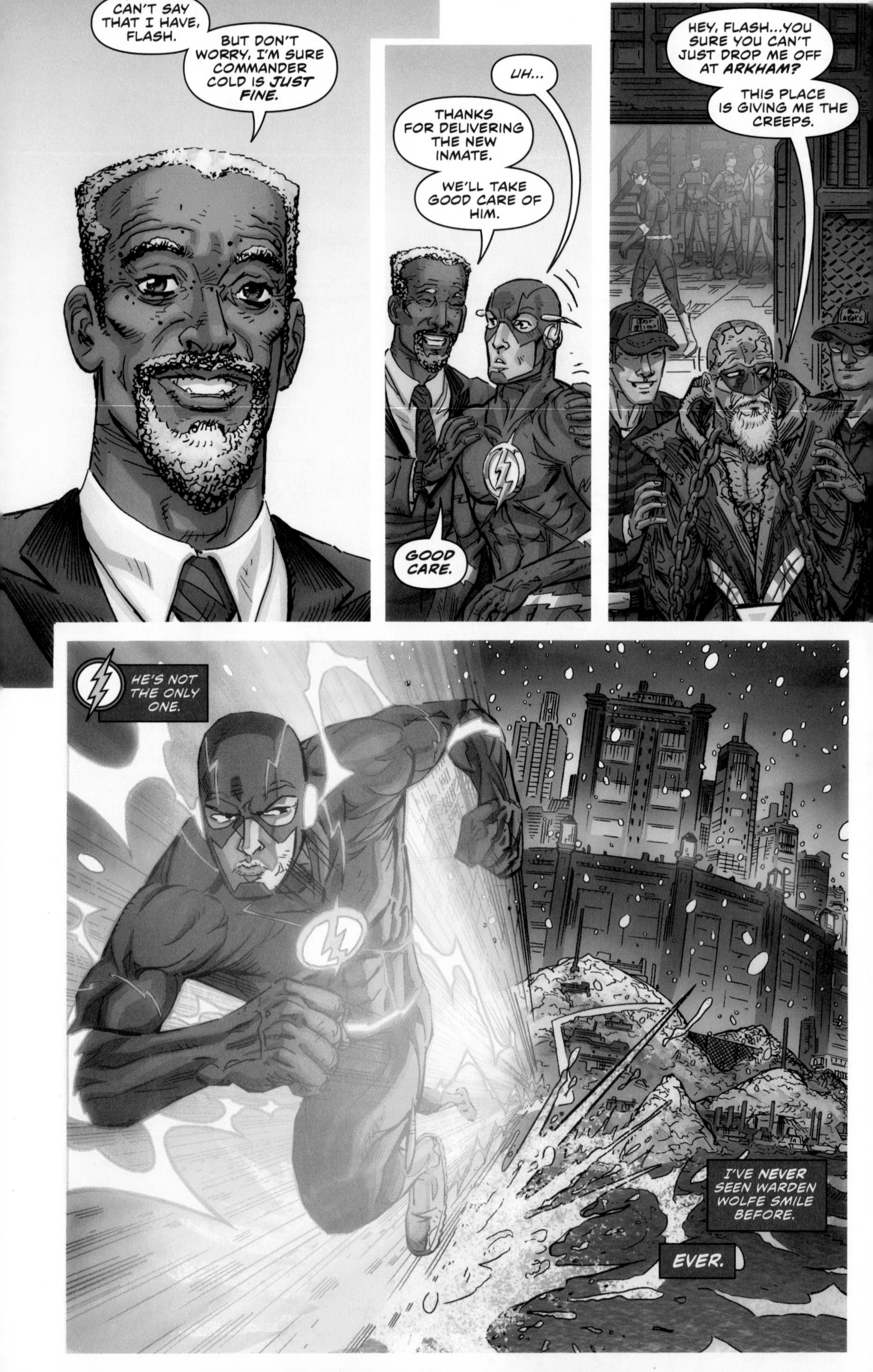
CAN'T SAY THAT I HAVE, FLASH.
BUT DON'T WORRY, I'M SURE COMMANDER COLD IS JUST FINE.
UH...
THANKS FOR DELIVERING THE NEW INMATE.
WE'LL TAKE GOOD CARE OF HIM.
GOOD CARE.
HEY, FLASH...YOU SURE YOU CAN'T JUST DROP ME OFF AT ARKHAM?
THIS PLACE IS GIVING ME THE CREEPS.
HE'S NOT THE ONLY ONE.
I'VE NEVER SEEN WARDEN WOLFE SMILE BEFORE.
EVER.

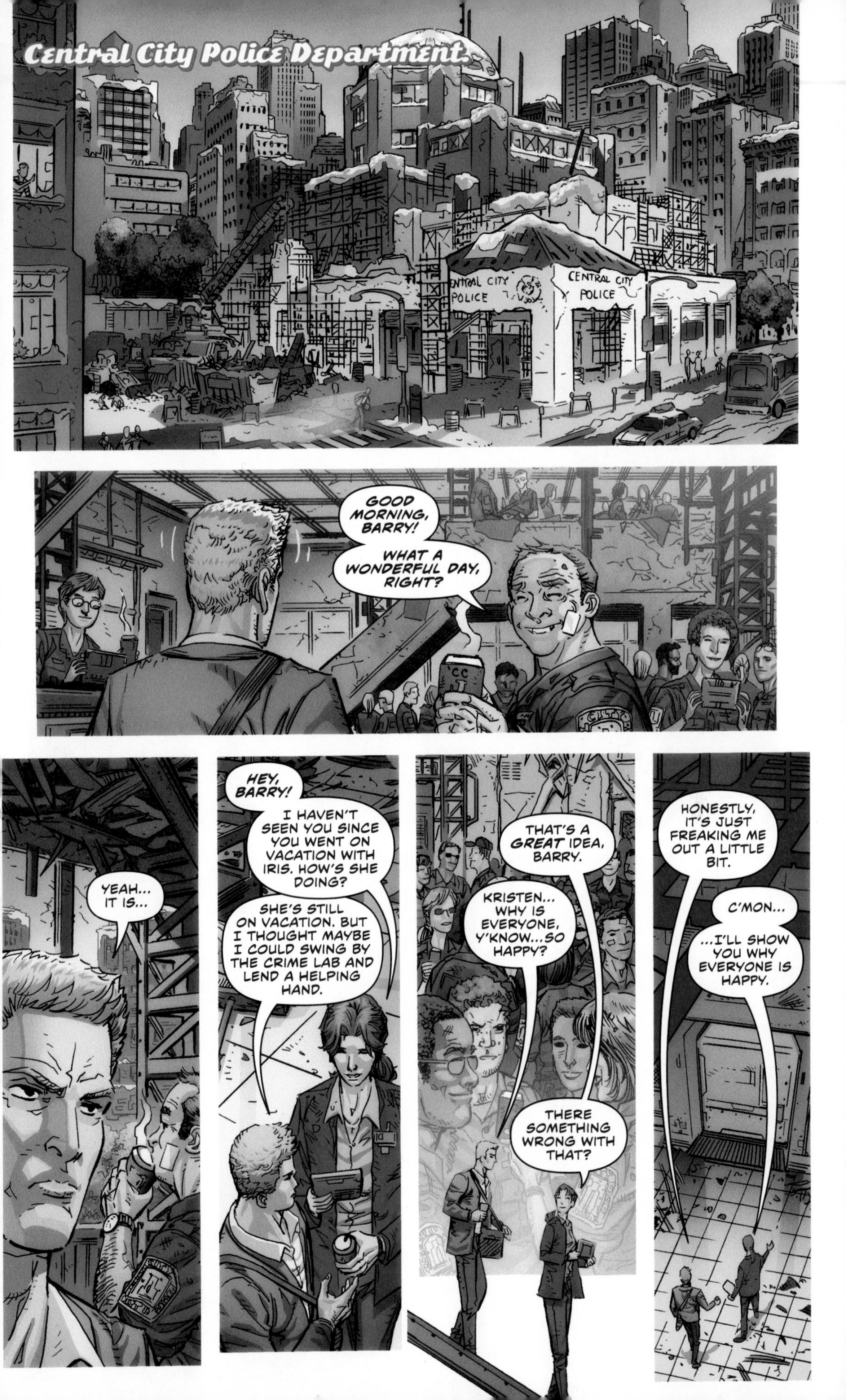
Central City Police Department.
CENTRAL CITY POLICE
CENTRAL CITY POLICE
GOOD MORNING, BARRY!
WHAT A WONDERFUL DAY, RIGHT?
YEAH... IT IS...
HEY, BARRY!
I HAVEN'T SEEN YOU SINCE YOU WENT ON VACATION WITH IRIS. HOW'S SHE DOING?
SHE'S STILL ON VACATION. BUT I THOUGHT MAYBE I COULD SWING BY THE CRIME LAB AND LEND A HELPING HAND.
THAT'S A GREAT IDEA, BARRY.
KRISTEN... WHY IS EVERYONE, Y'KNOW...SO HAPPY?
THERE SOMETHING WRONG WITH THAT?
HONESTLY, IT'S JUST FREAKING ME OUT A LITTLE BIT.
C'MON...
...I'LL SHOW YOU WHY EVERYONE IS HAPPY.

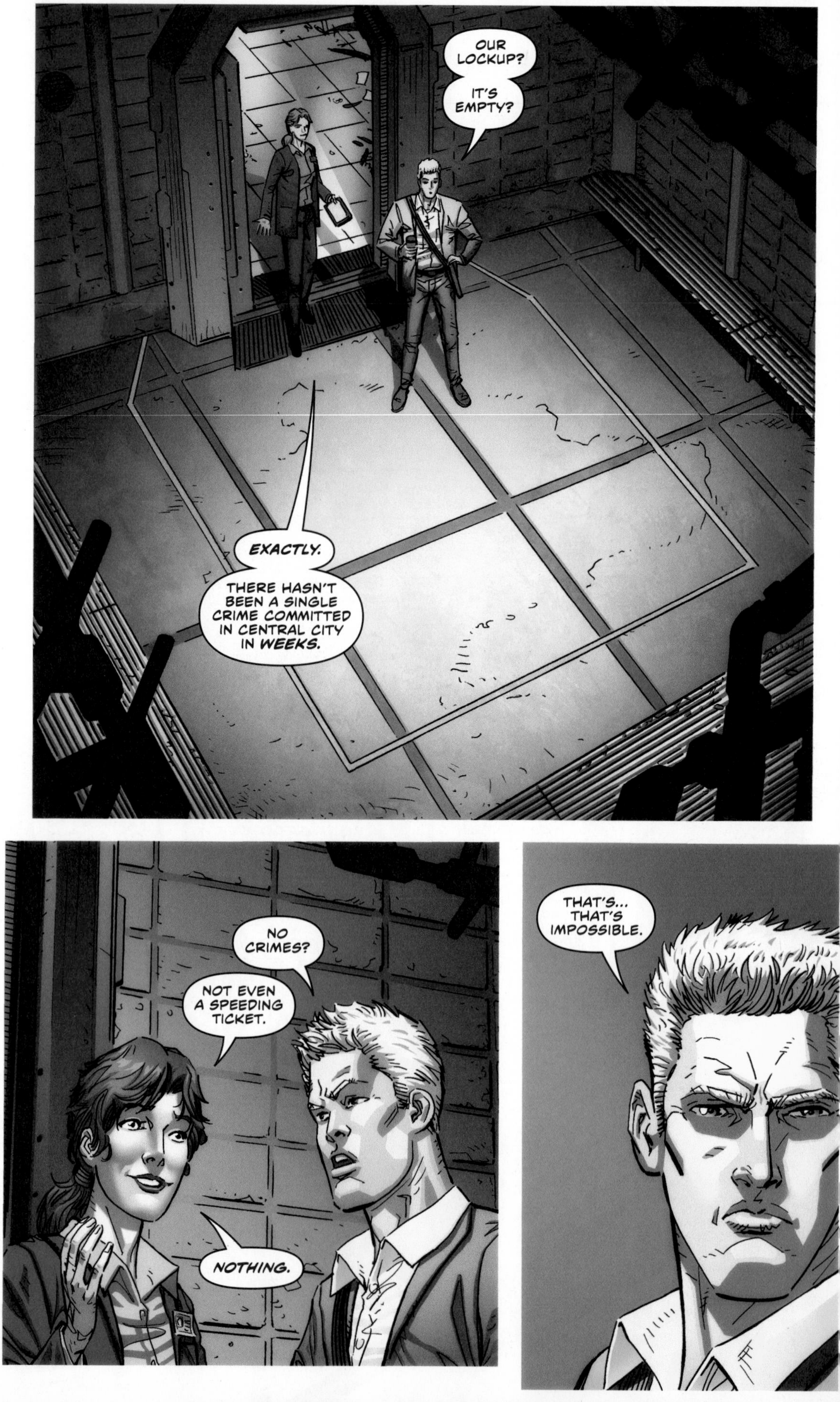
OUR LOCKUP?
IT'S EMPTY?
EXACTLY.
THERE HASN'T BEEN A SINGLE CRIME COMMITTED IN CENTRAL CITY IN *WEEKS.*
NO CRIMES?
NOT EVEN A SPEEDING TICKET.
NOTHING.
THAT'S... THAT'S IMPOSSIBLE.

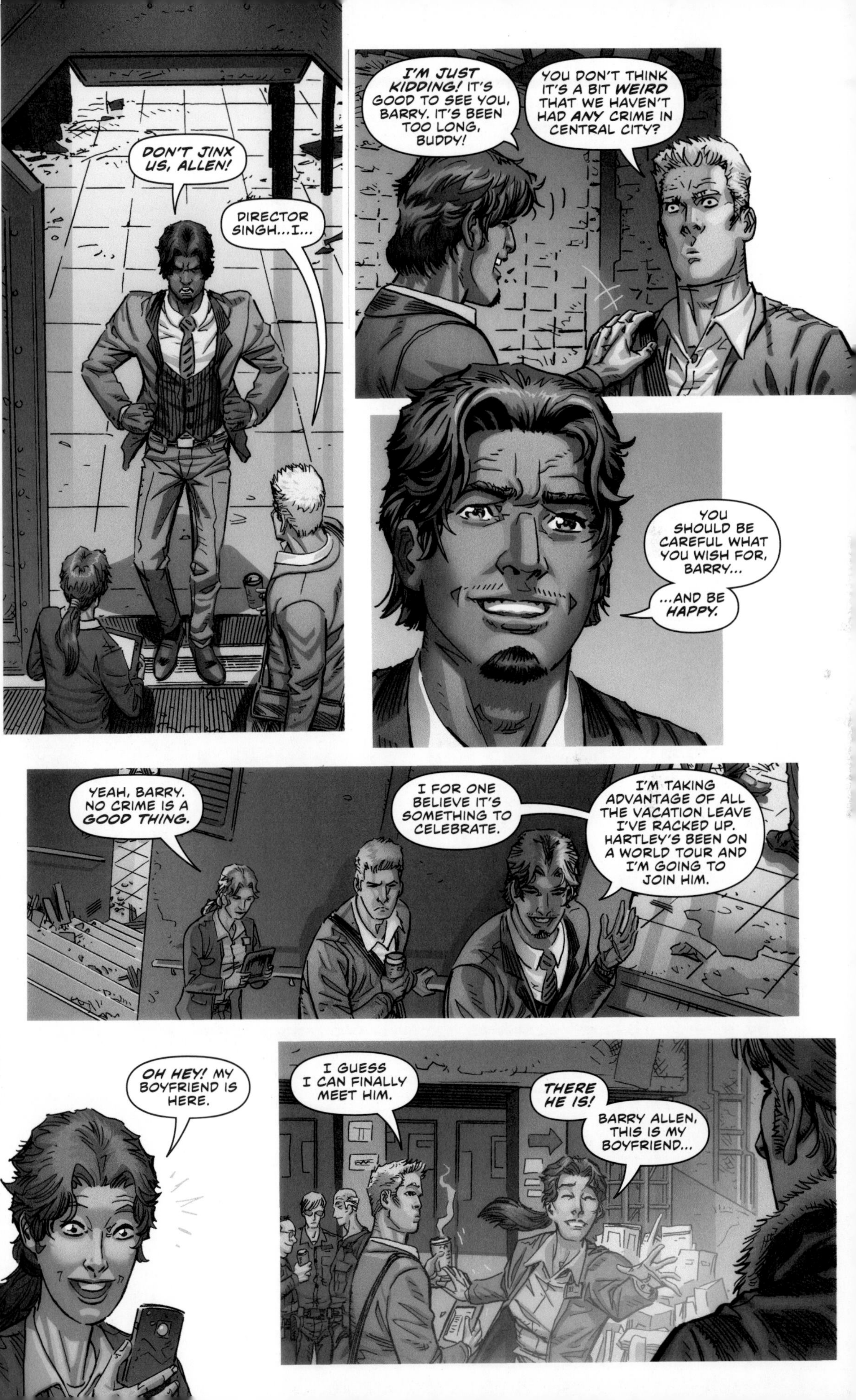
DON'T JINX US, ALLEN!
DIRECTOR SINGH...I...
I'M JUST KIDDING! IT'S GOOD TO SEE YOU, BARRY. IT'S BEEN TOO LONG, BUDDY!
YOU DON'T THINK IT'S A BIT WEIRD THAT WE HAVEN'T HAD ANY CRIME IN CENTRAL CITY?
YOU SHOULD BE CAREFUL WHAT YOU WISH FOR, BARRY...
...AND BE HAPPY.
YEAH, BARRY. NO CRIME IS A GOOD THING.
I FOR ONE BELIEVE IT'S SOMETHING TO CELEBRATE.
I'M TAKING ADVANTAGE OF ALL THE VACATION LEAVE I'VE RACKED UP. HARTLEY'S BEEN ON A WORLD TOUR AND I'M GOING TO JOIN HIM.
OH HEY! MY BOYFRIEND IS HERE.
I GUESS I CAN FINALLY MEET HIM.
THERE HE IS!
BARRY ALLEN, THIS IS MY BOYFRIEND...

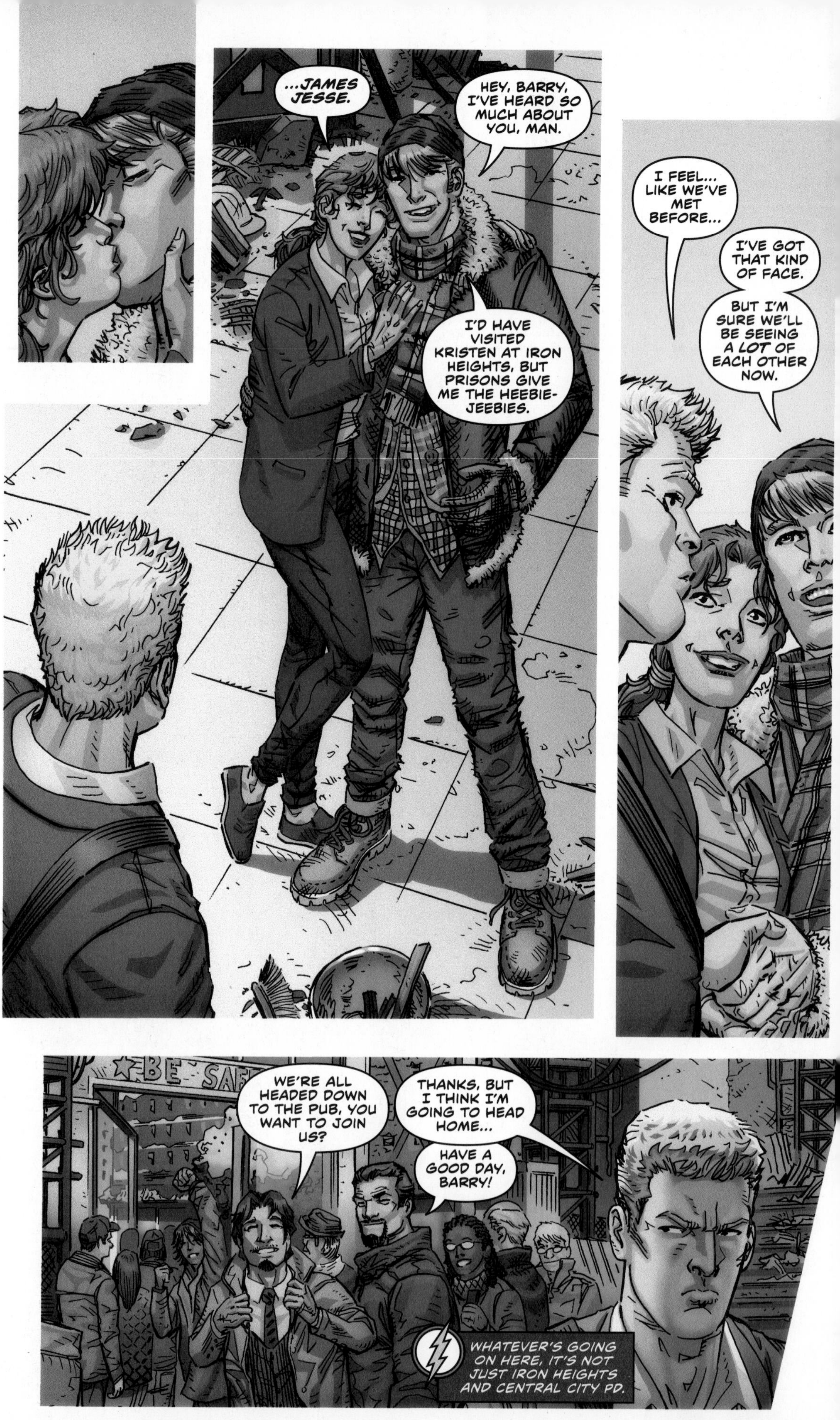
...JAMES JESSE.
HEY, BARRY, I'VE HEARD SO MUCH ABOUT YOU, MAN.
I'D HAVE VISITED KRISTEN AT IRON HEIGHTS, BUT PRISONS GIVE ME THE HEEBIE-JEEBIES.
I FEEL... LIKE WE'VE MET BEFORE...
I'VE GOT THAT KIND OF FACE.
BUT I'M SURE WE'LL BE SEEING A LOT OF EACH OTHER NOW.
WE'RE ALL HEADED DOWN TO THE PUB, YOU WANT TO JOIN US?
THANKS, BUT I THINK I'M GOING TO HEAD HOME...
HAVE A GOOD DAY, BARRY!
WHATEVER'S GOING ON HERE, IT'S NOT JUST IRON HEIGHTS AND CENTRAL CITY PD.

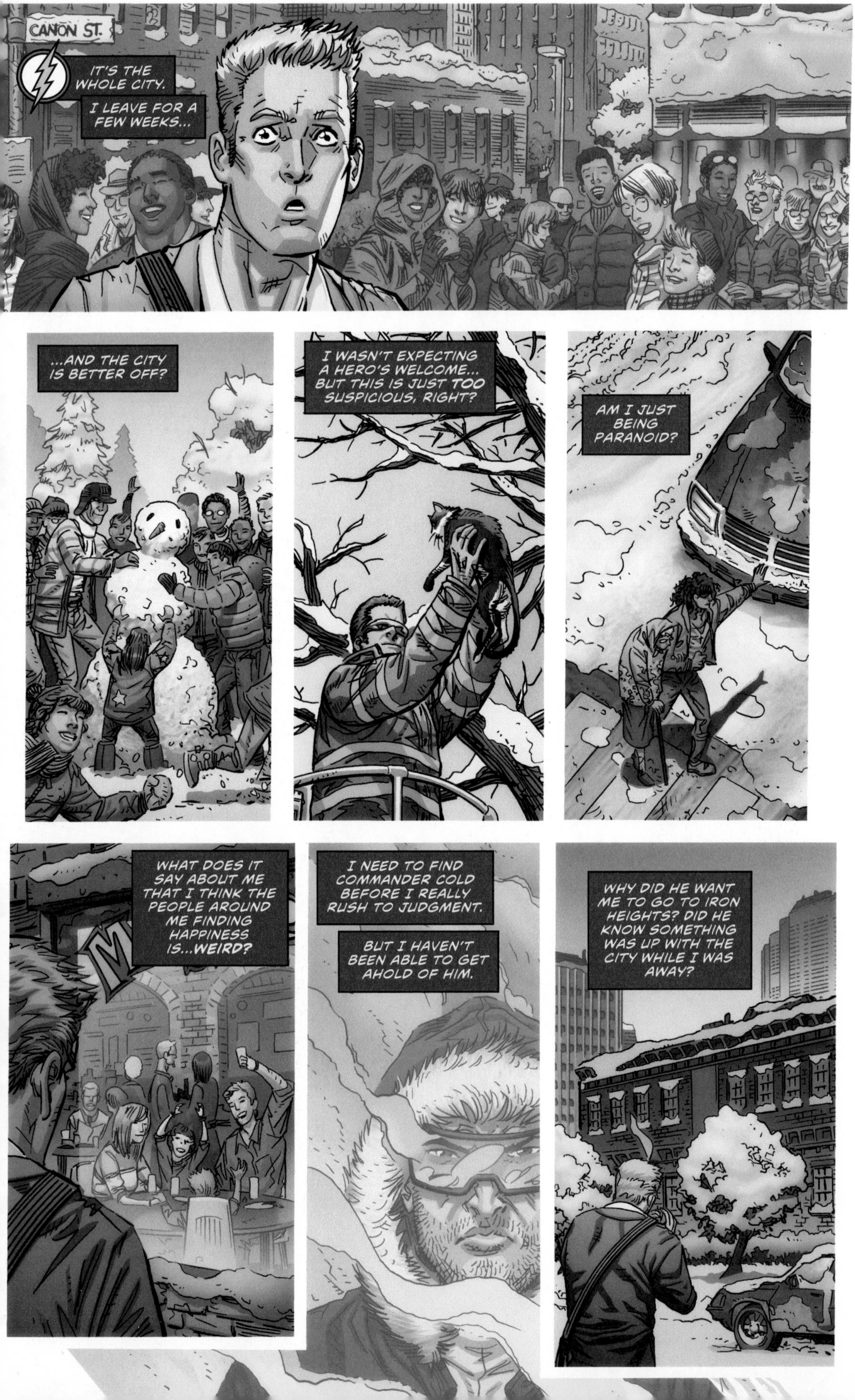
CANON ST.
IT'S THE WHOLE CITY.
I LEAVE FOR A FEW WEEKS...
...AND THE CITY IS BETTER OFF?
I WASN'T EXPECTING A HERO'S WELCOME... BUT THIS IS JUST TOO SUSPICIOUS, RIGHT?
AM I JUST BEING PARANOID?
WHAT DOES IT SAY ABOUT ME THAT I THINK THE PEOPLE AROUND ME FINDING HAPPINESS IS...WEIRD?
I NEED TO FIND COMMANDER COLD BEFORE I REALLY RUSH TO JUDGMENT.
BUT I HAVEN'T BEEN ABLE TO GET AHOLD OF HIM.
WHY DID HE WANT ME TO GO TO IRON HEIGHTS? DID HE KNOW SOMETHING WAS UP WITH THE CITY WHILE I WAS AWAY?

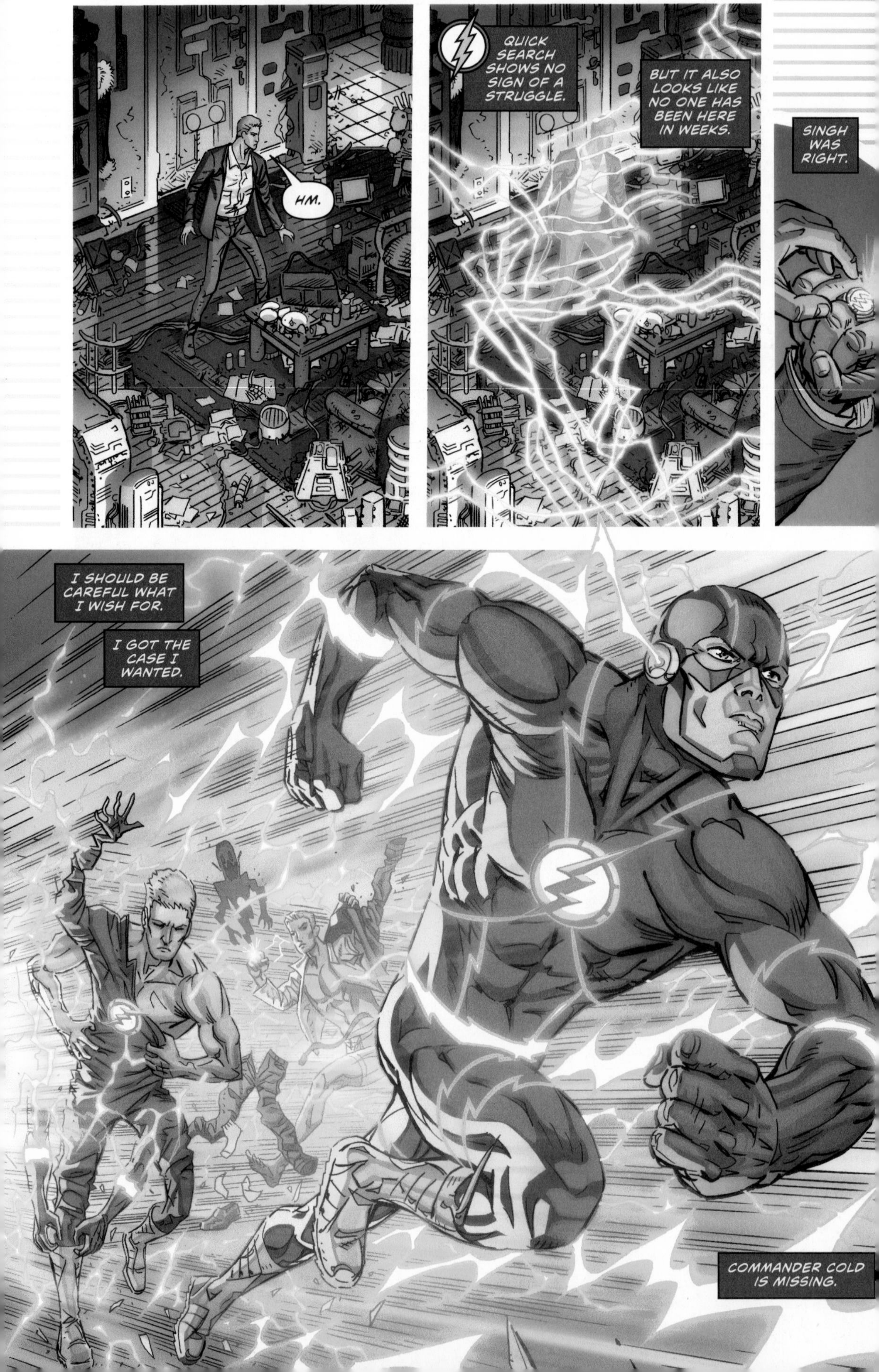
HM.
QUICK SEARCH SHOWS NO SIGN OF A STRUGGLE.
BUT IT ALSO LOOKS LIKE NO ONE HAS BEEN HERE IN WEEKS.
SINGH WAS RIGHT.
I SHOULD BE CAREFUL WHAT I WISH FOR.
I GOT THE CASE I WANTED.
COMMANDER COLD IS MISSING.

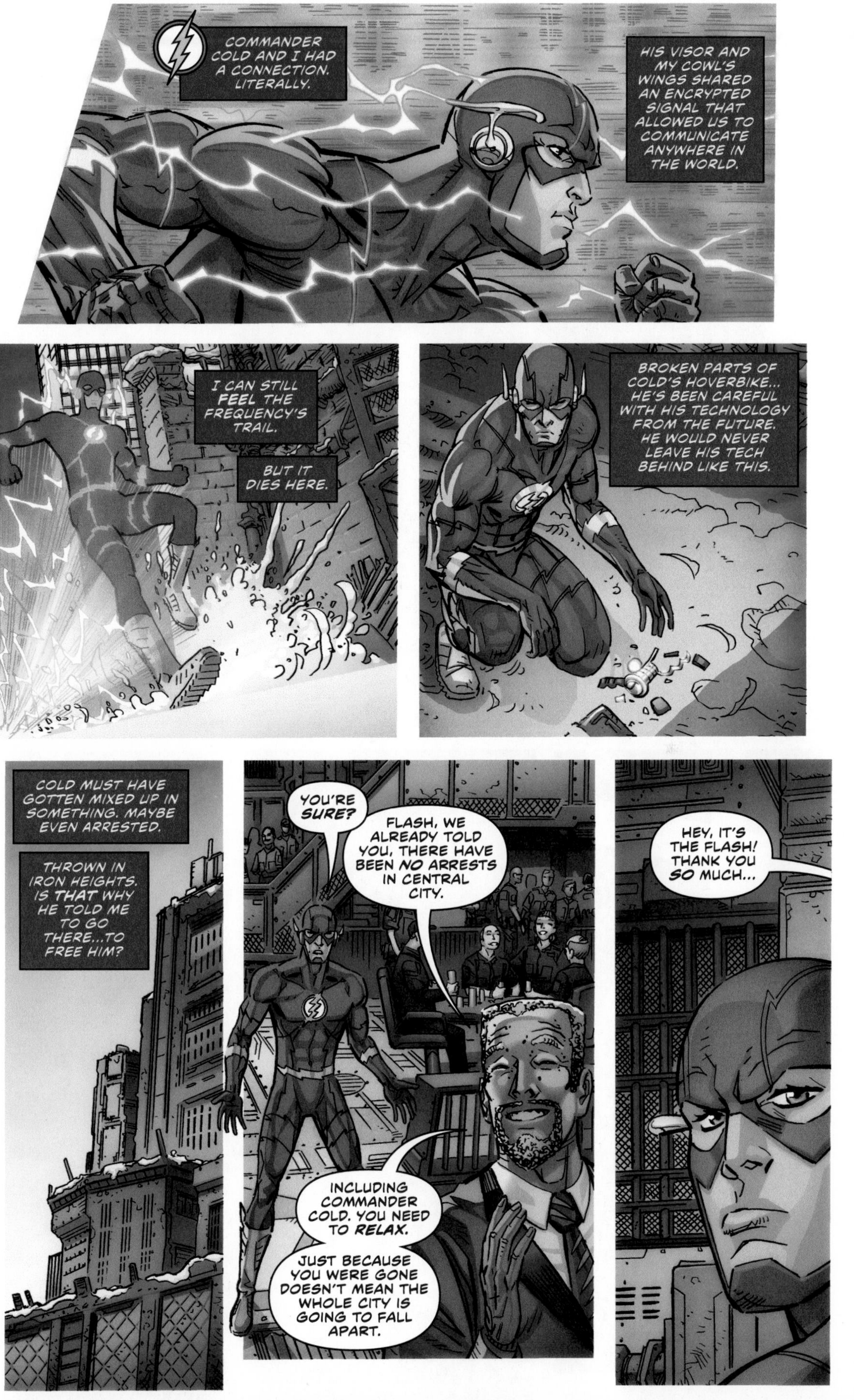

COMMANDER COLD AND I HAD A CONNECTION. LITERALLY.
HIS VISOR AND MY COWL'S WINGS SHARED AN ENCRYPTED SIGNAL THAT ALLOWED US TO COMMUNICATE ANYWHERE IN THE WORLD.
I CAN STILL FEEL THE FREQUENCY'S TRAIL.
BUT IT DIES HERE.
BROKEN PARTS OF COLD'S HOVERBIKE... HE'S BEEN CAREFUL WITH HIS TECHNOLOGY FROM THE FUTURE. HE WOULD NEVER LEAVE HIS TECH BEHIND LIKE THIS.
COLD MUST HAVE GOTTEN MIXED UP IN SOMETHING. MAYBE EVEN ARRESTED.
THROWN IN IRON HEIGHTS. IS THAT WHY HE TOLD ME TO GO THERE...TO FREE HIM?
YOU'RE SURE?
FLASH, WE ALREADY TOLD YOU, THERE HAVE BEEN NO ARRESTS IN CENTRAL CITY.
INCLUDING COMMANDER COLD. YOU NEED TO RELAX.
JUST BECAUSE YOU WERE GONE DOESN'T MEAN THE WHOLE CITY IS GOING TO FALL APART.
HEY, IT'S THE FLASH! THANK YOU SO MUCH...

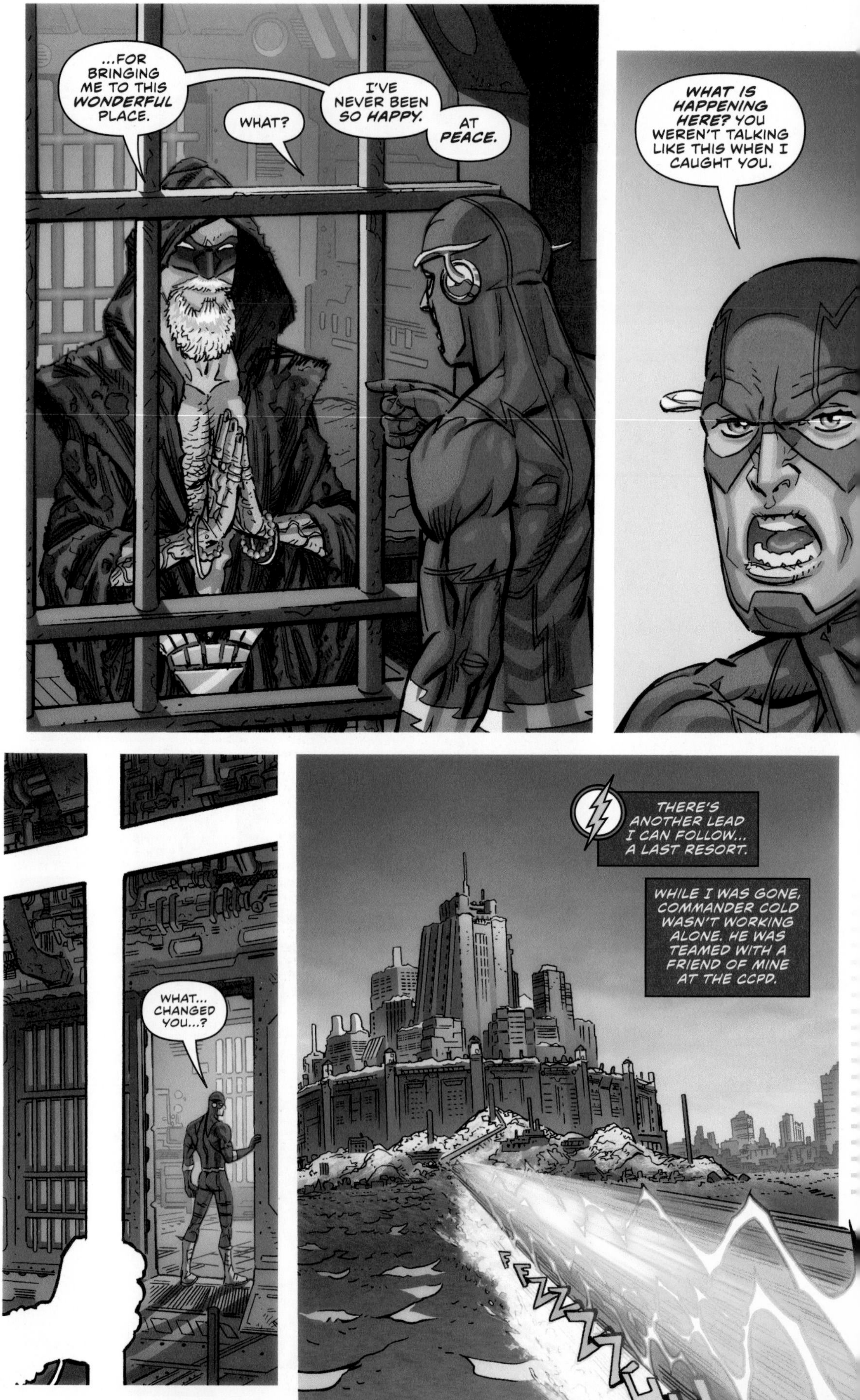
...FOR BRINGING ME TO THIS WONDERFUL PLACE.
WHAT?
I'VE NEVER BEEN SO HAPPY.
AT PEACE.
WHAT IS HAPPENING HERE? YOU WEREN'T TALKING LIKE THIS WHEN I CAUGHT YOU.
WHAT... CHANGED YOU...?
THERE'S ANOTHER LEAD I CAN FOLLOW... A LAST RESORT.
WHILE I WAS GONE, COMMANDER COLD WASN'T WORKING ALONE. HE WAS TEAMED WITH A FRIEND OF MINE AT THE CCPD.
FFZZZZHH

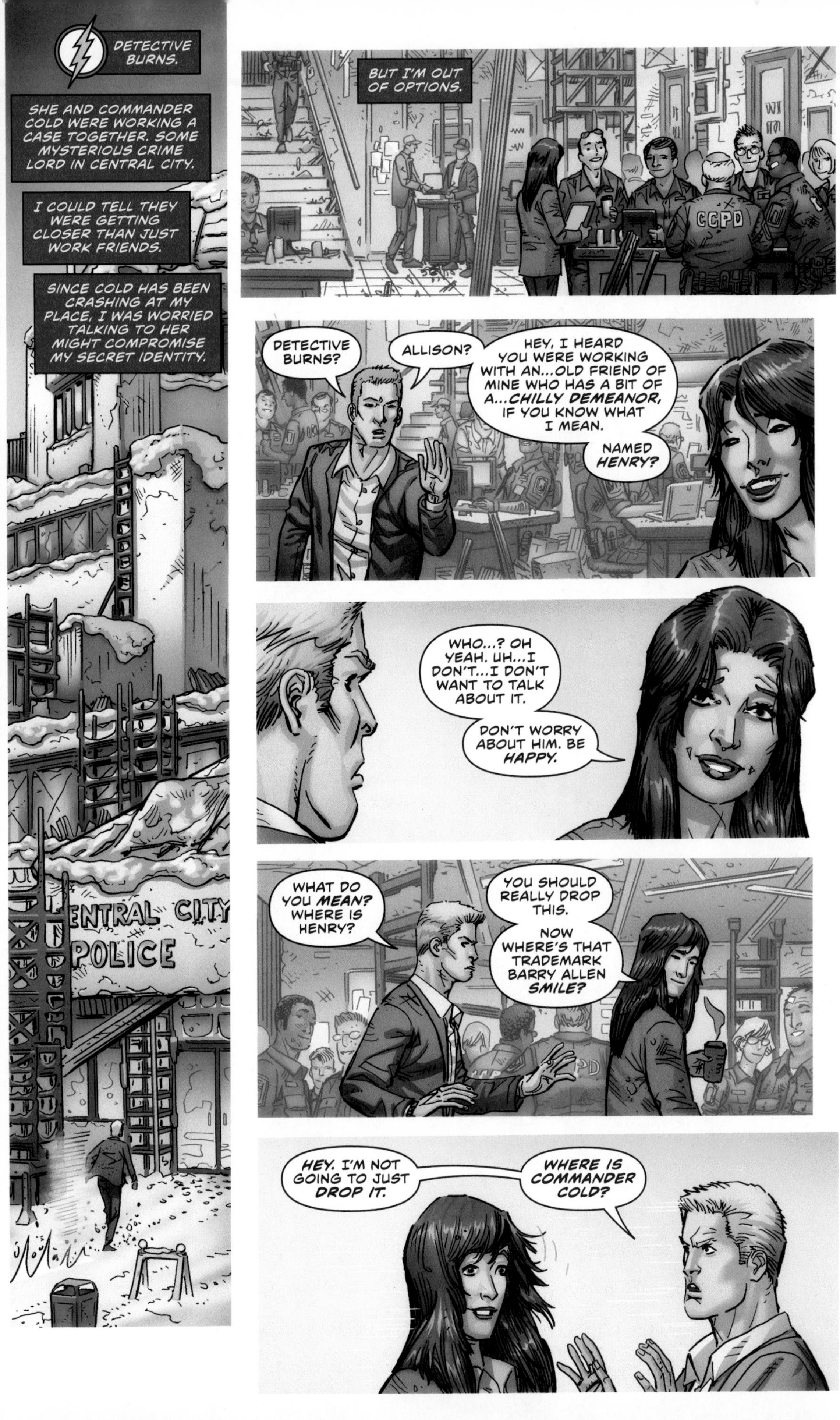
DETECTIVE BURNS.
SHE AND COMMANDER COLD WERE WORKING A CASE TOGETHER. SOME MYSTERIOUS CRIME LORD IN CENTRAL CITY.
I COULD TELL THEY WERE GETTING CLOSER THAN JUST WORK FRIENDS.
SINCE COLD HAS BEEN CRASHING AT MY PLACE, I WAS WORRIED TALKING TO HER MIGHT COMPROMISE MY SECRET IDENTITY.
CENTRAL CITY POLICE
BUT I'M OUT OF OPTIONS.
CCPD
DETECTIVE BURNS?
ALLISON?
HEY, I HEARD YOU WERE WORKING WITH AN...OLD FRIEND OF MINE WHO HAS A BIT OF A...CHILLY DEMEANOR, IF YOU KNOW WHAT I MEAN.
NAMED HENRY?
WHO...? OH YEAH. UH...I DON'T...I DON'T WANT TO TALK ABOUT IT.
DON'T WORRY ABOUT HIM. BE HAPPY.
WHAT DO YOU MEAN? WHERE IS HENRY?
YOU SHOULD REALLY DROP THIS.
NOW WHERE'S THAT TRADEMARK BARRY ALLEN SMILE?
HEY. I'M NOT GOING TO JUST DROP IT.
WHERE IS COMMANDER COLD?

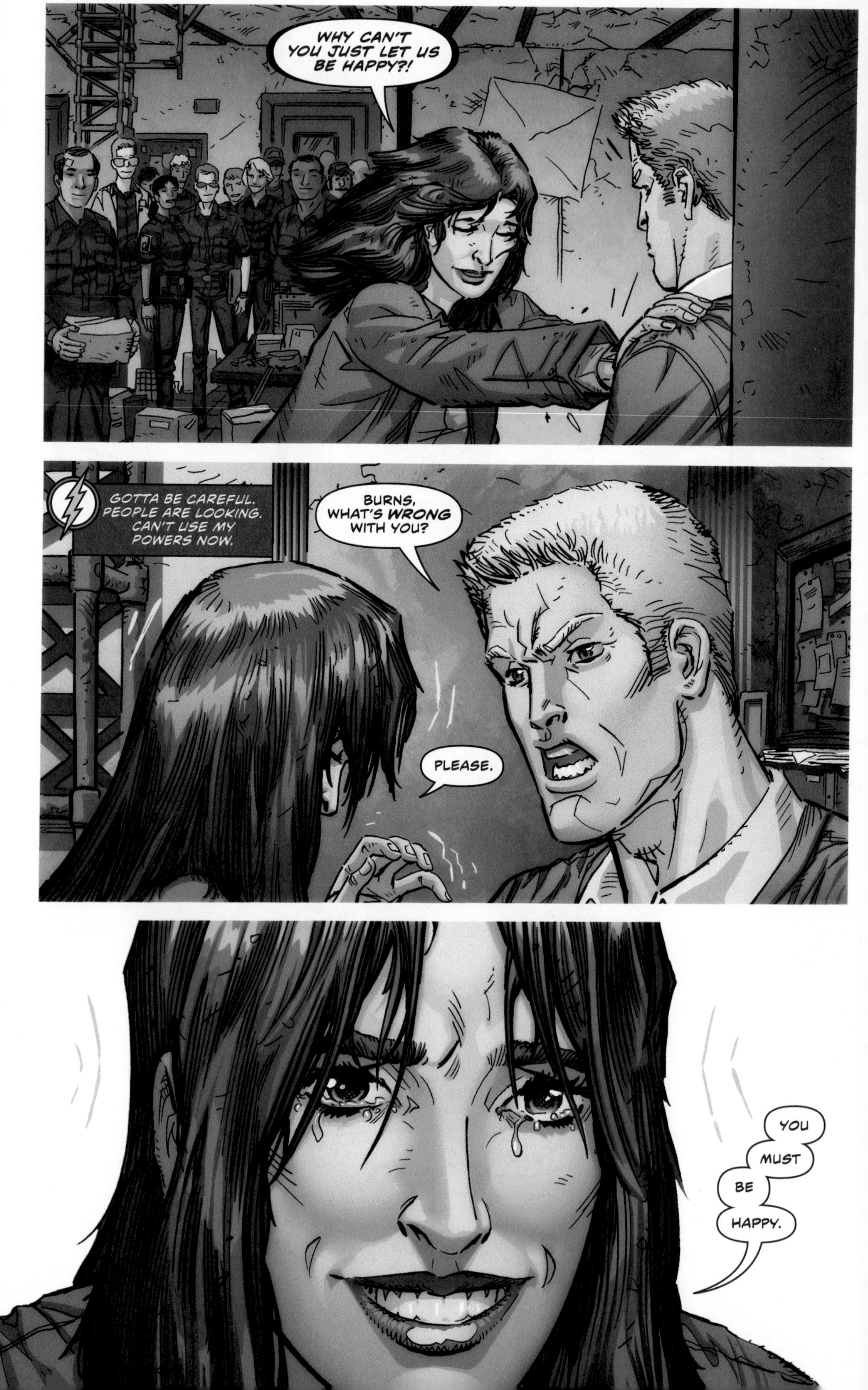
WHY CAN'T YOU JUST LET US BE HAPPY?!
GOTTA BE CAREFUL. PEOPLE ARE LOOKING. CAN'T USE MY POWERS NOW.
BURNS, WHAT'S *WRONG* WITH YOU?
PLEASE.
YOU
MUST
BE
HAPPY.

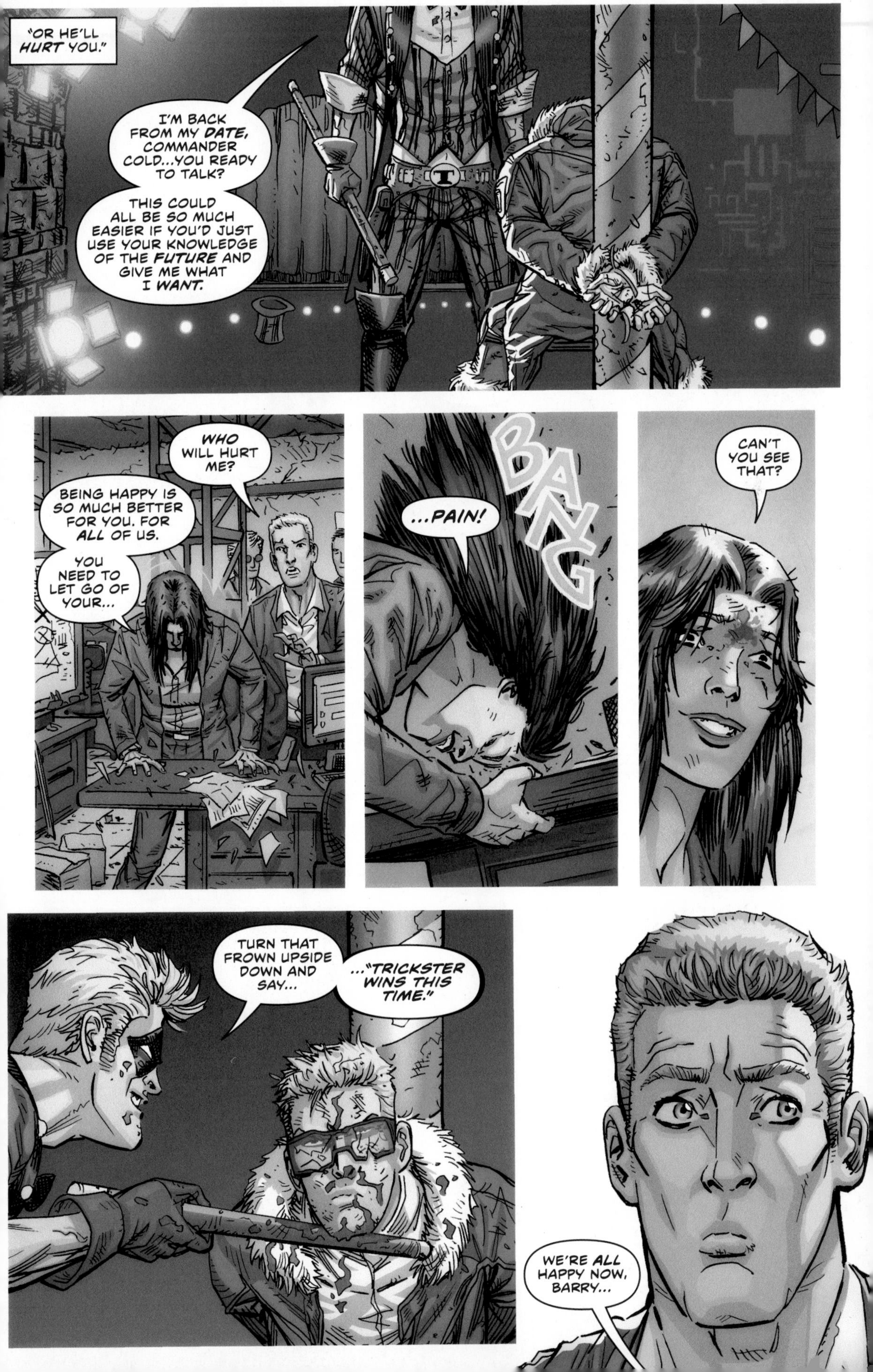
"OR HE'LL HURT YOU."
I'M BACK FROM MY DATE, COMMANDER COLD...YOU READY TO TALK?
THIS COULD ALL BE SO MUCH EASIER IF YOU'D JUST USE YOUR KNOWLEDGE OF THE FUTURE AND GIVE ME WHAT I WANT.
WHO WILL HURT ME?
BEING HAPPY IS SO MUCH BETTER FOR YOU. FOR ALL OF US.
YOU NEED TO LET GO OF YOUR...
...PAIN!
BANG
CAN'T YOU SEE THAT?
TURN THAT FROWN UPSIDE DOWN AND SAY...
..."TRICKSTER WINS THIS TIME."
WE'RE ALL HAPPY NOW, BARRY...

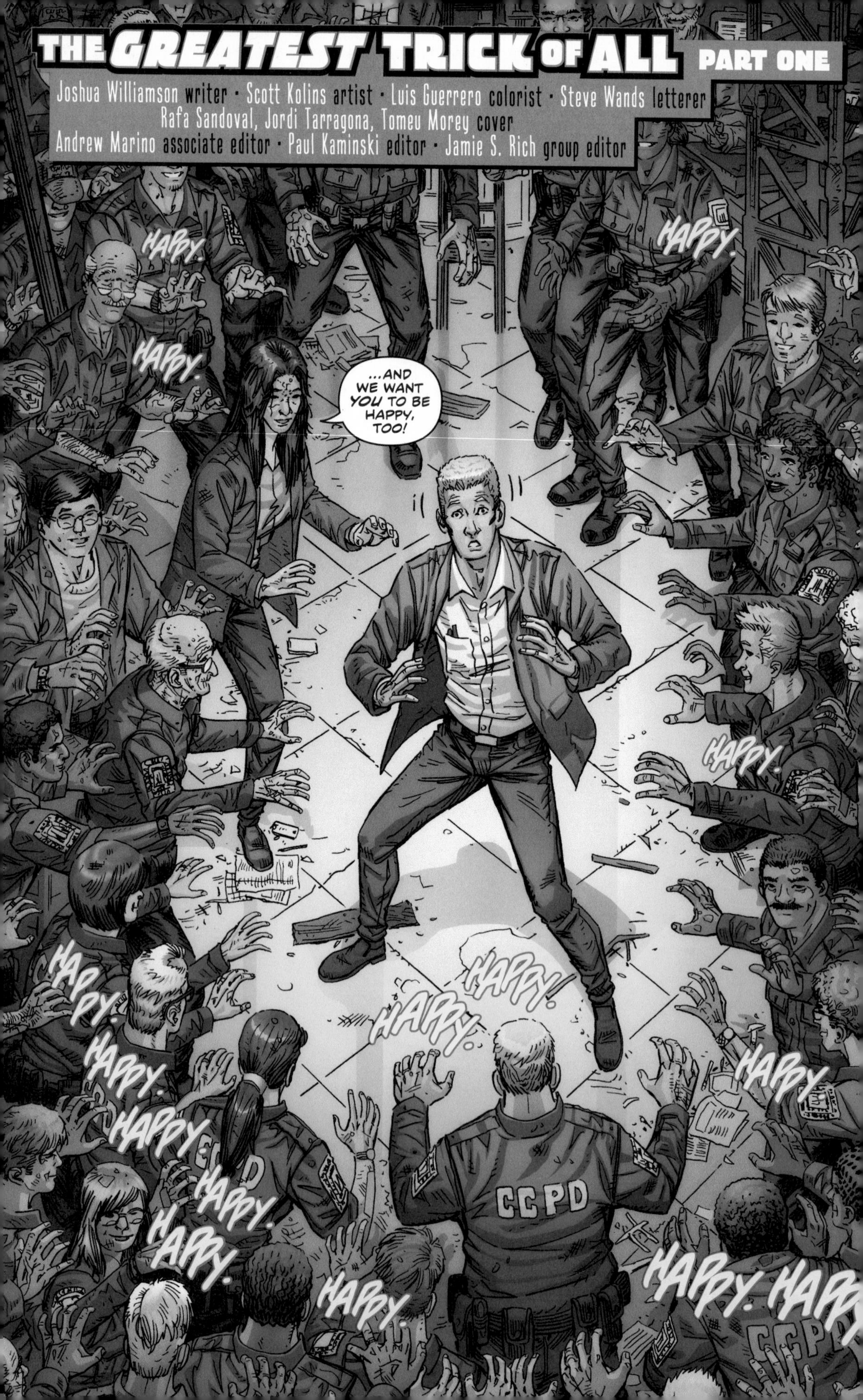
THE GREATEST TRICK OF ALL PART ONE
Joshua Williamson writer · Scott Kolins artist · Luis Guerrero colorist · Steve Wands letterer
Rafa Sandoval, Jordi Tarragona, Tomeu Morey cover
Andrew Marino associate editor · Paul Kaminski editor · Jamie S. Rich group editor
HAPPY.
HAPPY.
HAPPY.
...AND WE WANT YOU TO BE HAPPY, TOO!
HAPPY.
HAPPY.
HAPPY.
HAPPY.
HAPPY.
HAPPY.
HAPPY!
HAPPY.
HAPPY.
HAPPY.
HAPPY.
CCPD

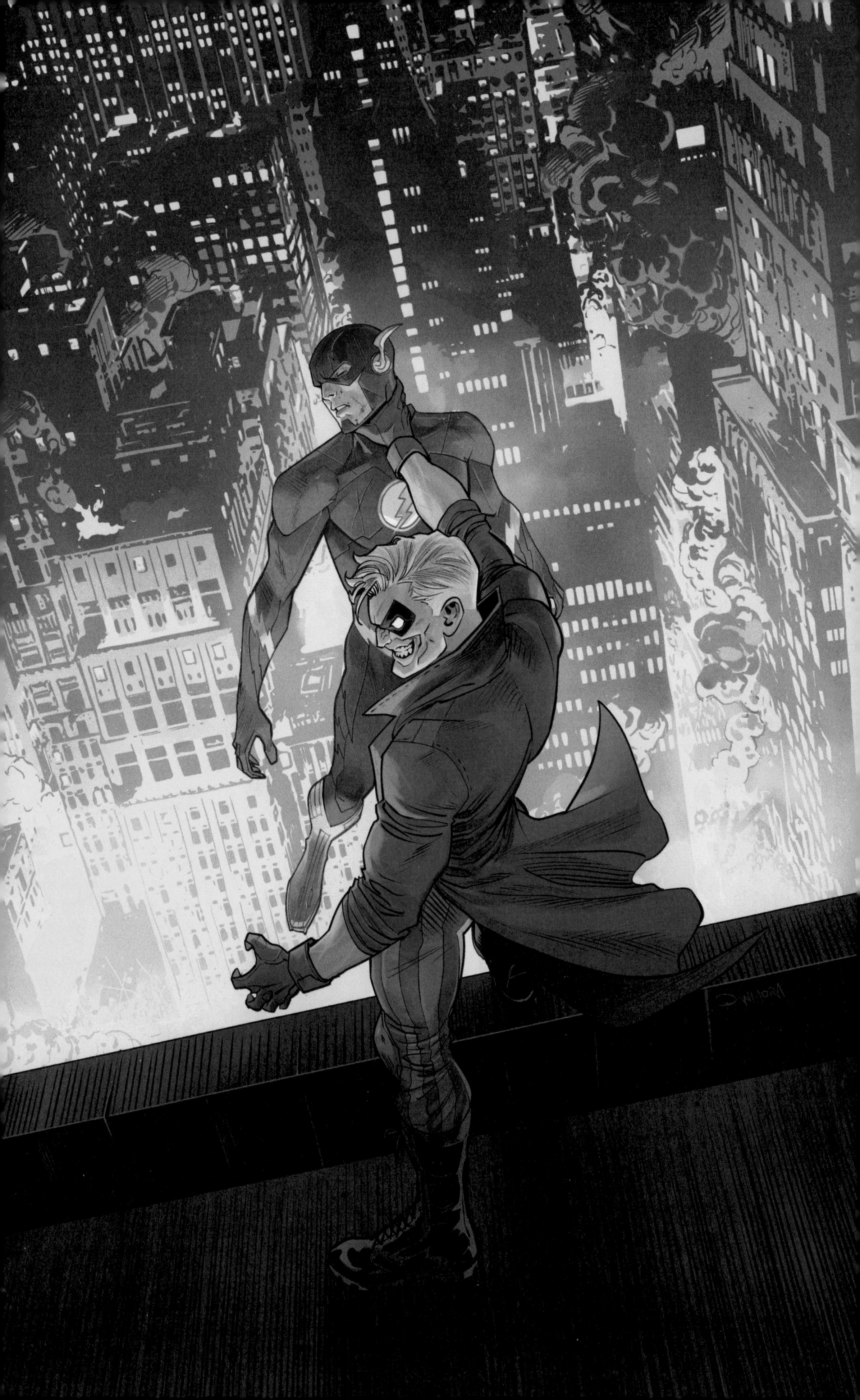

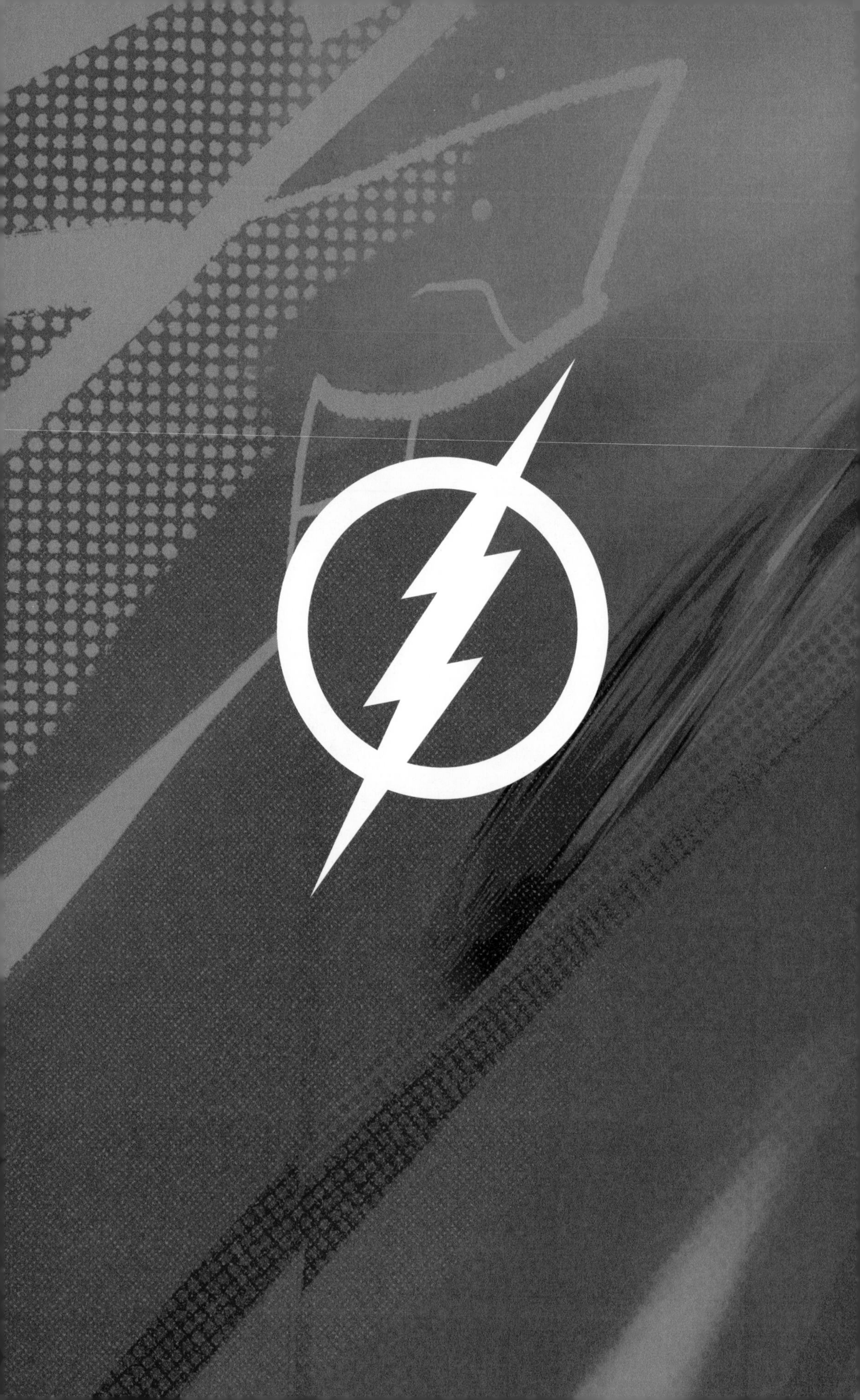

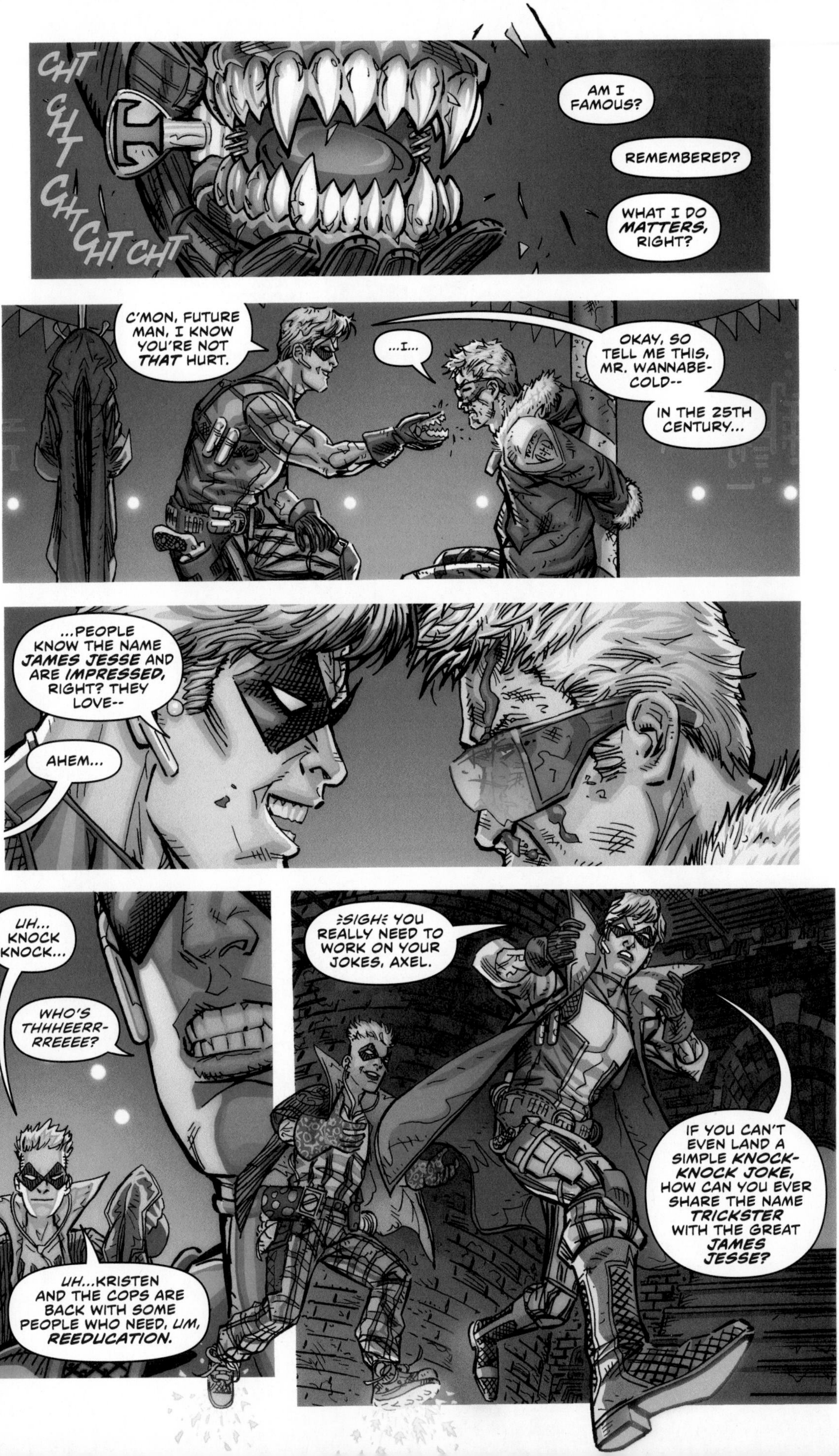
CHT CHT CHT CHT CHT CHT
AM I FAMOUS?
REMEMBERED?
WHAT I DO *MATTERS,* RIGHT?
C'MON, FUTURE MAN, I KNOW YOU'RE NOT *THAT* HURT.
...I...
OKAY, SO TELL ME THIS, MR. WANNABE-COLD--
IN THE 25TH CENTURY...
...PEOPLE KNOW THE NAME *JAMES JESSE* AND ARE *IMPRESSED,* RIGHT? THEY LOVE--
AHEM...
UH... KNOCK KNOCK...
WHO'S THHHEERR-RREEEE?
*UH...*KRISTEN AND THE COPS ARE BACK WITH SOME PEOPLE WHO NEED, *UM,* *REEDUCATION.*
SIGH YOU REALLY NEED TO WORK ON YOUR JOKES, AXEL.
IF YOU CAN'T EVEN LAND A SIMPLE *KNOCK-KNOCK JOKE,* HOW CAN YOU EVER SHARE THE NAME *TRICKSTER* WITH THE GREAT *JAMES JESSE?*

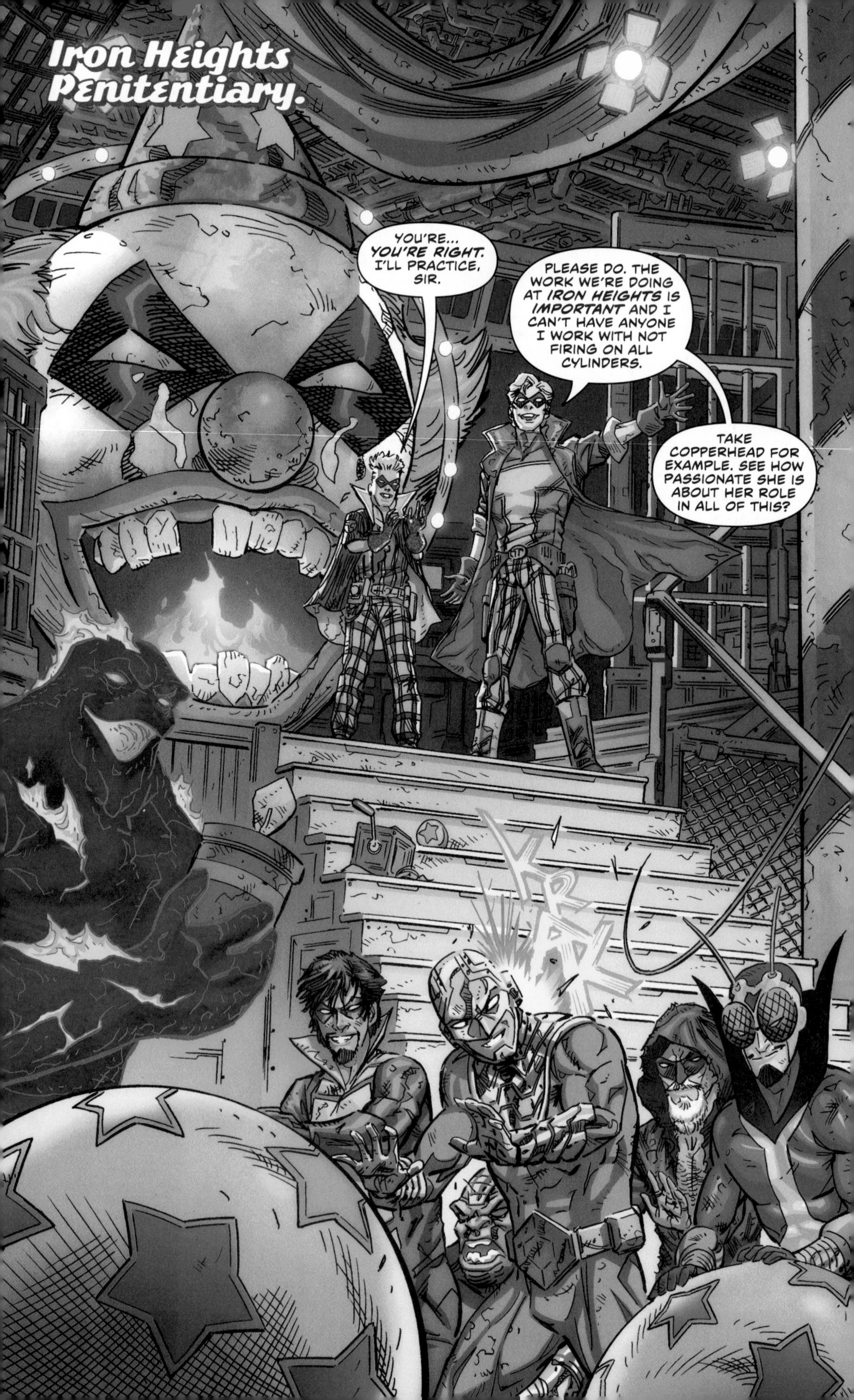
Iron Heights Penitentiary.
YOU'RE... YOU'RE RIGHT. I'LL PRACTICE, SIR.
PLEASE DO. THE WORK WE'RE DOING AT IRON HEIGHTS IS IMPORTANT AND I CAN'T HAVE ANYONE I WORK WITH NOT FIRING ON ALL CYLINDERS.
TAKE COPPERHEAD FOR EXAMPLE. SEE HOW PASSIONATE SHE IS ABOUT HER ROLE IN ALL OF THIS?

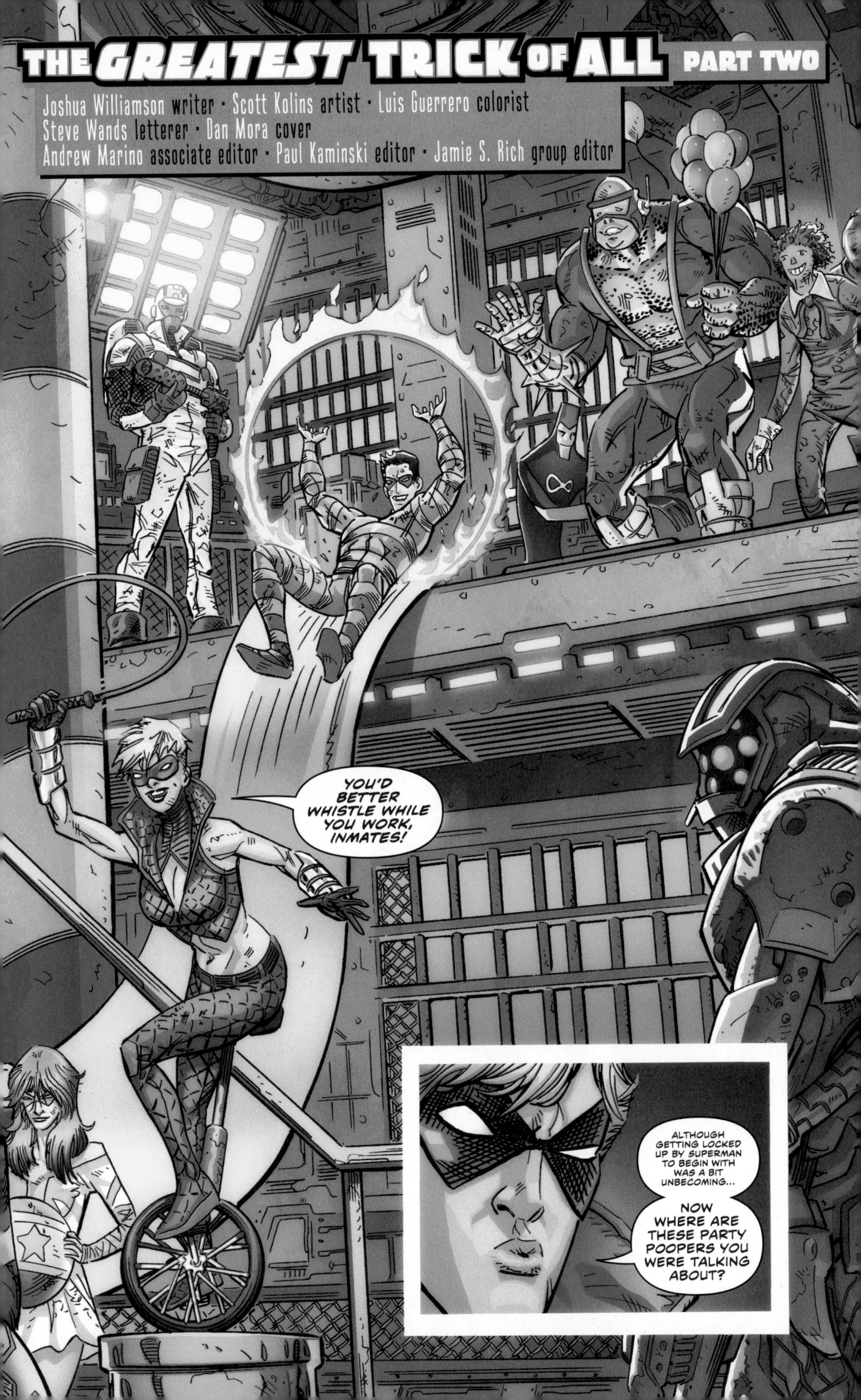
THE GREATEST TRICK OF ALL PART TWO
Joshua Williamson writer · Scott Kolins artist · Luis Guerrero colorist
Steve Wands letterer · Dan Mora cover
Andrew Marino associate editor · Paul Kaminski editor · Jamie S. Rich group editor
YOU'D BETTER WHISTLE WHILE YOU WORK, INMATES!
ALTHOUGH GETTING LOCKED UP BY SUPERMAN TO BEGIN WITH WAS A BIT UNBECOMING...
NOW WHERE ARE THESE PARTY POOPERS YOU WERE TALKING ABOUT?

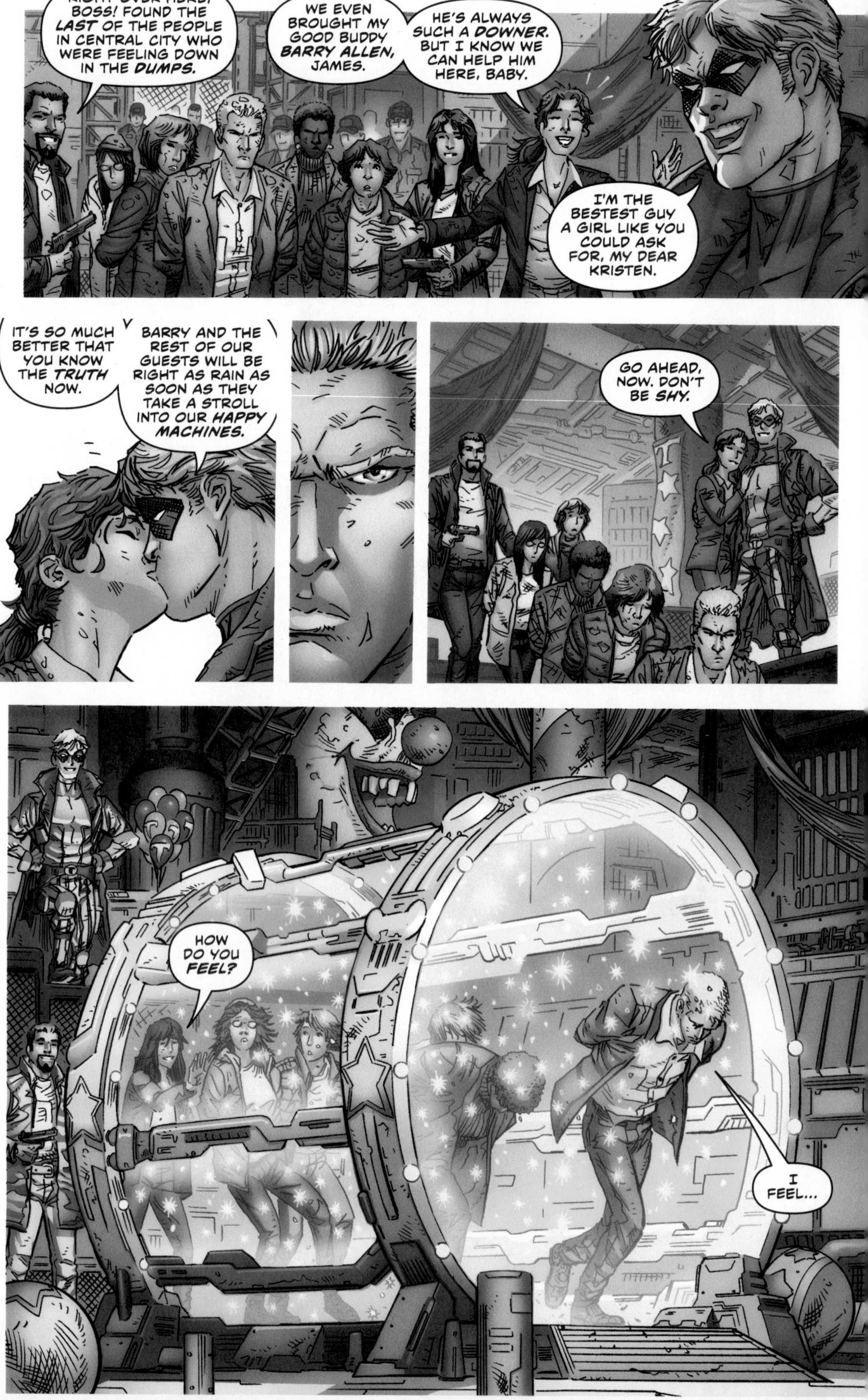
RIGHT OVER HERE, BOSS! FOUND THE LAST OF THE PEOPLE IN CENTRAL CITY WHO WERE FEELING DOWN IN THE DUMPS.
WE EVEN BROUGHT MY GOOD BUDDY BARRY ALLEN, JAMES.
HE'S ALWAYS SUCH A DOWNER. BUT I KNOW WE CAN HELP HIM HERE, BABY.
I'M THE BESTEST GUY A GIRL LIKE YOU COULD ASK FOR, MY DEAR KRISTEN.
IT'S SO MUCH BETTER THAT YOU KNOW THE TRUTH NOW.
BARRY AND THE REST OF OUR GUESTS WILL BE RIGHT AS RAIN AS SOON AS THEY TAKE A STROLL INTO OUR HAPPY MACHINES.
GO AHEAD, NOW. DON'T BE SHY.
HOW DO YOU FEEL?
I FEEL...

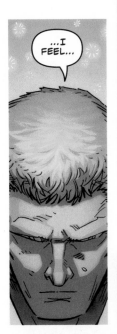

...I FEEL...

...HAPPY.

ISN'T THAT SO MUCH BETTER, BARRY?

DOESN'T IT FEEL *GREAT* TO BE *HAPPY*?

SO HAPPY.

OKIE DOKIE, FOLKS. FOLLOW ME AND WE'LL GET YOU BACK HOME SO YOU CAN KEEP ON LIVING A LIFE OF JOY AND HAPPINESS.

WE'RE WALKING, WE'RE WALKING.

SO HAPPY. SO SO SO...

...HAPPY...

EVERYONE IN CENTRAL CITY HAS FOUND HAPPINESS...

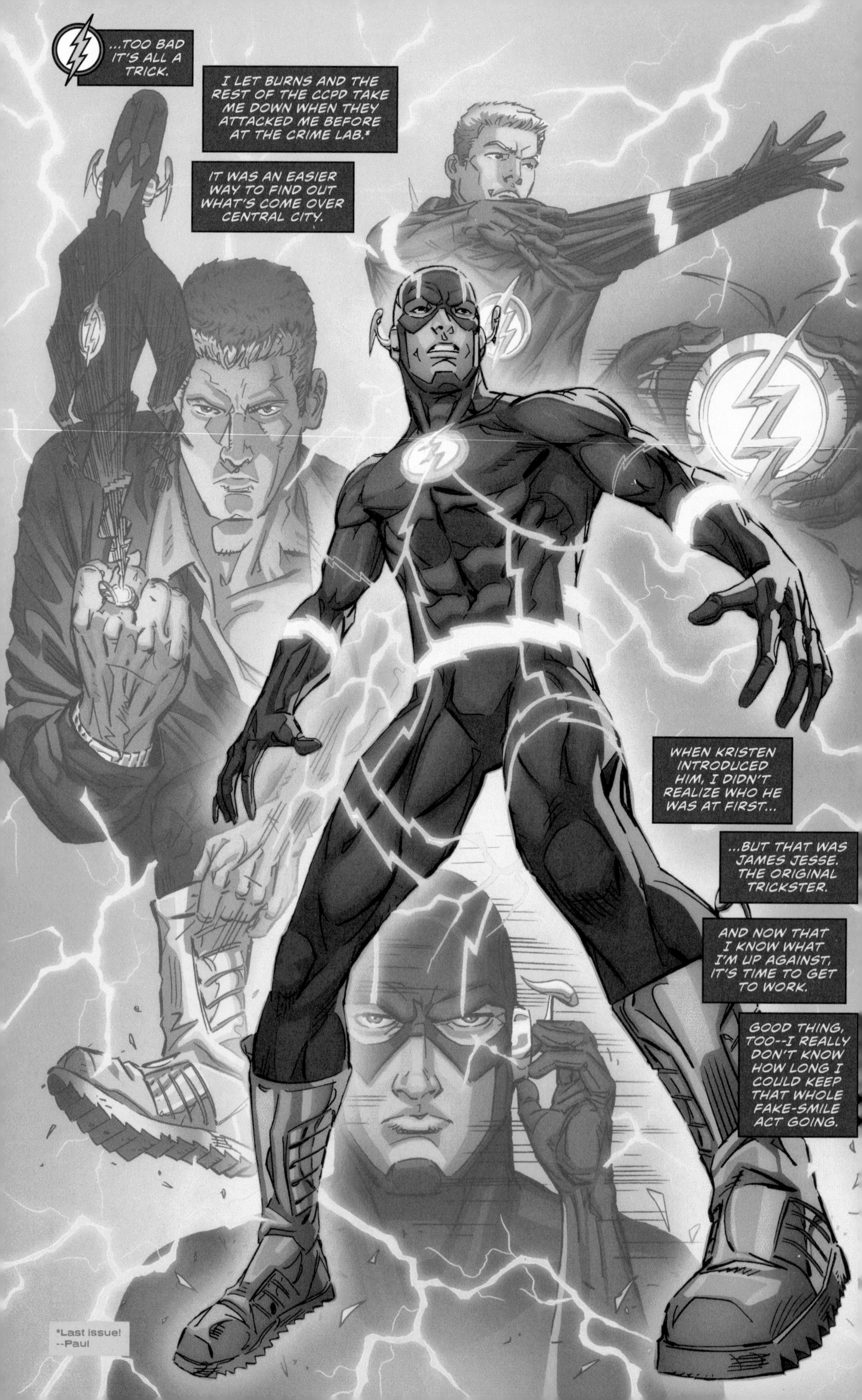
...TOO BAD IT'S ALL A TRICK.
I LET BURNS AND THE REST OF THE CCPD TAKE ME DOWN WHEN THEY ATTACKED ME BEFORE AT THE CRIME LAB.*
IT WAS AN EASIER WAY TO FIND OUT WHAT'S COME OVER CENTRAL CITY.
WHEN KRISTEN INTRODUCED HIM, I DIDN'T REALIZE WHO HE WAS AT FIRST...
...BUT THAT WAS JAMES JESSE. THE ORIGINAL TRICKSTER.
AND NOW THAT I KNOW WHAT I'M UP AGAINST, IT'S TIME TO GET TO WORK.
GOOD THING, TOO--I REALLY DON'T KNOW HOW LONG I COULD KEEP THAT WHOLE FAKE-SMILE ACT GOING.
*Last issue!
--Paul

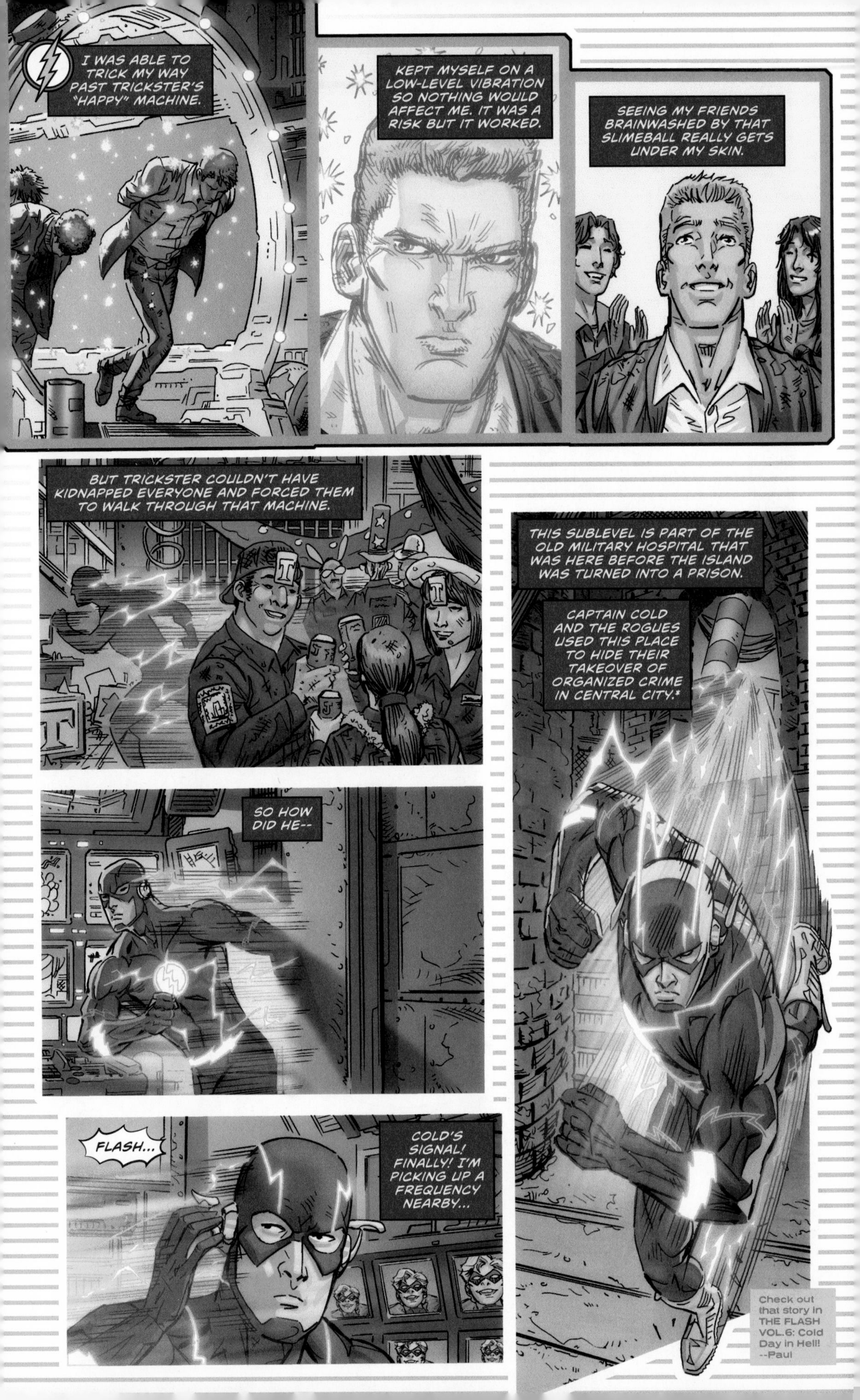
I WAS ABLE TO TRICK MY WAY PAST TRICKSTER'S "HAPPY" MACHINE.
KEPT MYSELF ON A LOW-LEVEL VIBRATION SO NOTHING WOULD AFFECT ME. IT WAS A RISK BUT IT WORKED.
SEEING MY FRIENDS BRAINWASHED BY THAT SLIMEBALL REALLY GETS UNDER MY SKIN.
BUT TRICKSTER COULDN'T HAVE KIDNAPPED EVERYONE AND FORCED THEM TO WALK THROUGH THAT MACHINE.
SO HOW DID HE--
FLASH...
COLD'S SIGNAL! FINALLY! I'M PICKING UP A FREQUENCY NEARBY...
THIS SUBLEVEL IS PART OF THE OLD MILITARY HOSPITAL THAT WAS HERE BEFORE THE ISLAND WAS TURNED INTO A PRISON.
CAPTAIN COLD AND THE ROGUES USED THIS PLACE TO HIDE THEIR TAKEOVER OF ORGANIZED CRIME IN CENTRAL CITY.*
Check out that story in THE FLASH VOL.6: Cold Day in Hell! --Paul

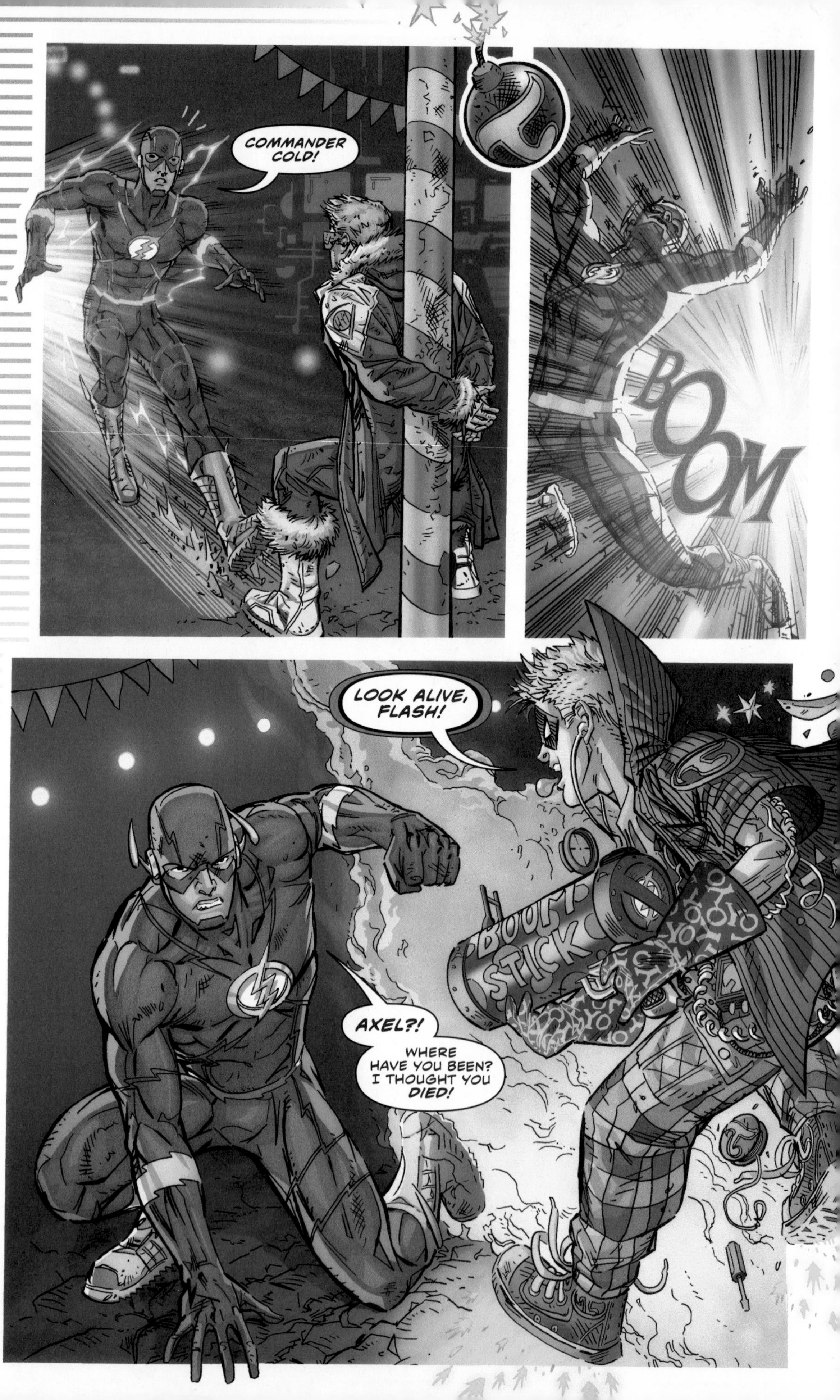
COMMANDER COLD!
BOOM
LOOK ALIVE, FLASH!
BOOM STICK
AXEL?!
WHERE HAVE YOU BEEN? I THOUGHT YOU DIED!

I *GOT BETTER.* AND LEARNED TO LET GO OF MY ANGER.

NOW I'M OVER THE MOON WITH *HAPPINESS.*

YOU SHOULD TRY IT SOMETIME!

WHEN DID YOU...

...START WORKING WITH JAMES JESSE?!

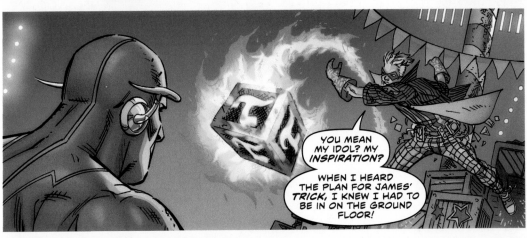

YOU MEAN MY IDOL? MY INSPIRATION?

WHEN I HEARD THE PLAN FOR JAMES' *TRICK,* I KNEW I HAD TO BE IN ON THE GROUND FLOOR!

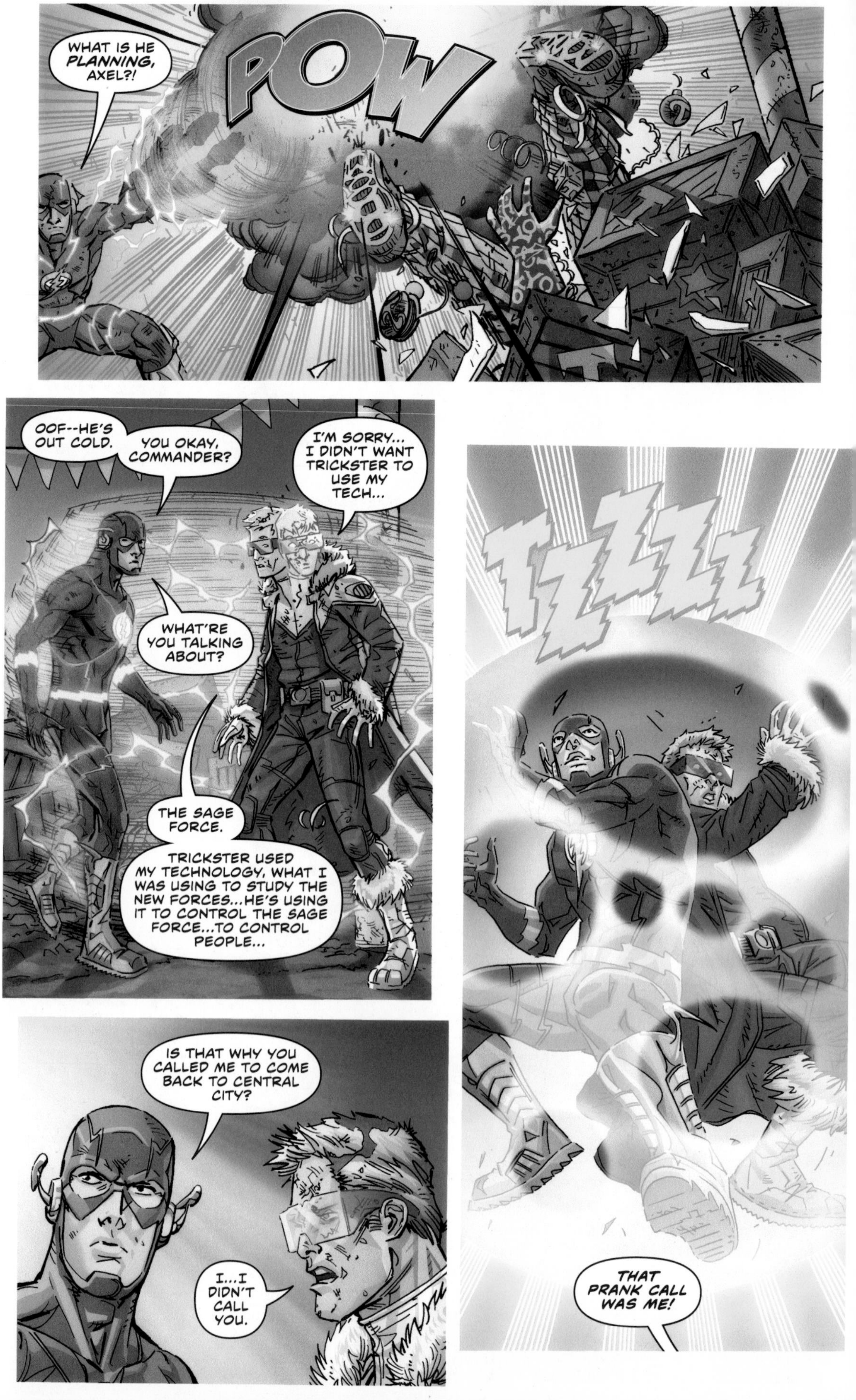

WHAT IS HE PLANNING, AXEL?!
POW
OOF--HE'S OUT COLD.
YOU OKAY, COMMANDER?
I'M SORRY... I DIDN'T WANT TRICKSTER TO USE MY TECH...
WHAT'RE YOU TALKING ABOUT?
THE SAGE FORCE.
TRICKSTER USED MY TECHNOLOGY, WHAT I WAS USING TO STUDY THE NEW FORCES...HE'S USING IT TO CONTROL THE SAGE FORCE...TO CONTROL PEOPLE...
IS THAT WHY YOU CALLED ME TO COME BACK TO CENTRAL CITY?
I...I DIDN'T CALL YOU.
TZZZZ
THAT PRANK CALL WAS ME!

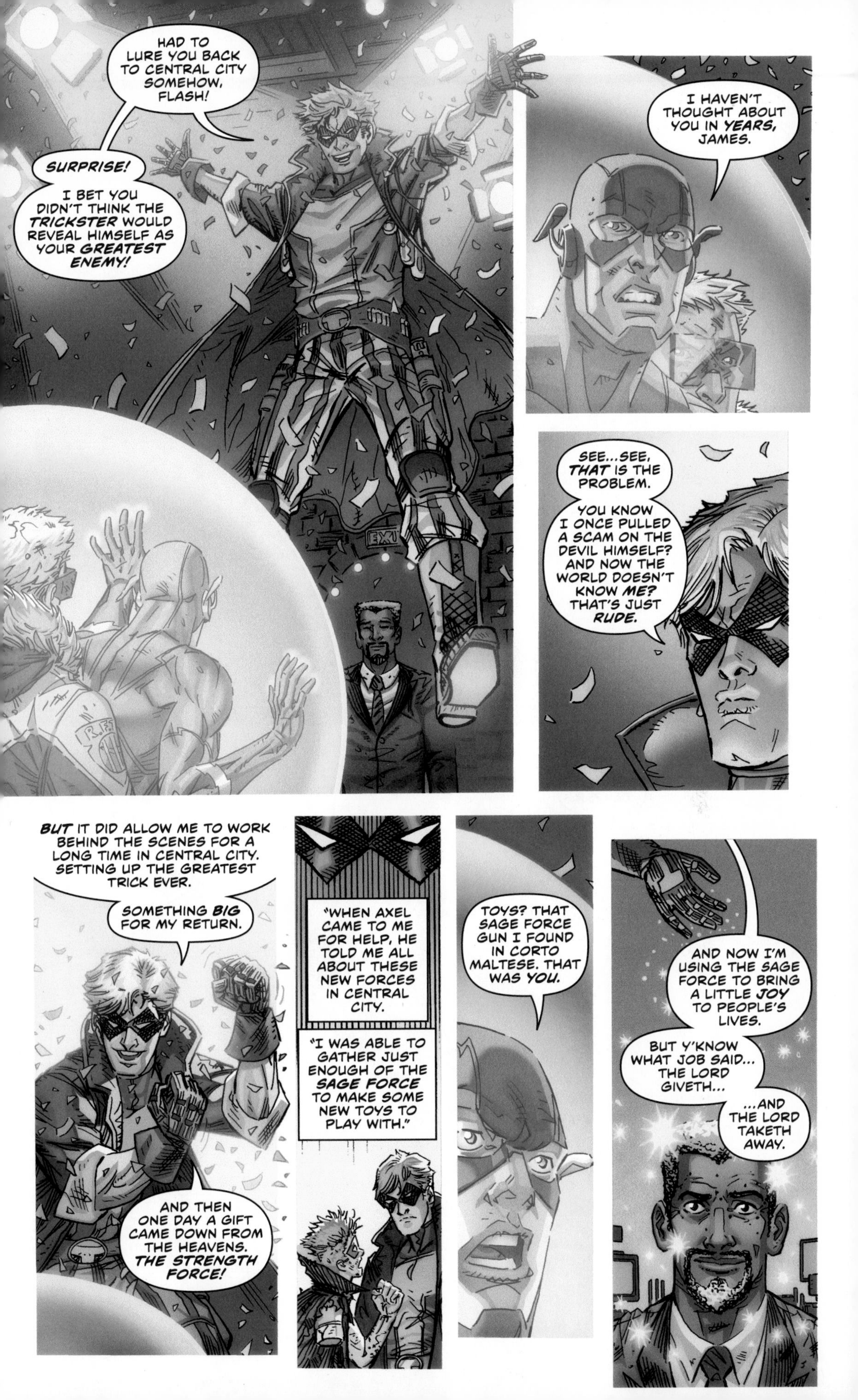
HAD TO LURE YOU BACK TO CENTRAL CITY SOMEHOW, FLASH!
SURPRISE!
I BET YOU DIDN'T THINK THE TRICKSTER WOULD REVEAL HIMSELF AS YOUR GREATEST ENEMY!
I HAVEN'T THOUGHT ABOUT YOU IN YEARS, JAMES.
SEE...SEE, THAT IS THE PROBLEM.
YOU KNOW I ONCE PULLED A SCAM ON THE DEVIL HIMSELF? AND NOW THE WORLD DOESN'T KNOW ME? THAT'S JUST RUDE.
BUT IT DID ALLOW ME TO WORK BEHIND THE SCENES FOR A LONG TIME IN CENTRAL CITY. SETTING UP THE GREATEST TRICK EVER.
SOMETHING BIG FOR MY RETURN.
AND THEN ONE DAY A GIFT CAME DOWN FROM THE HEAVENS. THE STRENGTH FORCE!
"WHEN AXEL CAME TO ME FOR HELP, HE TOLD ME ALL ABOUT THESE NEW FORCES IN CENTRAL CITY.
"I WAS ABLE TO GATHER JUST ENOUGH OF THE SAGE FORCE TO MAKE SOME NEW TOYS TO PLAY WITH."
TOYS? THAT SAGE FORCE GUN I FOUND IN CORTO MALTESE. THAT WAS YOU.
AND NOW I'M USING THE SAGE FORCE TO BRING A LITTLE JOY TO PEOPLE'S LIVES.
BUT Y'KNOW WHAT JOB SAID... THE LORD GIVETH...
...AND THE LORD TAKETH AWAY.

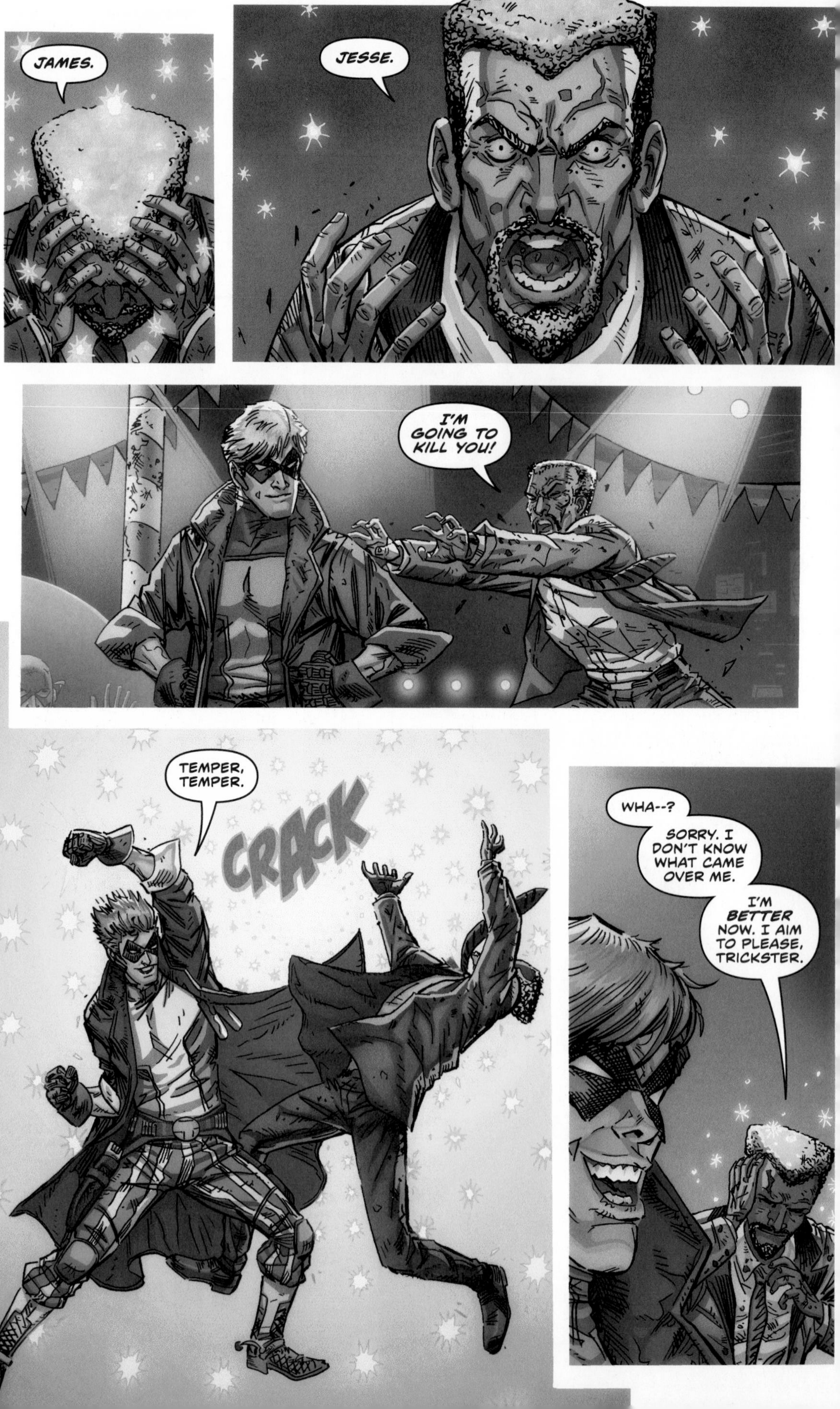
JAMES.
JESSE.
I'M GOING TO KILL YOU!
TEMPER, TEMPER.
CRACK
WHA--?
SORRY. I DON'T KNOW WHAT CAME OVER ME.
I'M *BETTER* NOW. I AIM TO PLEASE, TRICKSTER.

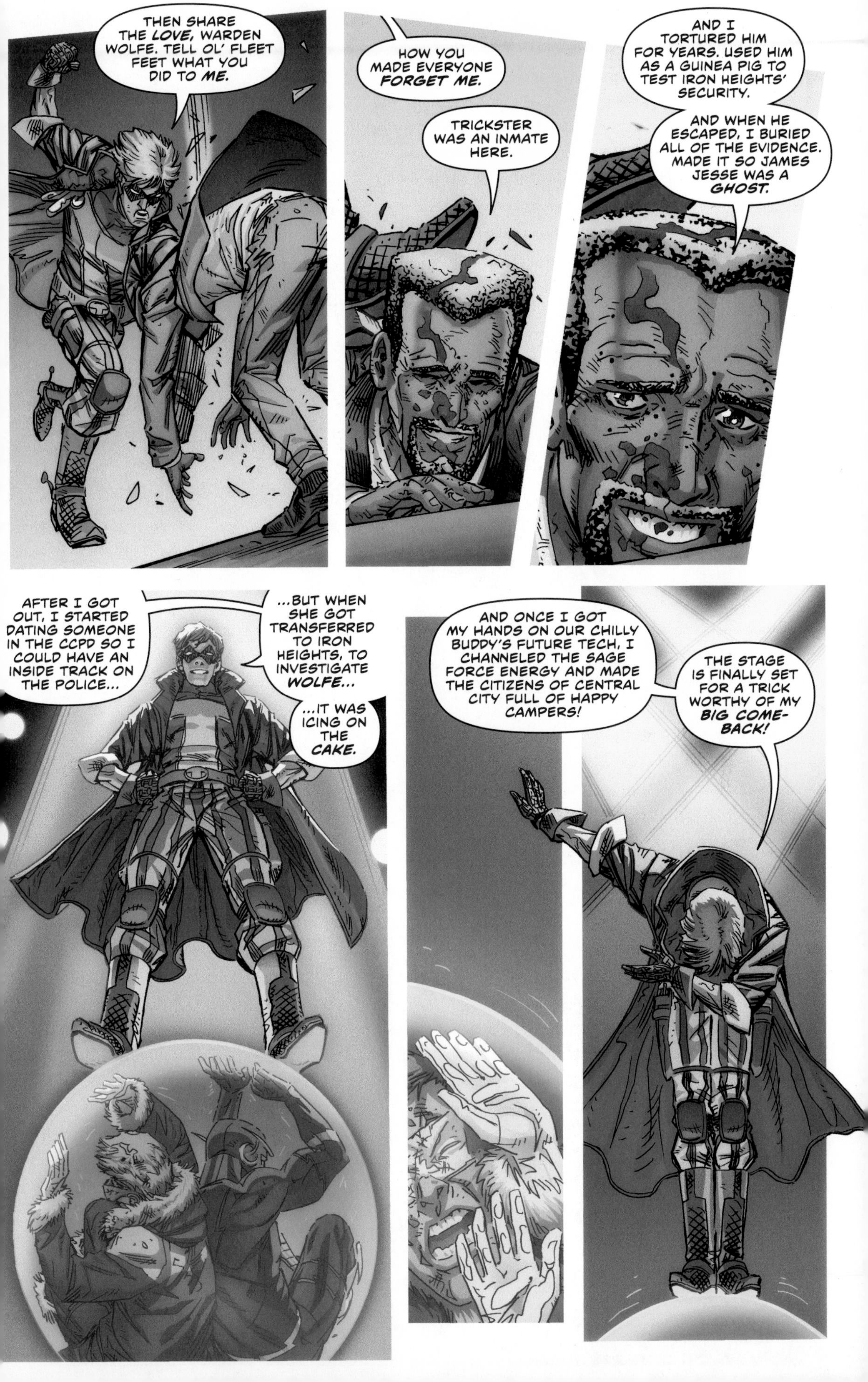
THEN SHARE THE LOVE, WARDEN WOLFE. TELL OL' FLEET FEET WHAT YOU DID TO ME.
HOW YOU MADE EVERYONE FORGET ME.
TRICKSTER WAS AN INMATE HERE.
AND I TORTURED HIM FOR YEARS. USED HIM AS A GUINEA PIG TO TEST IRON HEIGHTS' SECURITY.
AND WHEN HE ESCAPED, I BURIED ALL OF THE EVIDENCE. MADE IT SO JAMES JESSE WAS A GHOST.
AFTER I GOT OUT, I STARTED DATING SOMEONE IN THE CCPD SO I COULD HAVE AN INSIDE TRACK ON THE POLICE...
...BUT WHEN SHE GOT TRANSFERRED TO IRON HEIGHTS, TO INVESTIGATE WOLFE...
...IT WAS ICING ON THE CAKE.
AND ONCE I GOT MY HANDS ON OUR CHILLY BUDDY'S FUTURE TECH, I CHANNELED THE SAGE FORCE ENERGY AND MADE THE CITIZENS OF CENTRAL CITY FULL OF HAPPY CAMPERS!
THE STAGE IS FINALLY SET FOR A TRICK WORTHY OF MY BIG COME-BACK!

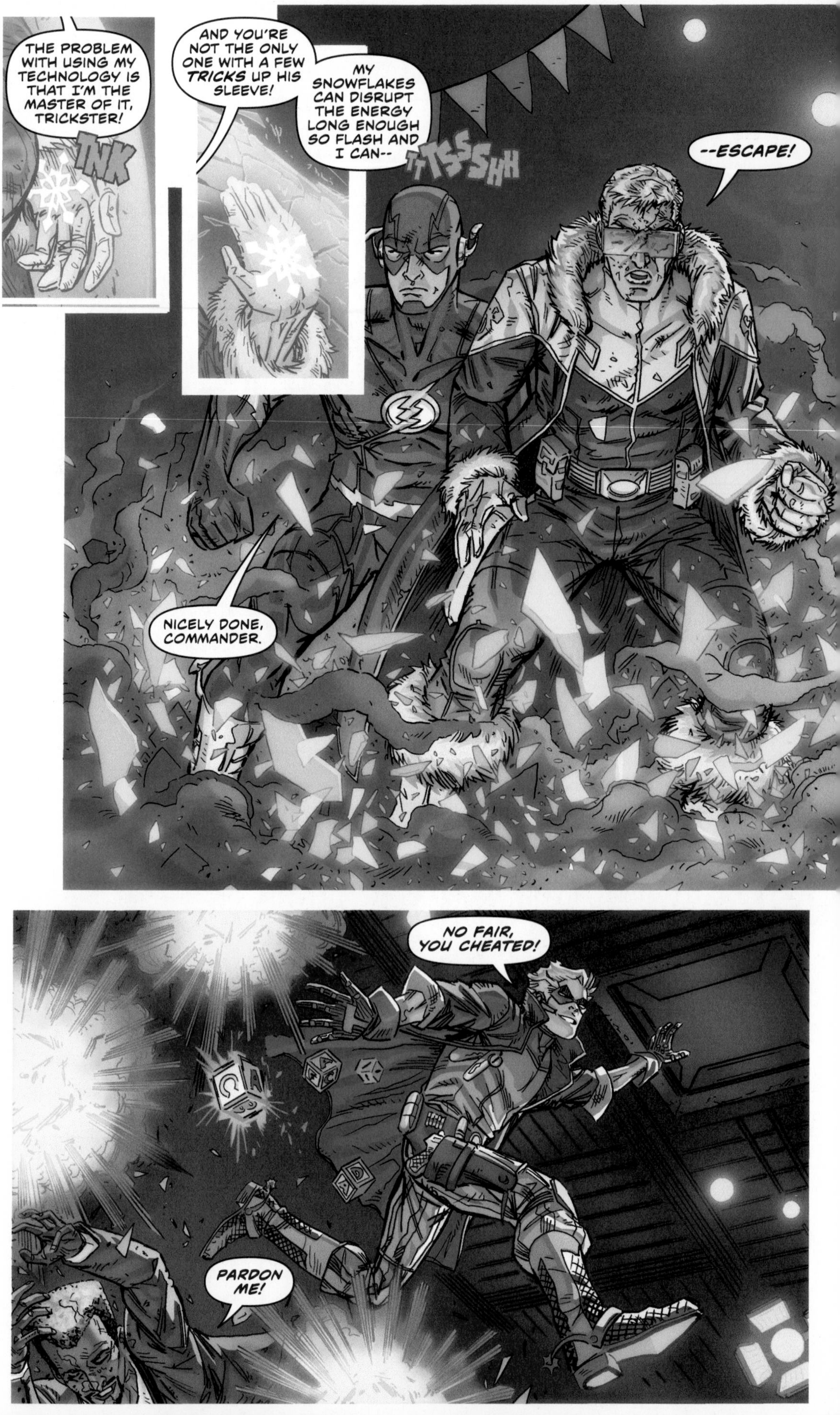
THE PROBLEM WITH USING MY TECHNOLOGY IS THAT I'M THE MASTER OF IT, TRICKSTER!
TNK
AND YOU'RE NOT THE ONLY ONE WITH A FEW TRICKS UP HIS SLEEVE!
MY SNOWFLAKES CAN DISRUPT THE ENERGY LONG ENOUGH SO FLASH AND I CAN--
TTTSSSHH
--ESCAPE!
NICELY DONE, COMMANDER.
NO FAIR, YOU CHEATED!
PARDON ME!

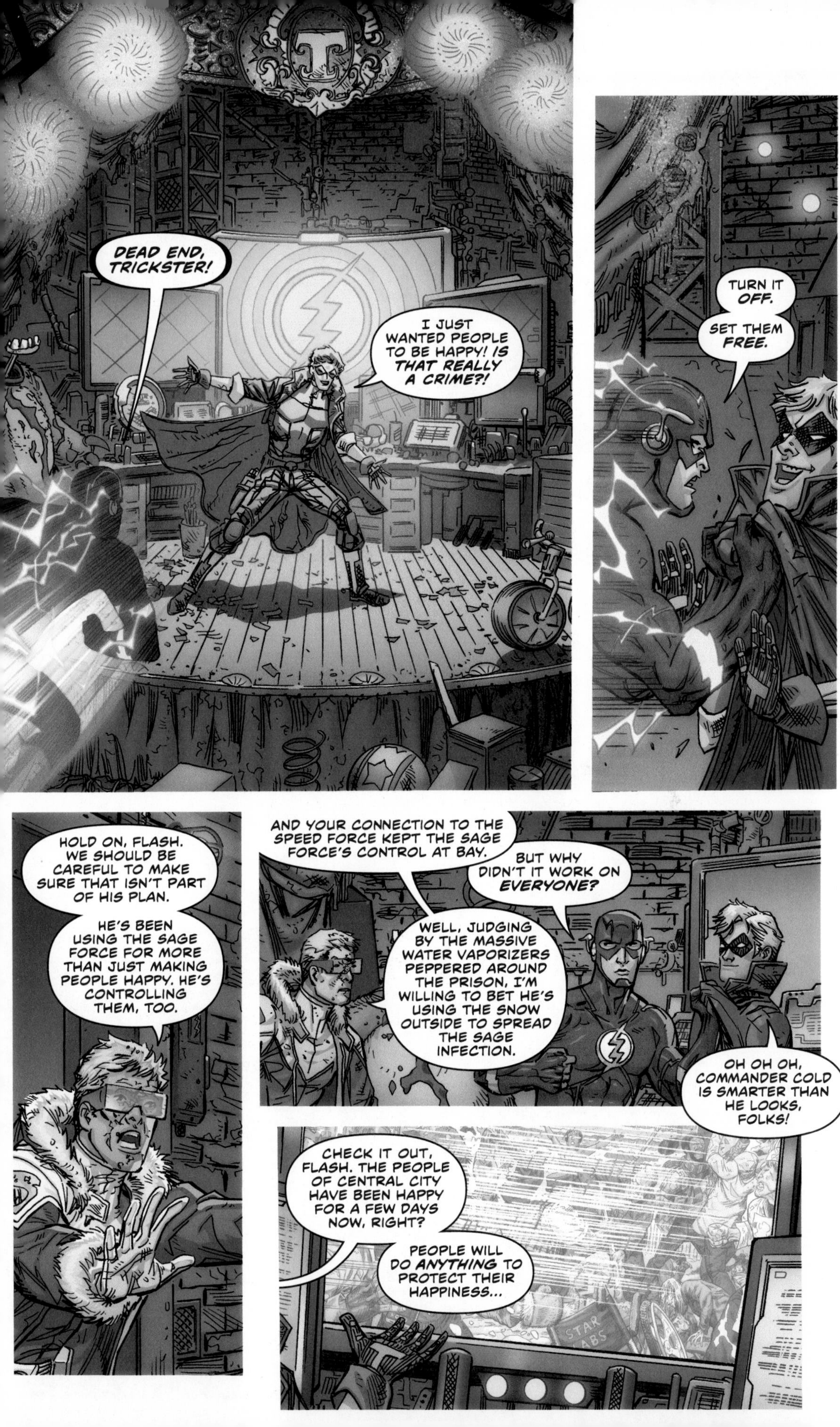
DEAD END, TRICKSTER!
I JUST WANTED PEOPLE TO BE HAPPY! IS THAT REALLY A CRIME?!
TURN IT OFF.
SET THEM FREE.
HOLD ON, FLASH. WE SHOULD BE CAREFUL TO MAKE SURE THAT ISN'T PART OF HIS PLAN.
HE'S BEEN USING THE SAGE FORCE FOR MORE THAN JUST MAKING PEOPLE HAPPY. HE'S CONTROLLING THEM, TOO.
AND YOUR CONNECTION TO THE SPEED FORCE KEPT THE SAGE FORCE'S CONTROL AT BAY.
BUT WHY DIDN'T IT WORK ON EVERYONE?
WELL, JUDGING BY THE MASSIVE WATER VAPORIZERS PEPPERED AROUND THE PRISON, I'M WILLING TO BET HE'S USING THE SNOW OUTSIDE TO SPREAD THE SAGE INFECTION.
OH OH OH, COMMANDER COLD IS SMARTER THAN HE LOOKS, FOLKS!
CHECK IT OUT, FLASH. THE PEOPLE OF CENTRAL CITY HAVE BEEN HAPPY FOR A FEW DAYS NOW, RIGHT?
PEOPLE WILL DO ANYTHING TO PROTECT THEIR HAPPINESS...
STAR LABS

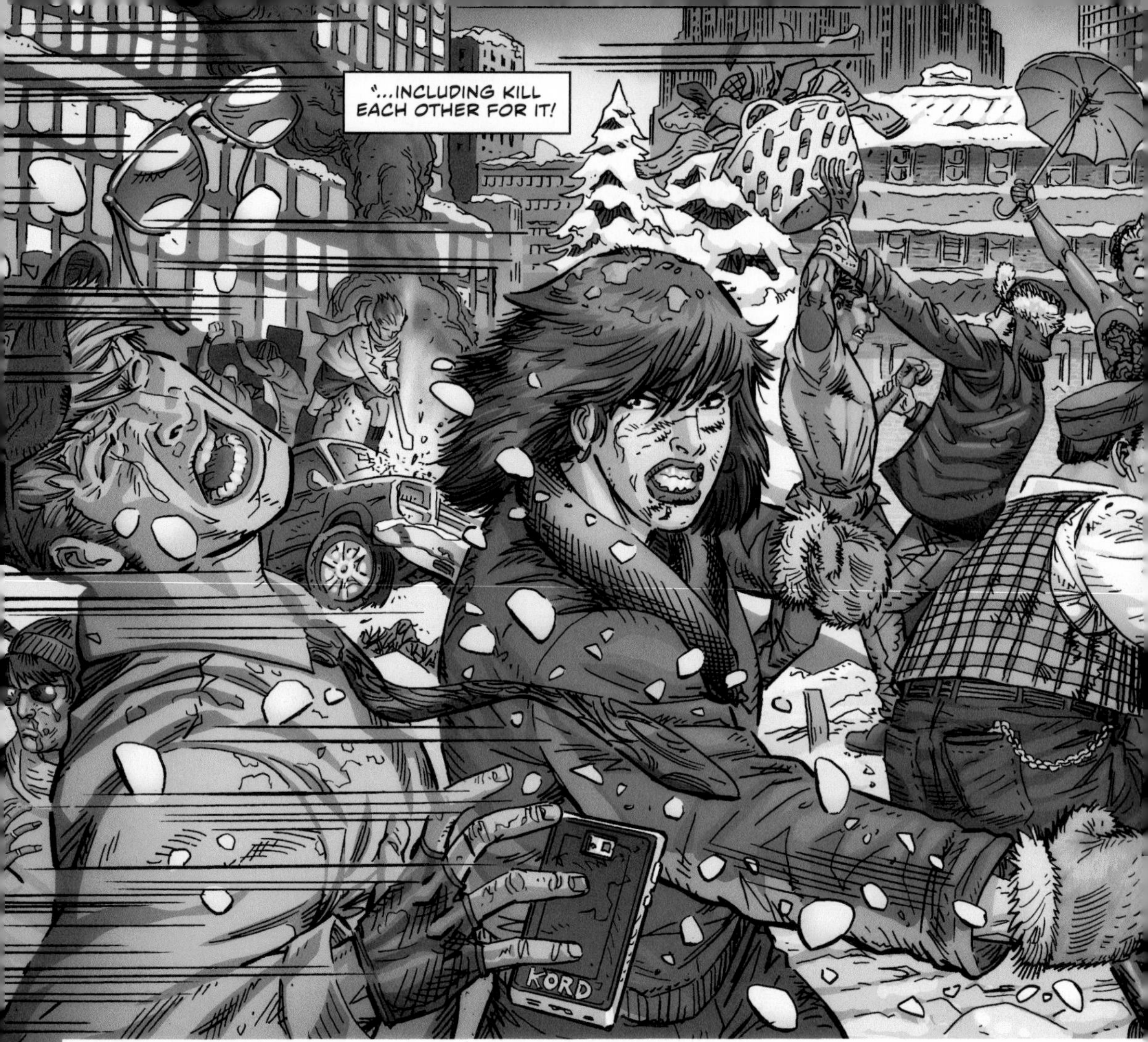
"...INCLUDING KILL EACH OTHER FOR IT!
KORD

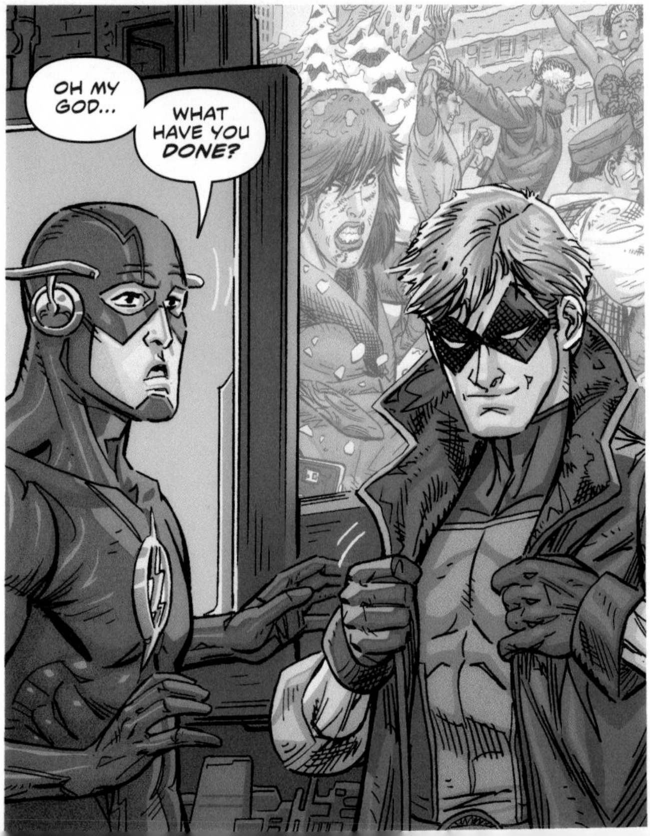
OH MY GOD...
WHAT HAVE YOU DONE?

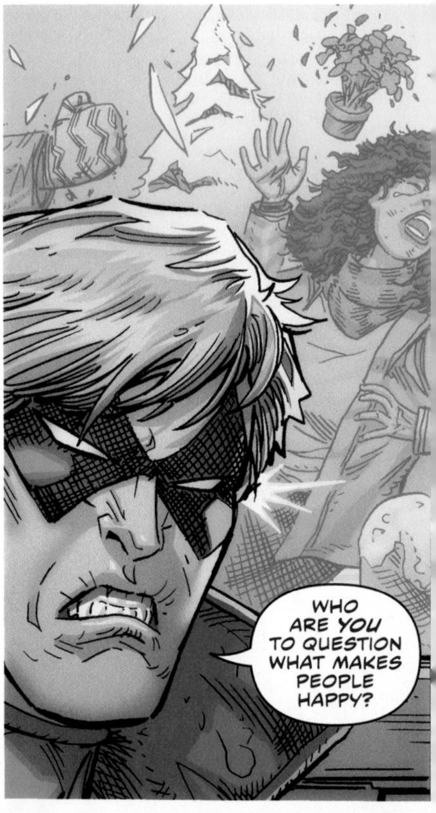
WHO ARE YOU TO QUESTION WHAT MAKES PEOPLE HAPPY?

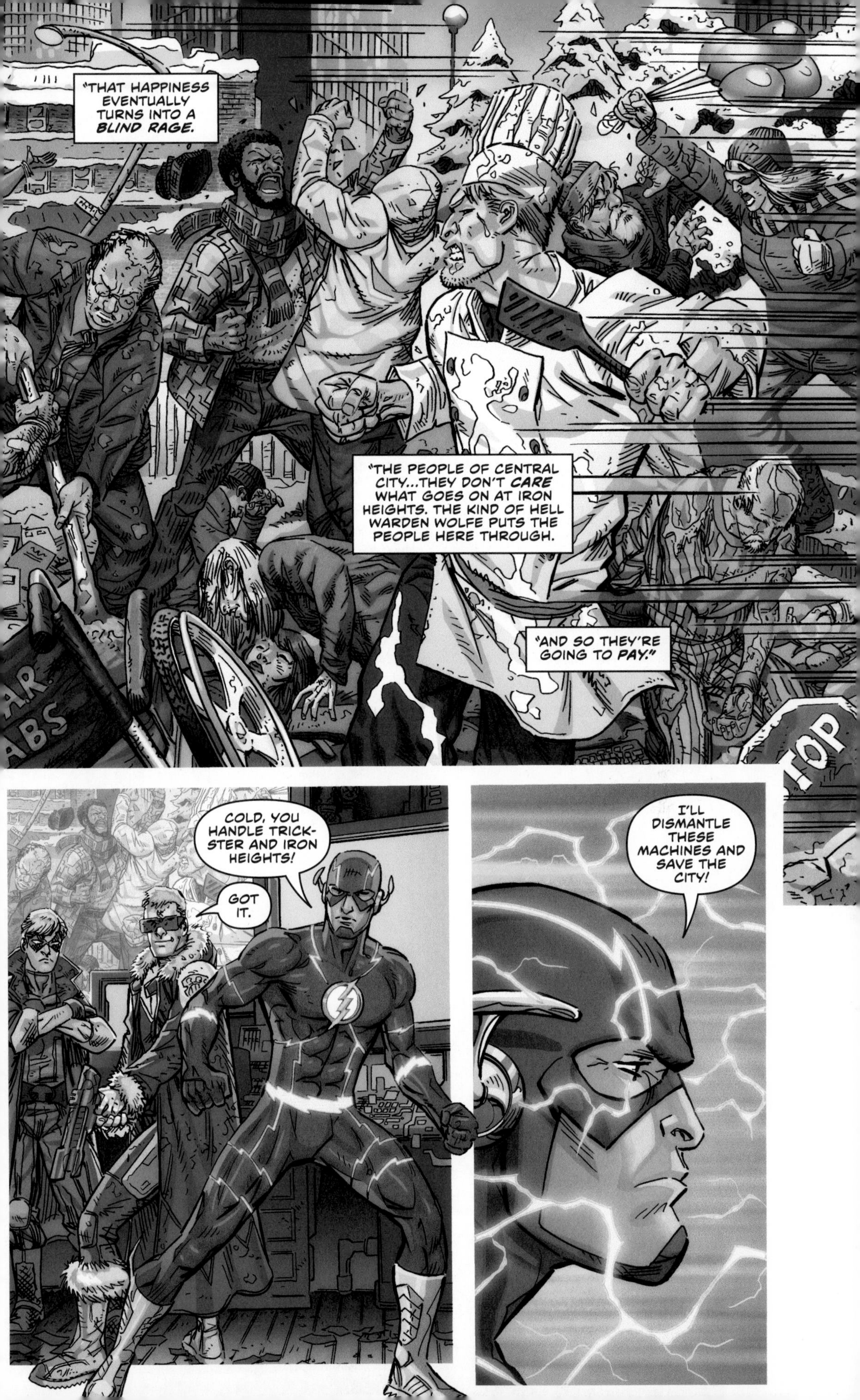
"THAT HAPPINESS EVENTUALLY TURNS INTO A *BLIND RAGE*.
"THE PEOPLE OF CENTRAL CITY...THEY DON'T *CARE* WHAT GOES ON AT IRON HEIGHTS. THE KIND OF HELL WARDEN WOLFE PUTS THE PEOPLE HERE THROUGH.
"AND SO THEY'RE GOING TO *PAY*."
COLD, YOU HANDLE TRICK-STER AND IRON HEIGHTS!
GOT IT.
I'LL DISMANTLE THESE MACHINES AND SAVE THE CITY!

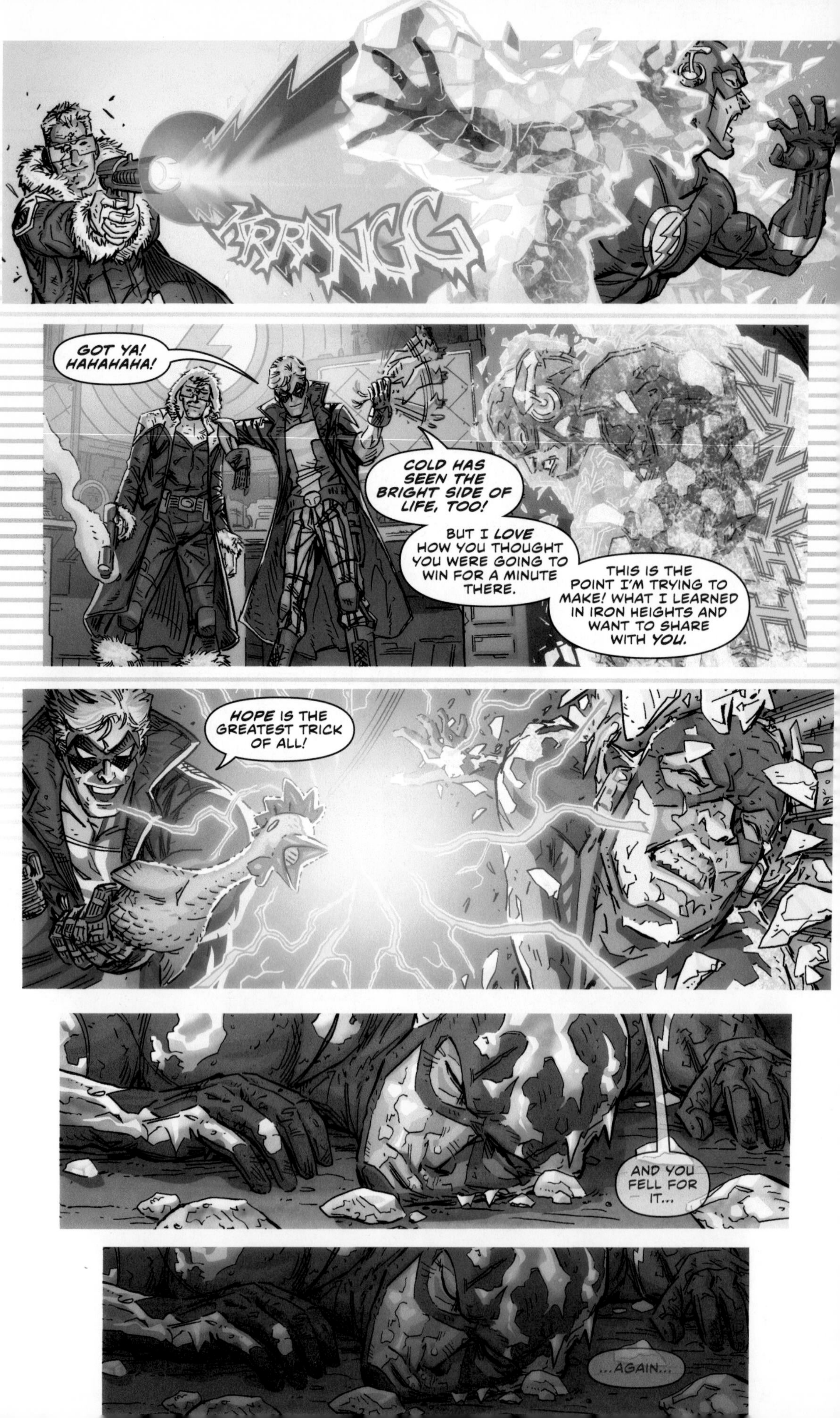
KRRRNGG
GOT YA! HAHAHAHA!
COLD HAS SEEN THE BRIGHT SIDE OF LIFE, TOO!
BUT I LOVE HOW YOU THOUGHT YOU WERE GOING TO WIN FOR A MINUTE THERE.
THIS IS THE POINT I'M TRYING TO MAKE! WHAT I LEARNED IN IRON HEIGHTS AND WANT TO SHARE WITH YOU.
HOPE IS THE GREATEST TRICK OF ALL!
AND YOU FELL FOR IT...
...AGAIN...

TTPPPPTTTT

...WHAT...?

HE'S ALIVE!

TRICKSTER... WHAT'RE YOU...

DOING? WATCHING MY TRICK UNFOLD.

YOU SEE, I THOUGHT ABOUT ALL KINDS OF REVENGE. AND LET ME TELL YA...LIVING WELL WAS NOT GONNA CUT IT!

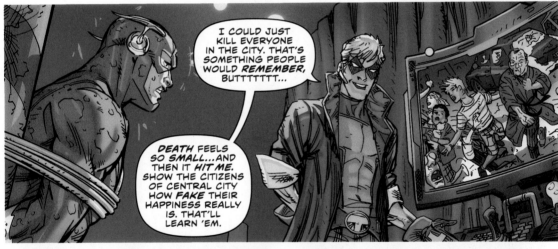

I COULD JUST KILL EVERYONE IN THE CITY. THAT'S SOMETHING PEOPLE WOULD *REMEMBER*, BUTTTTTT...

DEATH FEELS SO *SMALL*...AND THEN IT *HIT ME*. SHOW THE CITIZENS OF CENTRAL CITY HOW *FAKE* THEIR HAPPINESS REALLY IS. THAT'LL LEARN 'EM.

THESE RESTRAINTS CAN'T HOLD ME, TRICKSTER!

I'LL SAVE THE PEOPLE FROM YOUR SICK *GAMES*.

HOW ARE YOU GOING TO DO THAT, FLASH?

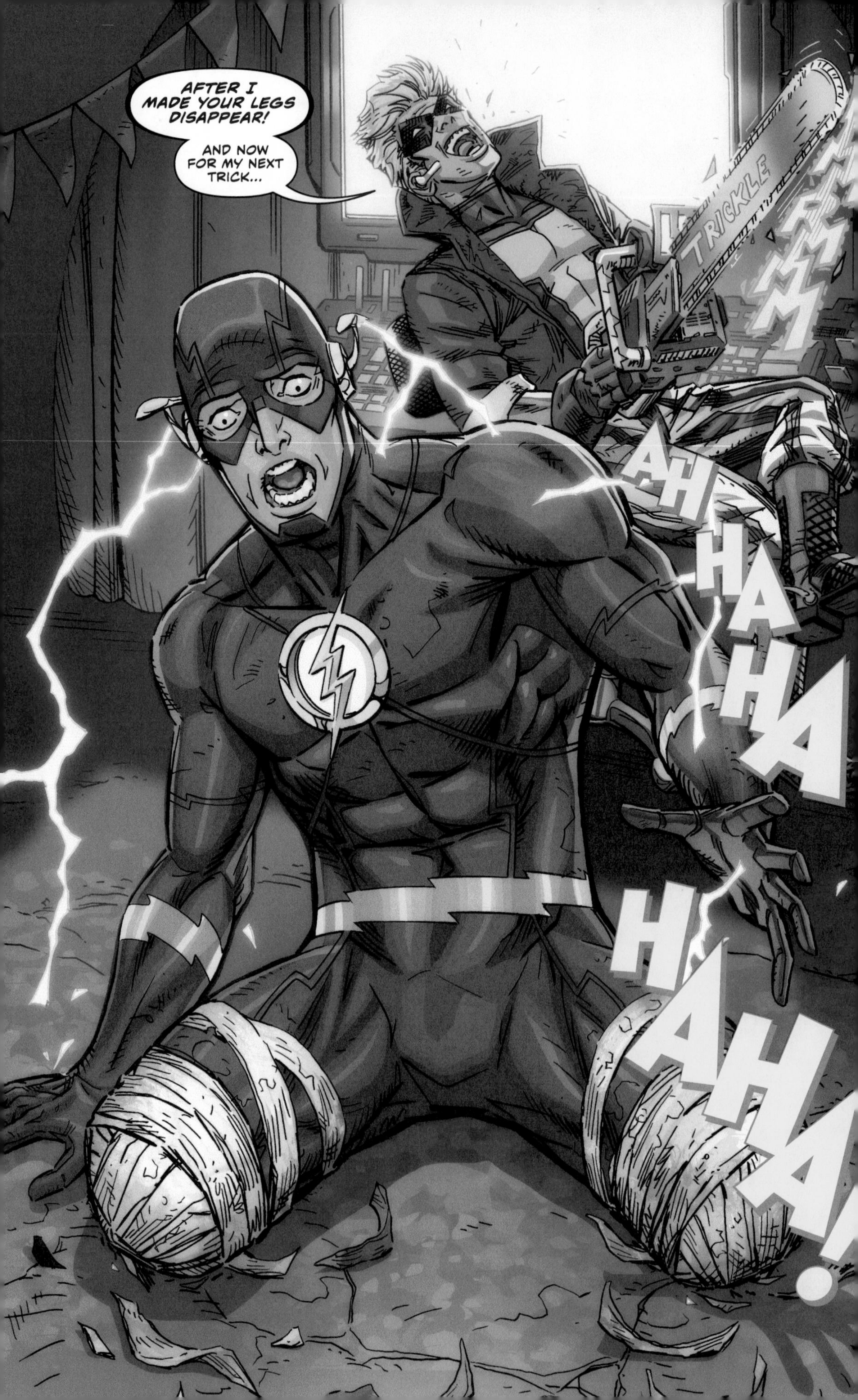
AFTER I MADE YOUR LEGS DISAPPEAR!
AND NOW FOR MY NEXT TRICK...
TRICKLE
AHHAHAHAHAHAHA!

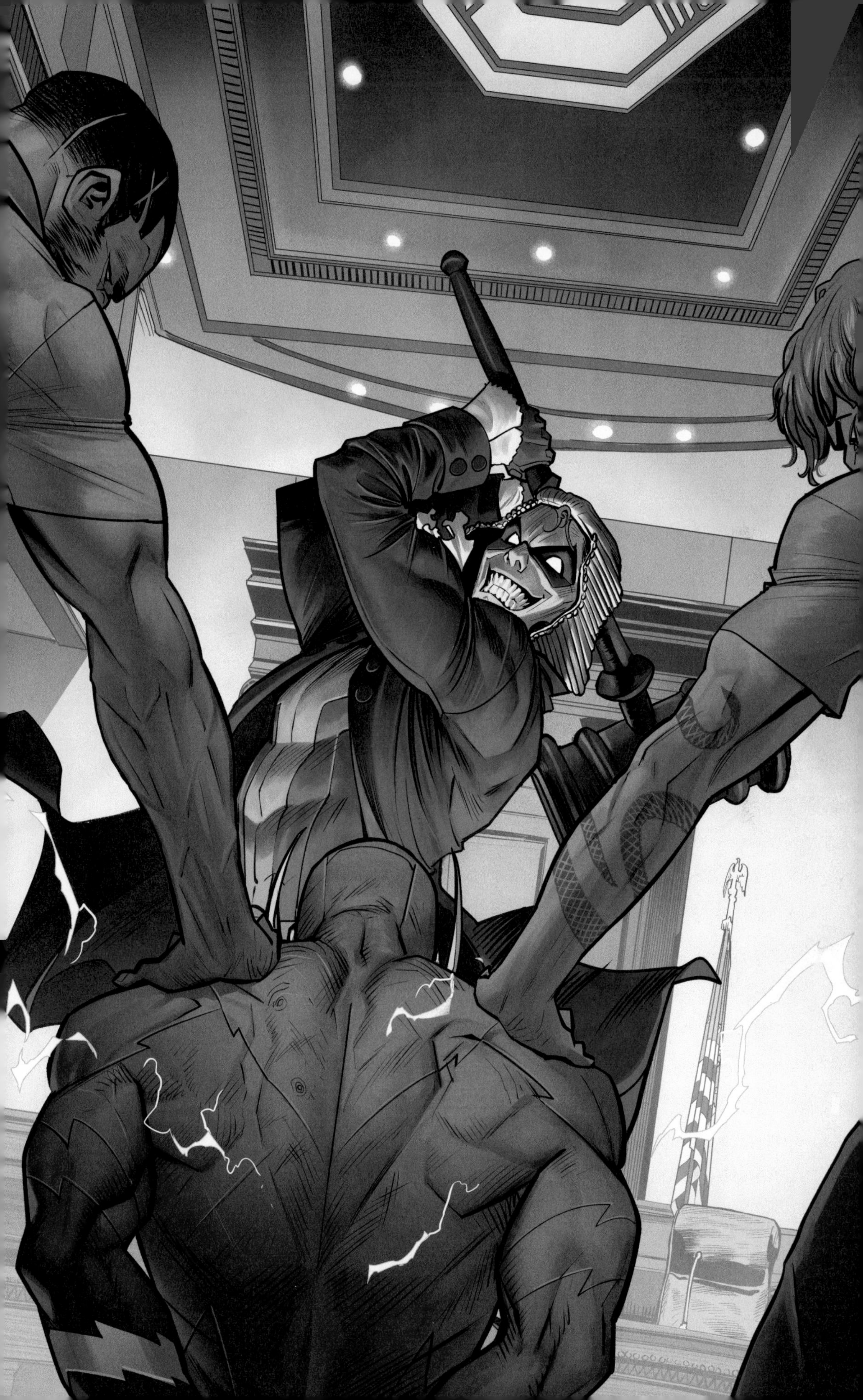

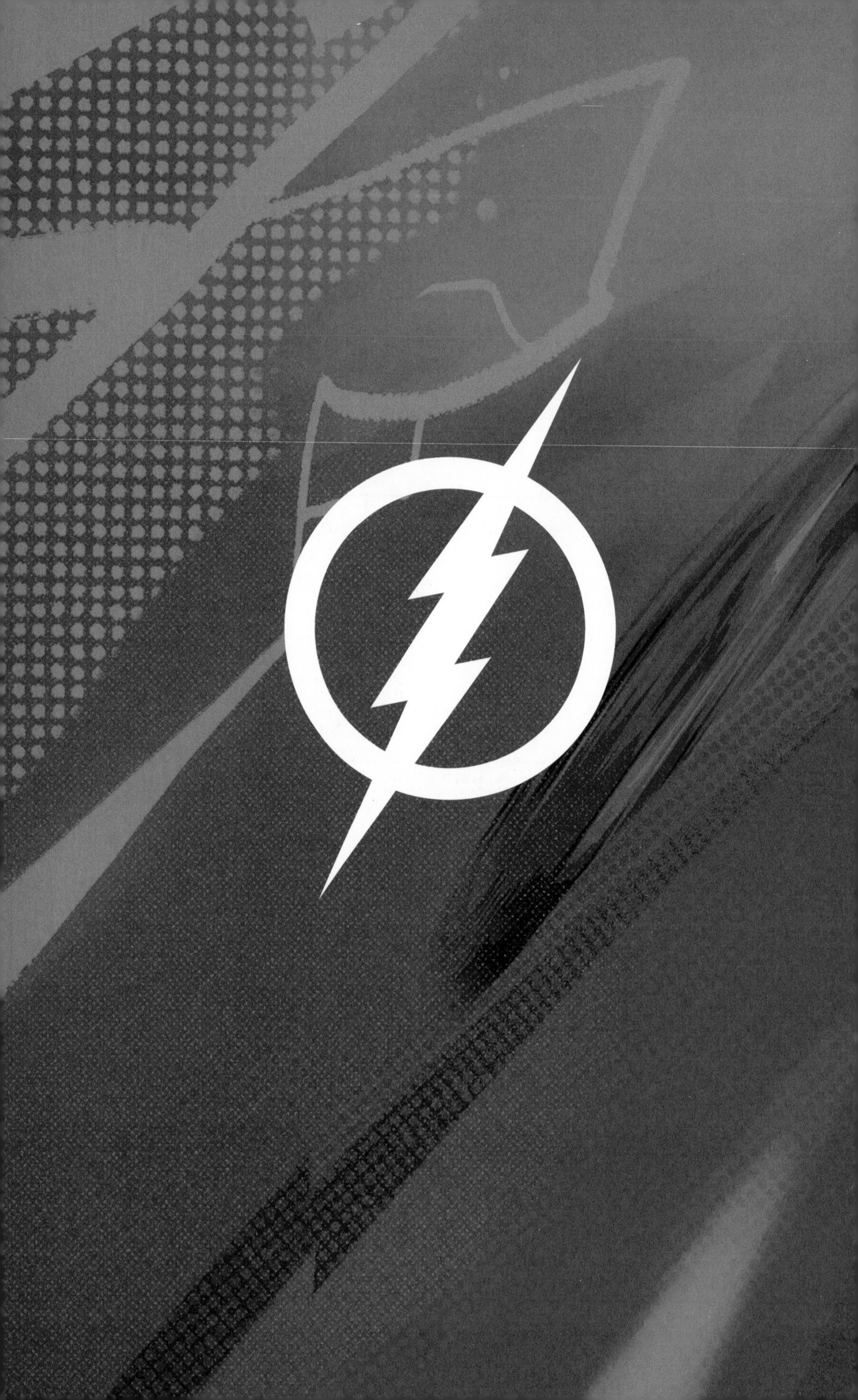

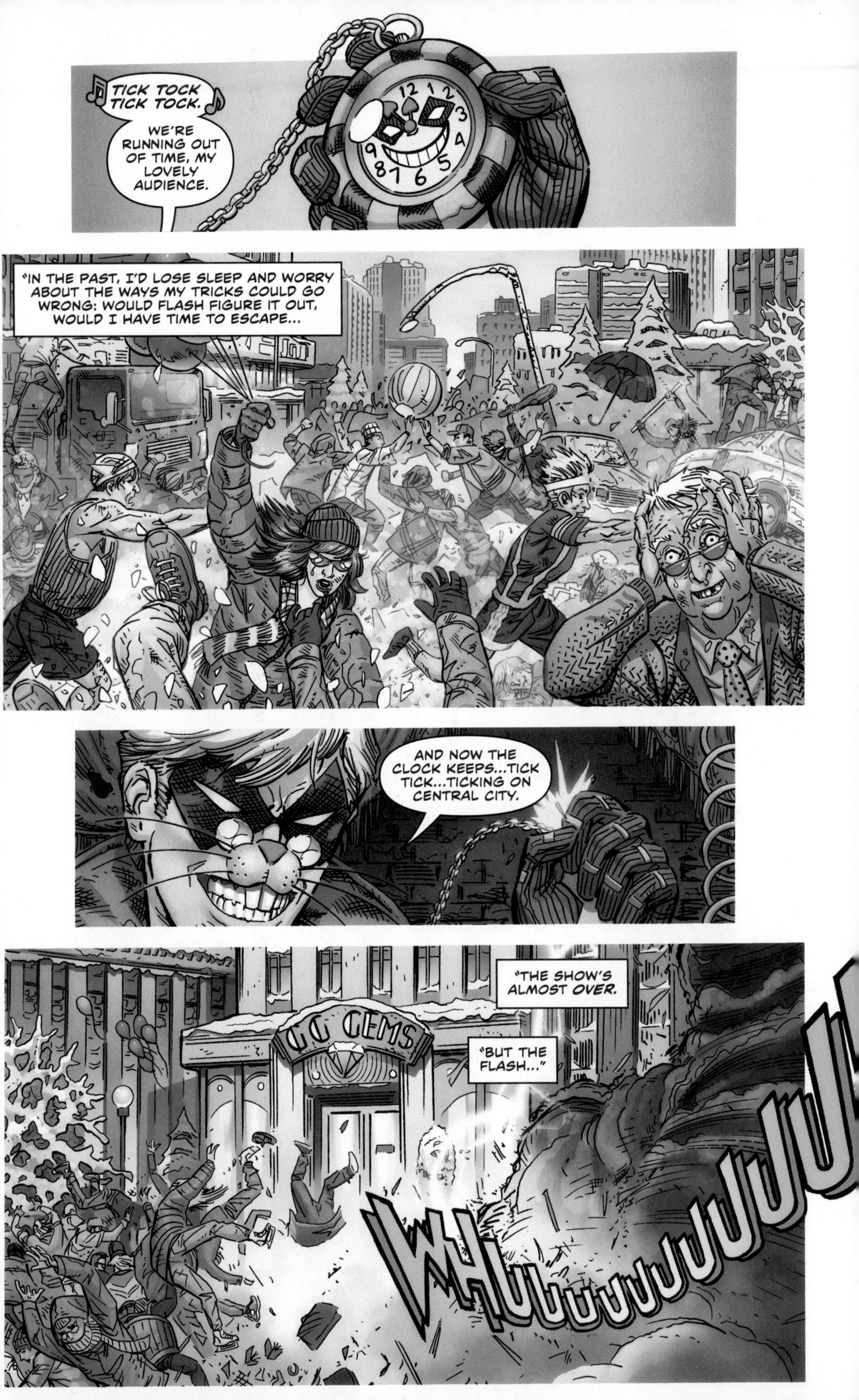
TICK TOCK TICK TOCK.
WE'RE RUNNING OUT OF TIME, MY LOVELY AUDIENCE.
"IN THE PAST, I'D LOSE SLEEP AND WORRY ABOUT THE WAYS MY TRICKS COULD GO WRONG: WOULD FLASH FIGURE IT OUT, WOULD I HAVE TIME TO ESCAPE...
AND NOW THE CLOCK KEEPS...TICK TICK...TICKING ON CENTRAL CITY.
"THE SHOW'S ALMOST OVER.
"BUT THE FLASH..."
CC GEMS
WHUUUUUUUUUU

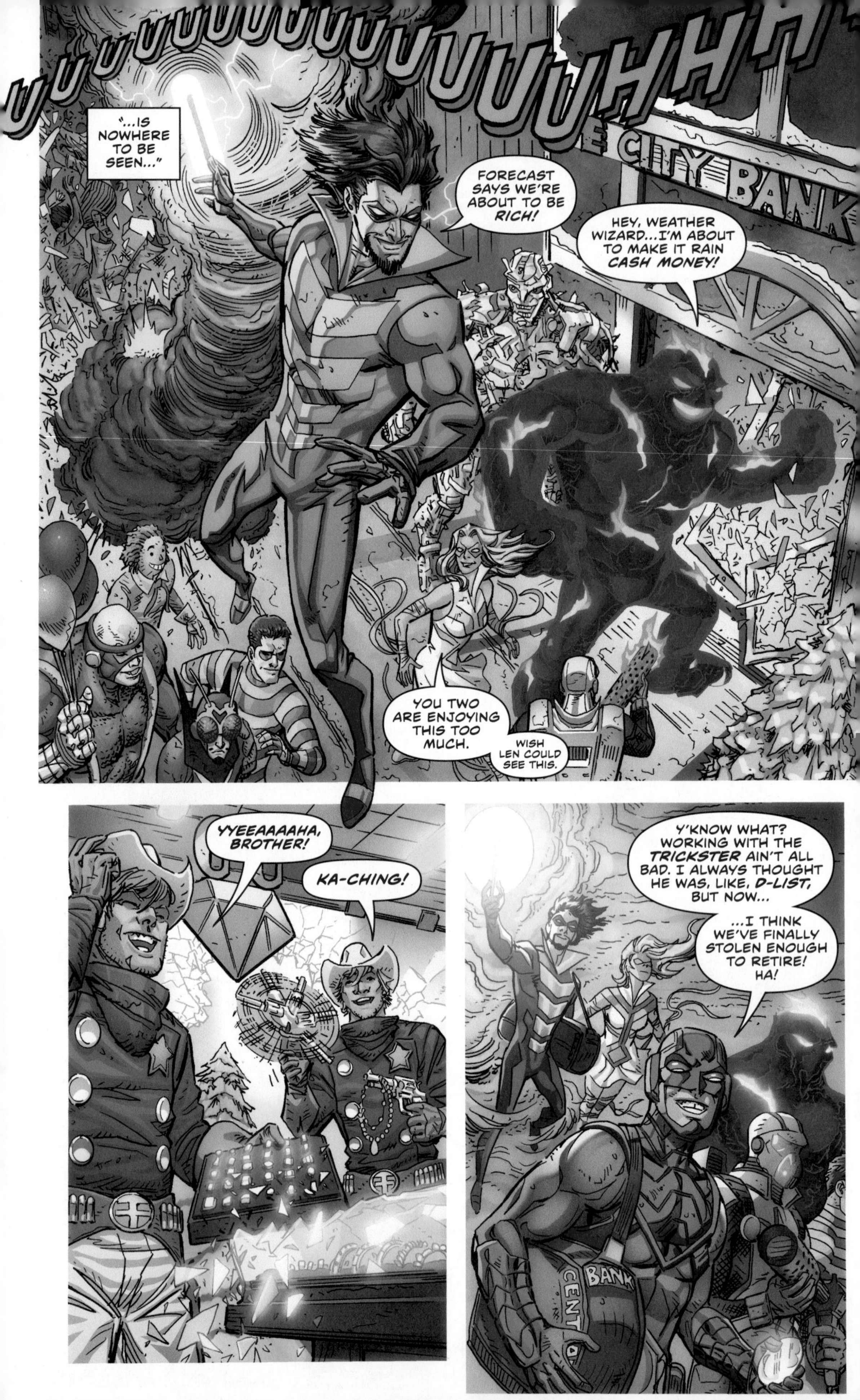
UUUUUUUUUUUUUUUUUUUUHHH
"...IS NOWHERE TO BE SEEN..."
E CITY BANK
FORECAST SAYS WE'RE ABOUT TO BE *RICH!*
HEY, WEATHER WIZARD...I'M ABOUT TO MAKE IT RAIN *CASH MONEY!*
YOU TWO ARE ENJOYING THIS TOO MUCH.
WISH LEN COULD SEE THIS.
YYEEAAAAAHA, BROTHER!
KA-CHING!
Y'KNOW WHAT? WORKING WITH THE *TRICKSTER* AIN'T ALL BAD. I ALWAYS THOUGHT HE WAS, LIKE, *D-LIST,* BUT NOW...
...I THINK WE'VE FINALLY STOLEN ENOUGH TO RETIRE! HA!
BANK
CENT

AS LONG AS TRICKSTER GETS HIS CUT, YOU'LL BE ABLE TO DO MORE THAN JUST RETIRE, MIRROR MASTER.

THIS IS THE START OF A WHOLE NEW ERA FOR THE ROGUES.

JUST KEEP THE TREASURE COMING.

OUR TRANSPORTS ARE NEARLY FULL, TRICKSTER.

WE'RE READY TO HIT THE OPEN SEAS WITH OUR PRIZES.

THANK YOU, COPPERHEAD!

AFTER TODAY THE WORLD WILL REMEMBER JAMES JESSE!

HELL, THEY'LL WRITE SONGS ABOUT ME!

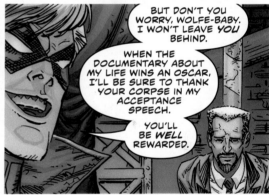

BUT DON'T YOU WORRY, WOLFE-BABY. I WON'T LEAVE YOU BEHIND.

WHEN THE DOCUMENTARY ABOUT MY LIFE WINS AN OSCAR, I'LL BE SURE TO THANK YOUR CORPSE IN MY ACCEPTANCE SPEECH.

YOU'LL BE WELL REWARDED.

HEY, BOSS, I FOUND THOSE PEOPLE YOU WANTED...

OH JOY!

YOU'RE NOT WORRIED ABOUT THE FLASH?

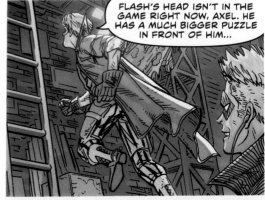

FLASH'S HEAD ISN'T IN THE GAME RIGHT NOW, AXEL. HE HAS A MUCH BIGGER PUZZLE IN FRONT OF HIM...

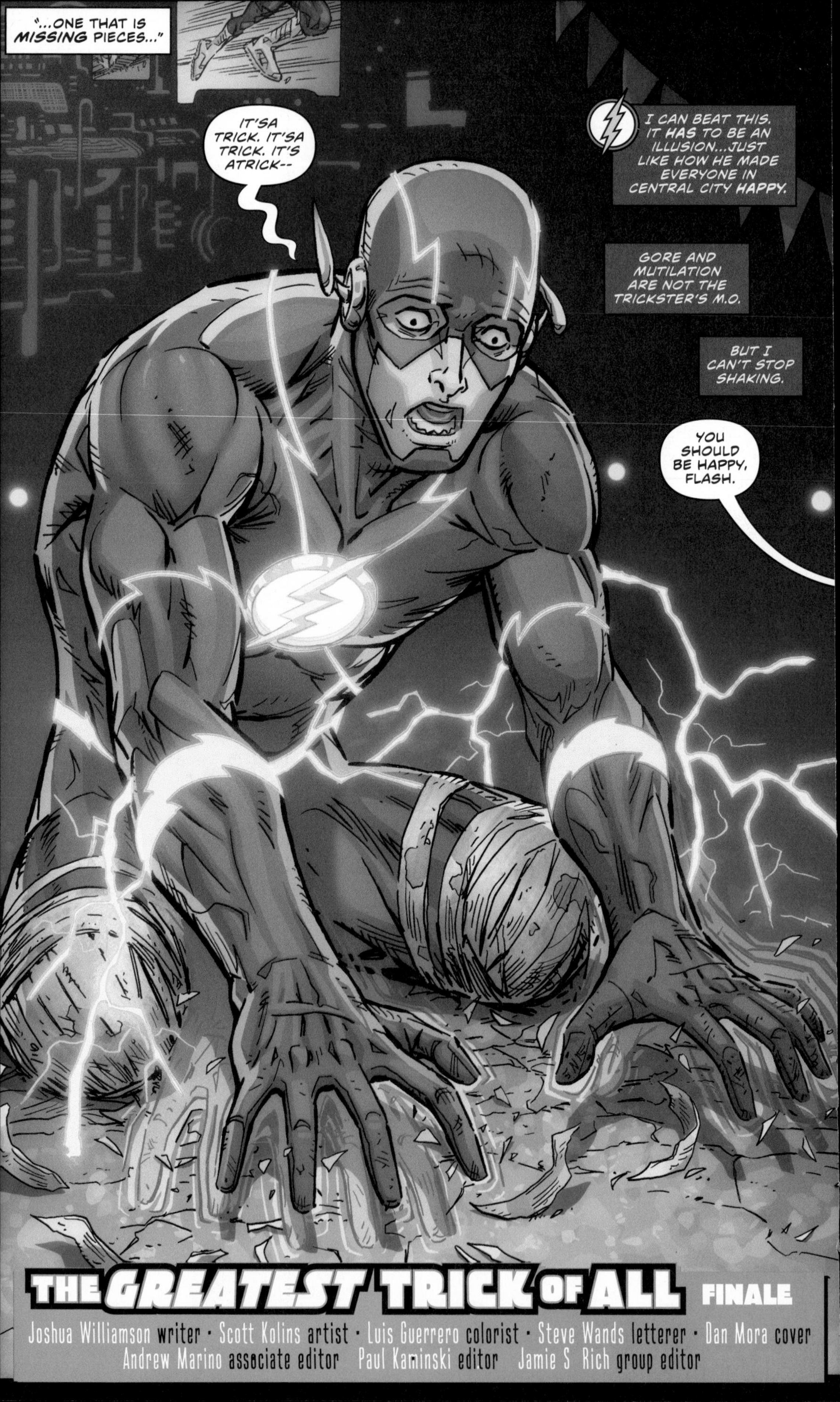
"...ONE THAT IS MISSING PIECES..."
IT'SA TRICK. IT'SA TRICK. IT'S ATRICK--
I CAN BEAT THIS. IT HAS TO BE AN ILLUSION...JUST LIKE HOW HE MADE EVERYONE IN CENTRAL CITY HAPPY.
GORE AND MUTILATION ARE NOT THE TRICKSTER'S M.O.
BUT I CAN'T STOP SHAKING.
YOU SHOULD BE HAPPY, FLASH.
THE GREATEST TRICK OF ALL FINALE
Joshua Williamson writer · Scott Kolins artist · Luis Guerrero colorist · Steve Wands letterer · Dan Mora cover
Andrew Marino associate editor Paul Kaminski editor Jamie S. Rich group editor

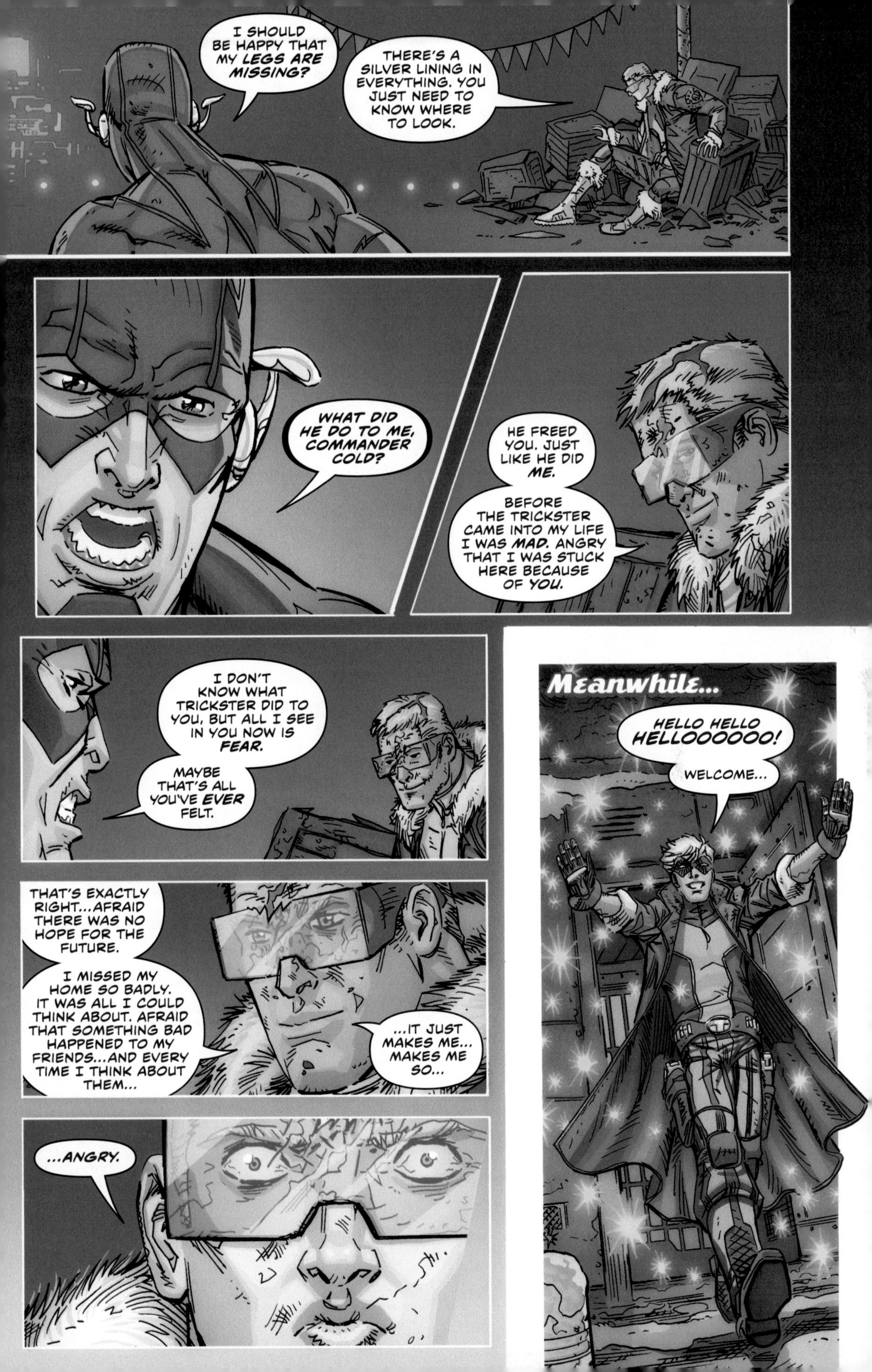
I SHOULD BE HAPPY THAT MY LEGS ARE MISSING?
THERE'S A SILVER LINING IN EVERYTHING. YOU JUST NEED TO KNOW WHERE TO LOOK.
WHAT DID HE DO TO ME, COMMANDER COLD?
HE FREED YOU. JUST LIKE HE DID ME.
BEFORE THE TRICKSTER CAME INTO MY LIFE I WAS MAD. ANGRY THAT I WAS STUCK HERE BECAUSE OF YOU.
I DON'T KNOW WHAT TRICKSTER DID TO YOU, BUT ALL I SEE IN YOU NOW IS FEAR.
MAYBE THAT'S ALL YOU'VE EVER FELT.
THAT'S EXACTLY RIGHT...AFRAID THERE WAS NO HOPE FOR THE FUTURE.
I MISSED MY HOME SO BADLY. IT WAS ALL I COULD THINK ABOUT. AFRAID THAT SOMETHING BAD HAPPENED TO MY FRIENDS...AND EVERY TIME I THINK ABOUT THEM...
...IT JUST MAKES ME... MAKES ME SO...
...ANGRY.
Meanwhile...
HELLO HELLO HELLOOOOOO!
WELCOME...

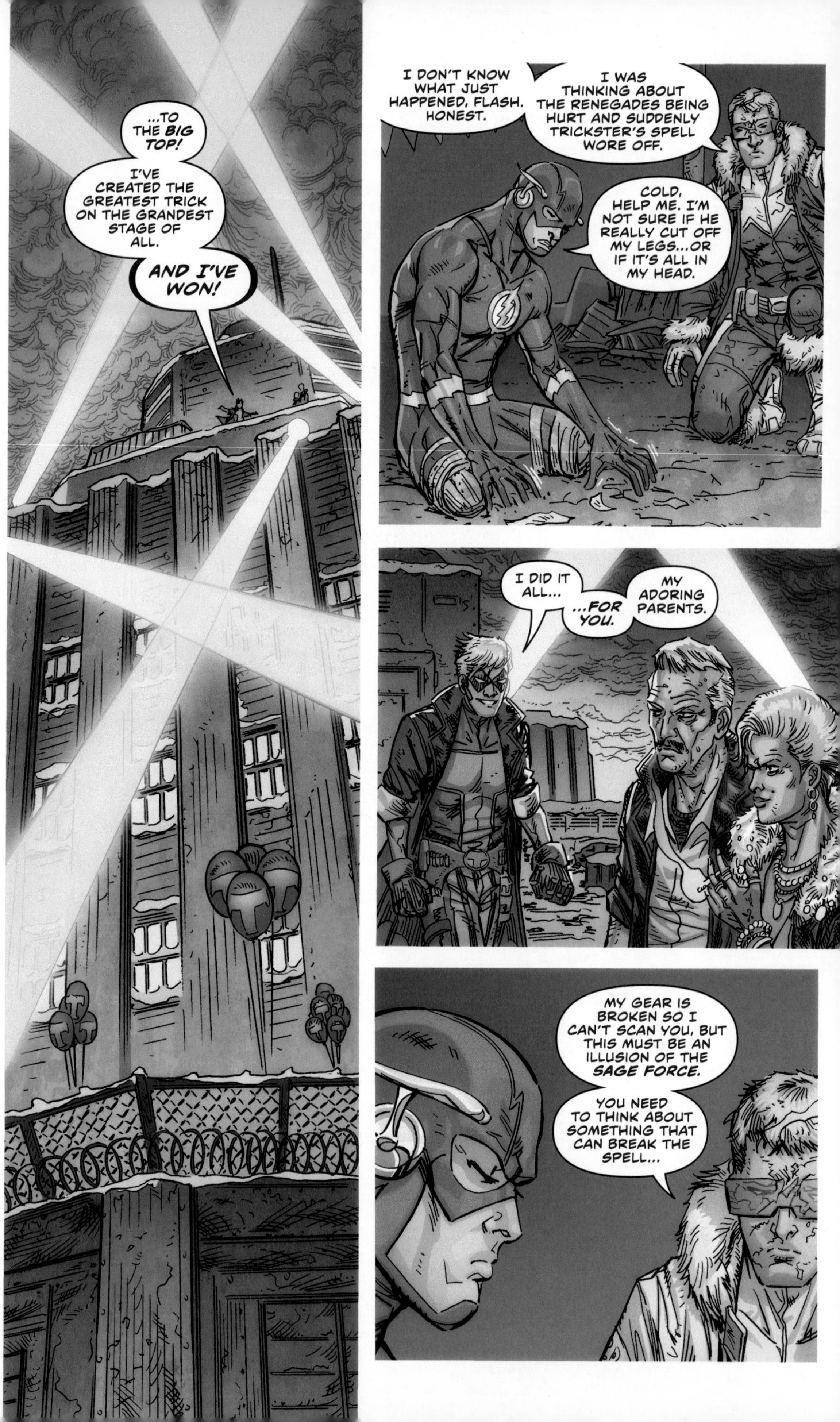
...TO THE BIG TOP!
I'VE CREATED THE GREATEST TRICK ON THE GRANDEST STAGE OF ALL.
AND I'VE WON!
I DON'T KNOW WHAT JUST HAPPENED, FLASH. HONEST.
I WAS THINKING ABOUT THE RENEGADES BEING HURT AND SUDDENLY TRICKSTER'S SPELL WORE OFF.
COLD, HELP ME. I'M NOT SURE IF HE REALLY CUT OFF MY LEGS...OR IF IT'S ALL IN MY HEAD.
I DID IT ALL...
...FOR YOU.
MY ADORING PARENTS.
MY GEAR IS BROKEN SO I CAN'T SCAN YOU, BUT THIS MUST BE AN ILLUSION OF THE SAGE FORCE.
YOU NEED TO THINK ABOUT SOMETHING THAT CAN BREAK THE SPELL...

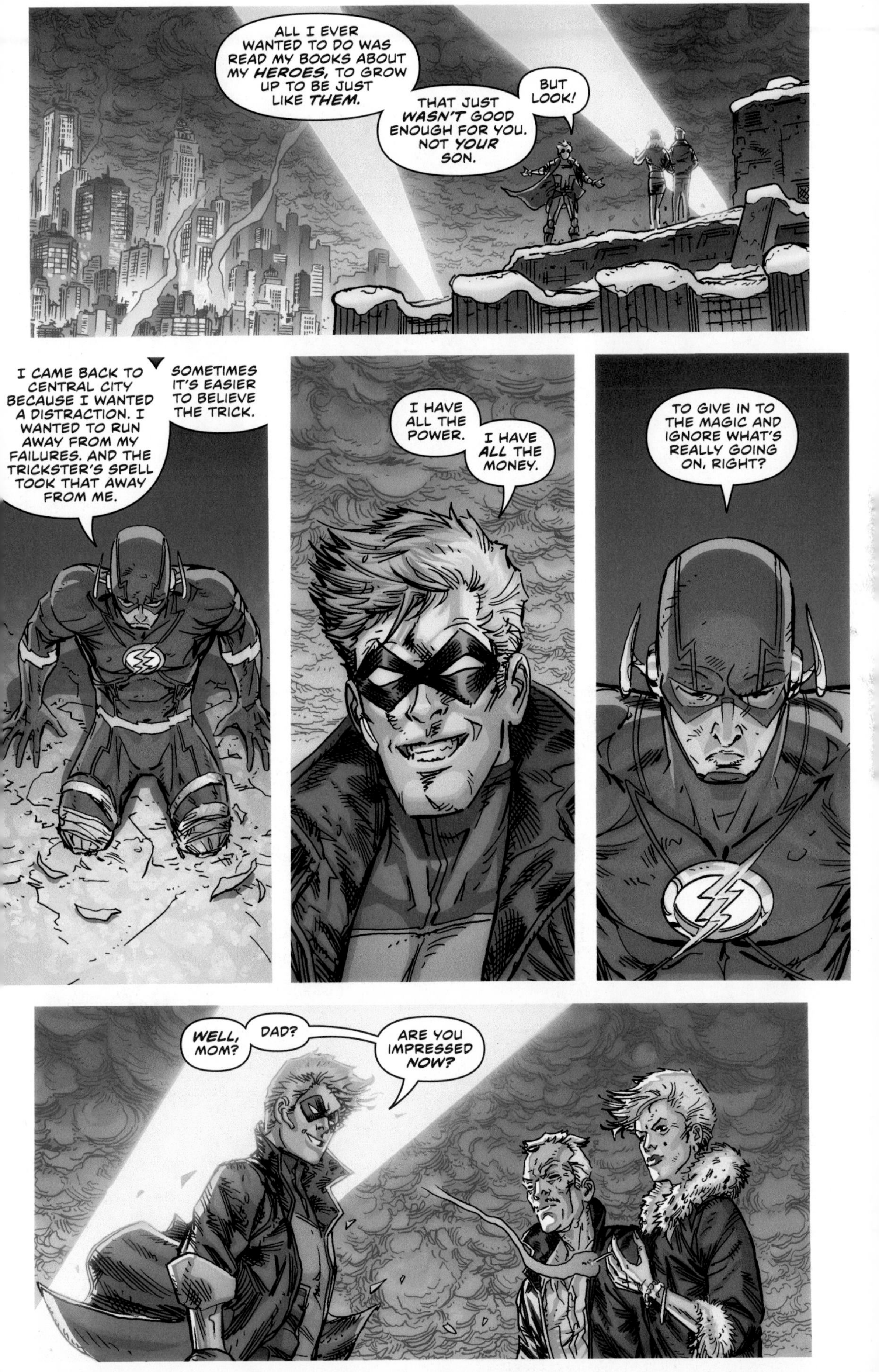
ALL I EVER WANTED TO DO WAS READ MY BOOKS ABOUT MY *HEROES,* TO GROW UP TO BE JUST LIKE *THEM.*
THAT JUST *WASN'T* GOOD ENOUGH FOR YOU. NOT *YOUR* SON.
BUT LOOK!
I CAME BACK TO CENTRAL CITY BECAUSE I WANTED A DISTRACTION. I WANTED TO RUN AWAY FROM MY FAILURES. AND THE TRICKSTER'S SPELL TOOK THAT AWAY FROM ME.
SOMETIMES IT'S EASIER TO BELIEVE THE TRICK.
I HAVE ALL THE POWER.
I HAVE *ALL* THE MONEY.
TO GIVE IN TO THE MAGIC AND IGNORE WHAT'S REALLY GOING ON, RIGHT?
WELL, MOM?
DAD?
ARE YOU IMPRESSED *NOW?*

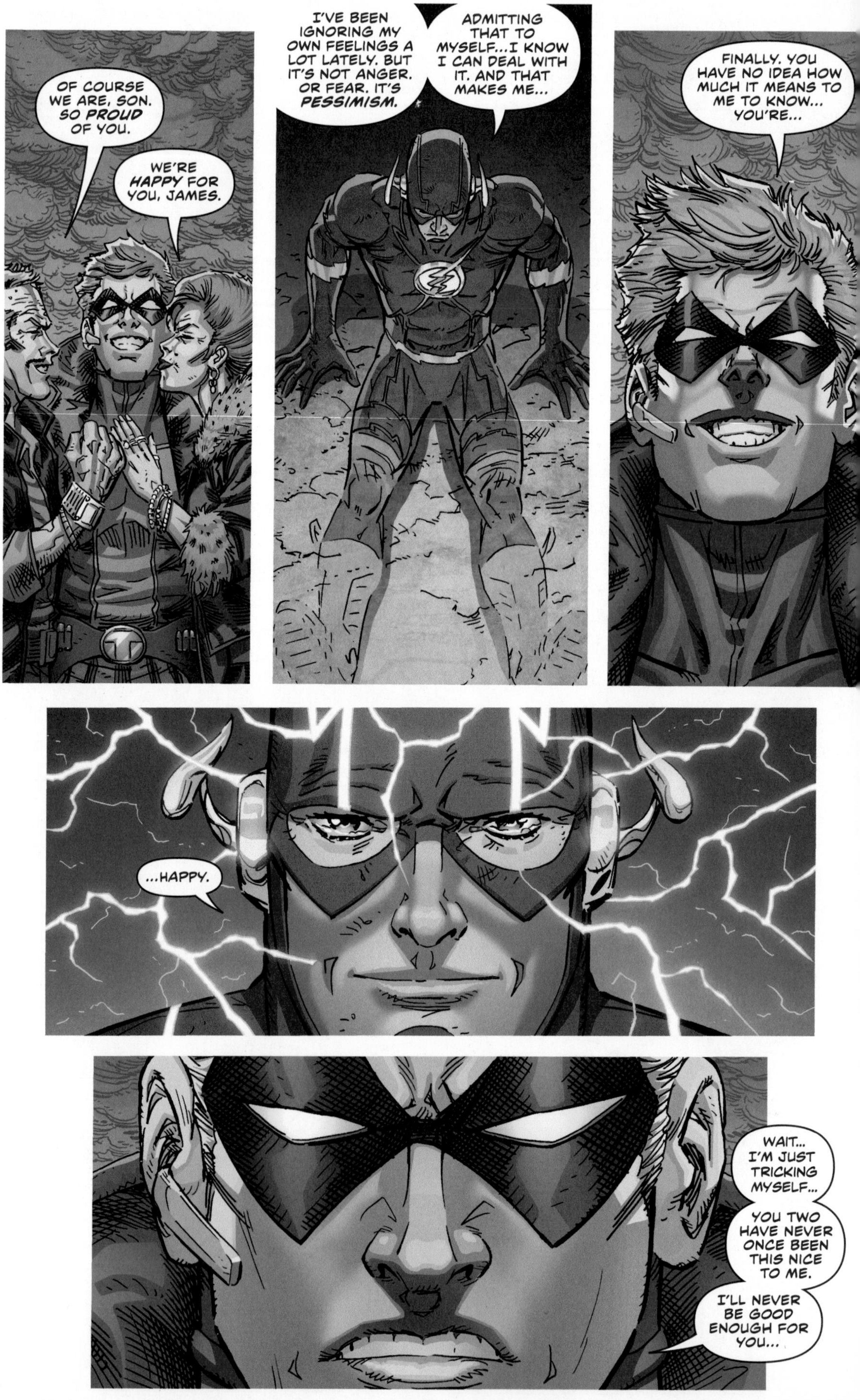
OF COURSE WE ARE, SON. SO PROUD OF YOU.
WE'RE HAPPY FOR YOU, JAMES.
I'VE BEEN IGNORING MY OWN FEELINGS A LOT LATELY. BUT IT'S NOT ANGER. OR FEAR. IT'S PESSIMISM.
ADMITTING THAT TO MYSELF...I KNOW I CAN DEAL WITH IT. AND THAT MAKES ME...
FINALLY. YOU HAVE NO IDEA HOW MUCH IT MEANS TO ME TO KNOW... YOU'RE...
...HAPPY.
WAIT... I'M JUST TRICKING MYSELF...
YOU TWO HAVE NEVER ONCE BEEN THIS NICE TO ME.
I'LL NEVER BE GOOD ENOUGH FOR YOU...

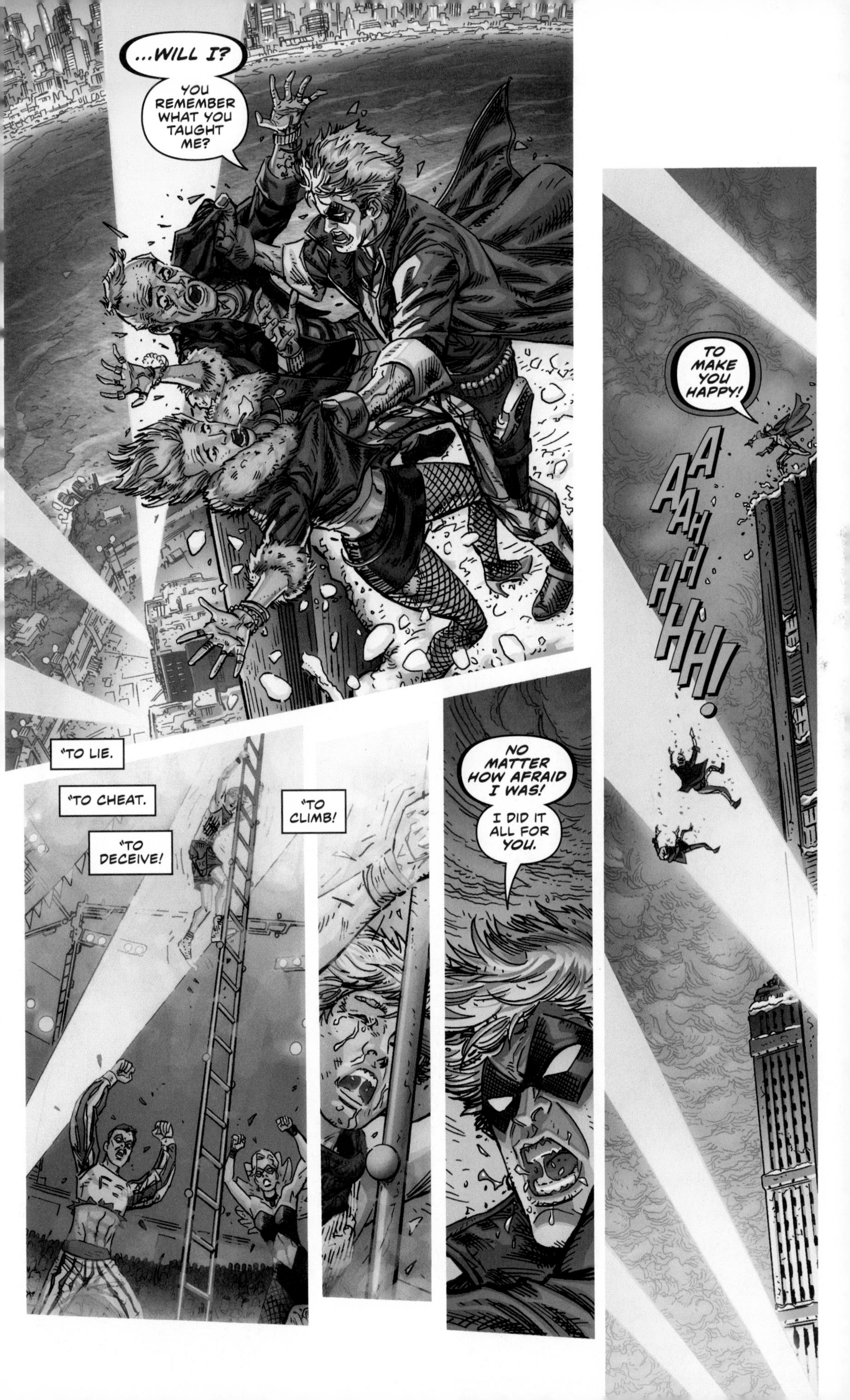
...WILL I?
YOU REMEMBER WHAT YOU TAUGHT ME?
TO MAKE YOU HAPPY!
AAAHHHHHH!
"TO LIE.
"TO CHEAT.
"TO DECEIVE!
"TO CLIMB!
NO MATTER HOW AFRAID I WAS!
I DID IT ALL FOR YOU.

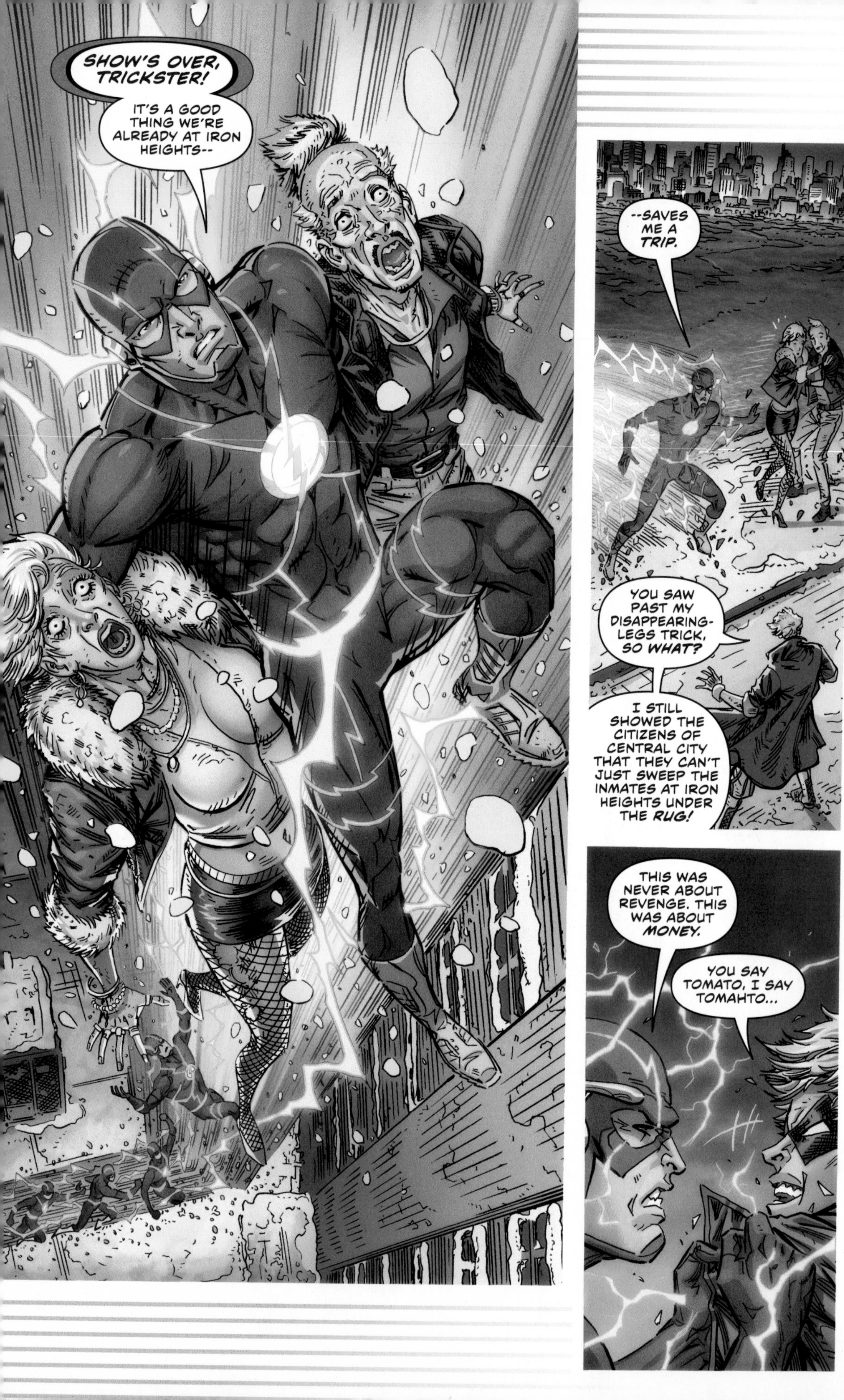
SHOW'S OVER, TRICKSTER!
IT'S A GOOD THING WE'RE ALREADY AT IRON HEIGHTS--
--SAVES ME A TRIP.
YOU SAW PAST MY DISAPPEARING-LEGS TRICK, SO WHAT?
I STILL SHOWED THE CITIZENS OF CENTRAL CITY THAT THEY CAN'T JUST SWEEP THE INMATES AT IRON HEIGHTS UNDER THE RUG!
THIS WAS NEVER ABOUT REVENGE. THIS WAS ABOUT MONEY.
YOU SAY TOMATO, I SAY TOMAHTO...

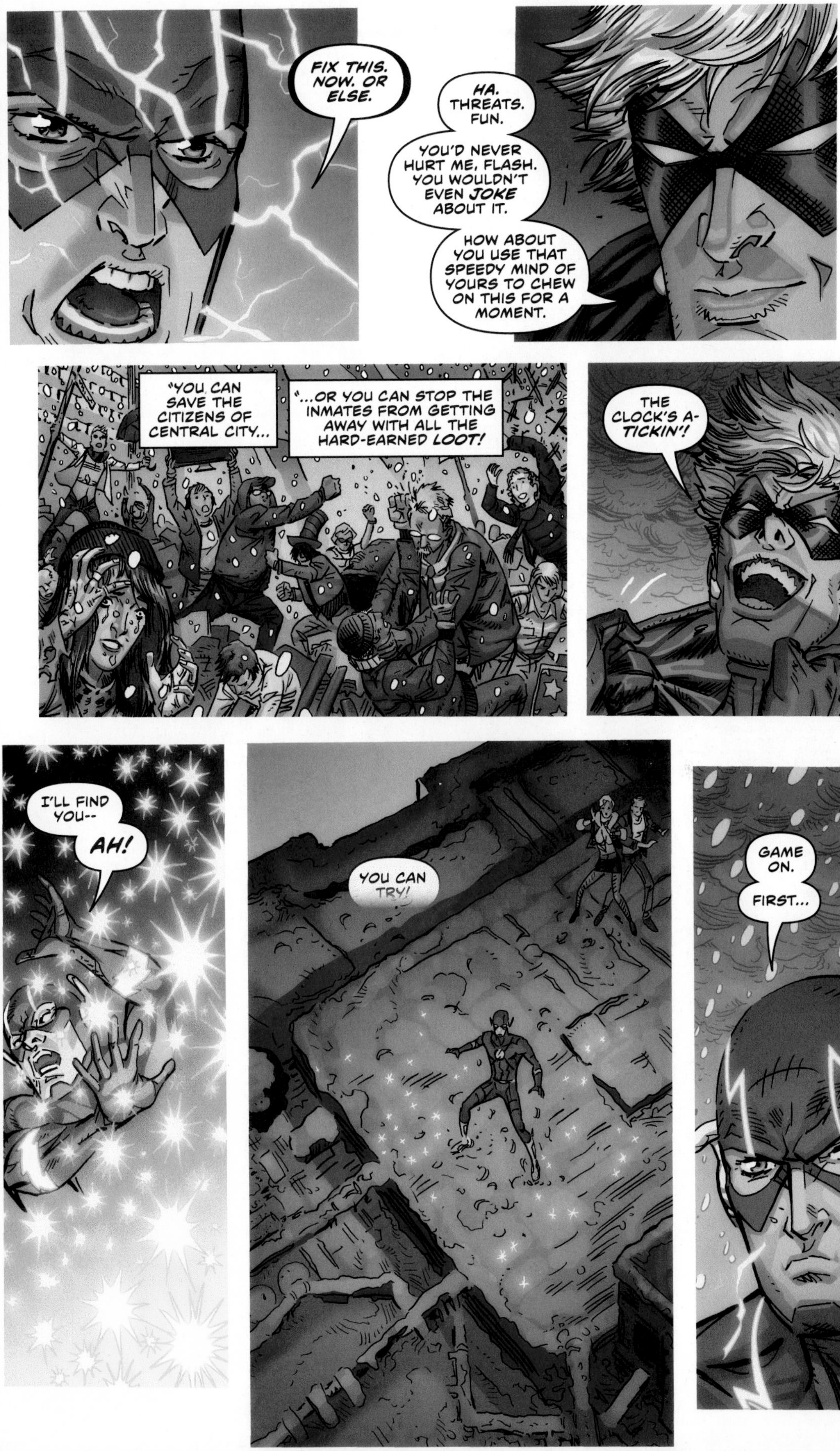
FIX THIS. NOW. OR ELSE.
HA. THREATS. FUN.
YOU'D NEVER HURT ME, FLASH. YOU WOULDN'T EVEN JOKE ABOUT IT.
HOW ABOUT YOU USE THAT SPEEDY MIND OF YOURS TO CHEW ON THIS FOR A MOMENT.
"YOU CAN SAVE THE CITIZENS OF CENTRAL CITY...
"...OR YOU CAN STOP THE INMATES FROM GETTING AWAY WITH ALL THE HARD-EARNED LOOT!
THE CLOCK'S A-TICKIN'!
I'LL FIND YOU-- AH!
YOU CAN TRY!
GAME ON.
FIRST...

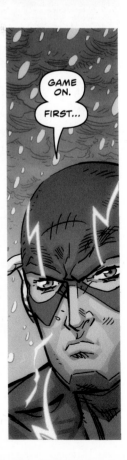

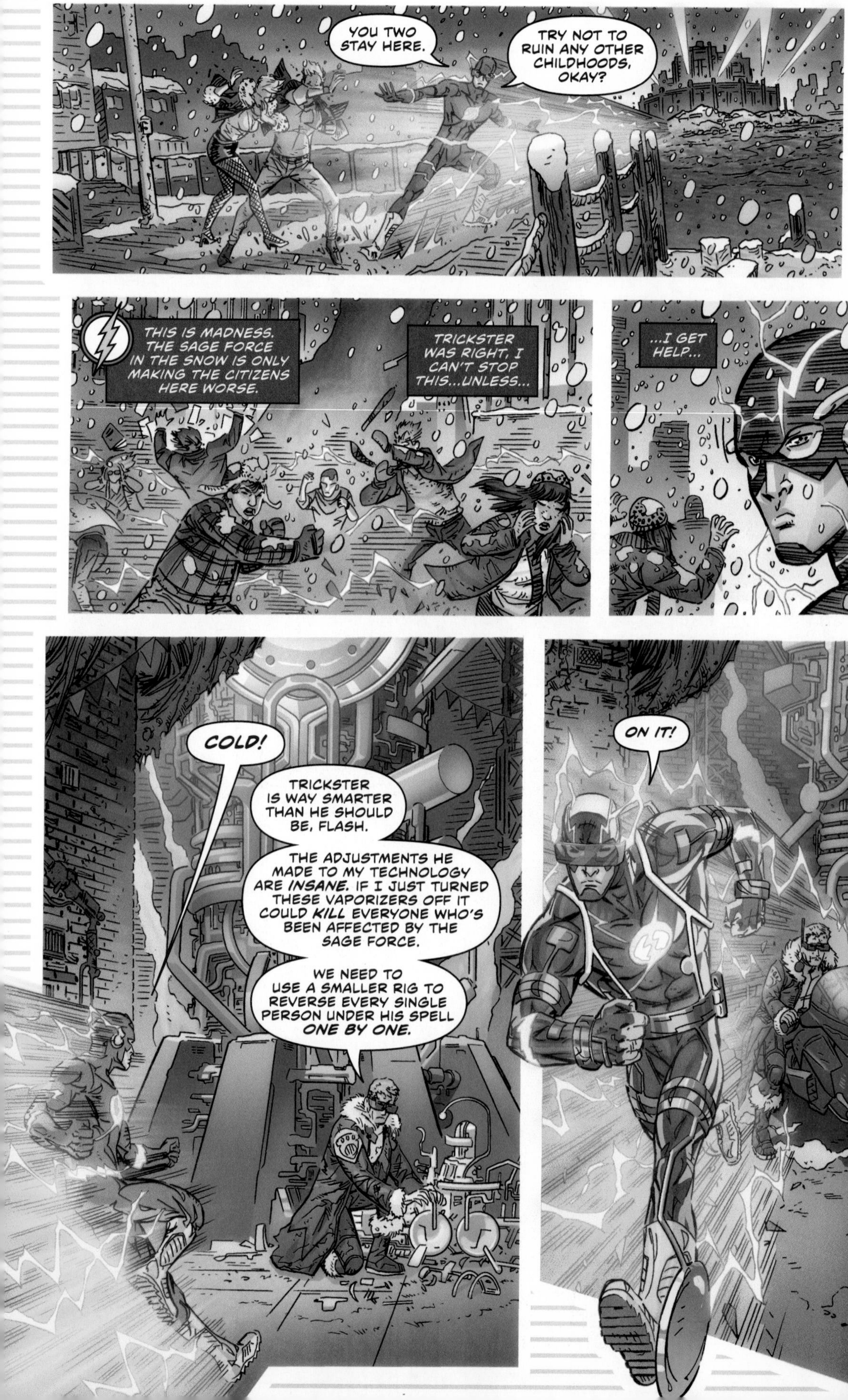
YOU TWO STAY HERE.
TRY NOT TO RUIN ANY OTHER CHILDHOODS, OKAY?
THIS IS MADNESS. THE SAGE FORCE IN THE SNOW IS ONLY MAKING THE CITIZENS HERE WORSE.
TRICKSTER WAS RIGHT, I CAN'T STOP THIS...UNLESS...
...I GET HELP...
COLD!
TRICKSTER IS WAY SMARTER THAN HE SHOULD BE, FLASH.
THE ADJUSTMENTS HE MADE TO MY TECHNOLOGY ARE INSANE. IF I JUST TURNED THESE VAPORIZERS OFF IT COULD KILL EVERYONE WHO'S BEEN AFFECTED BY THE SAGE FORCE.
WE NEED TO USE A SMALLER RIG TO REVERSE EVERY SINGLE PERSON UNDER HIS SPELL ONE BY ONE.
ON IT!

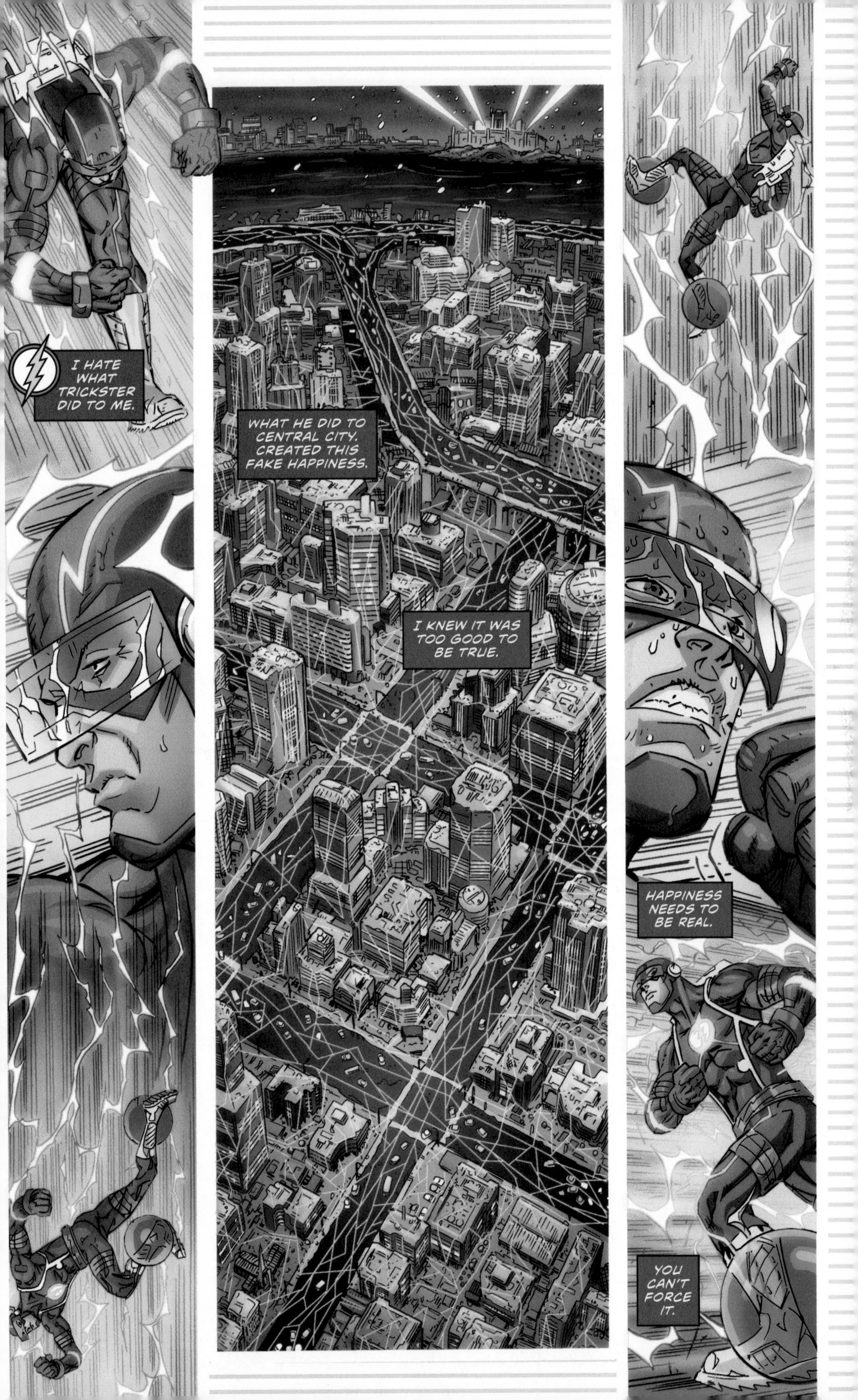

I HATE WHAT TRICKSTER DID TO ME.
WHAT HE DID TO CENTRAL CITY. CREATED THIS FAKE HAPPINESS.
I KNEW IT WAS TOO GOOD TO BE TRUE.
HAPPINESS NEEDS TO BE REAL.
YOU CAN'T FORCE IT.

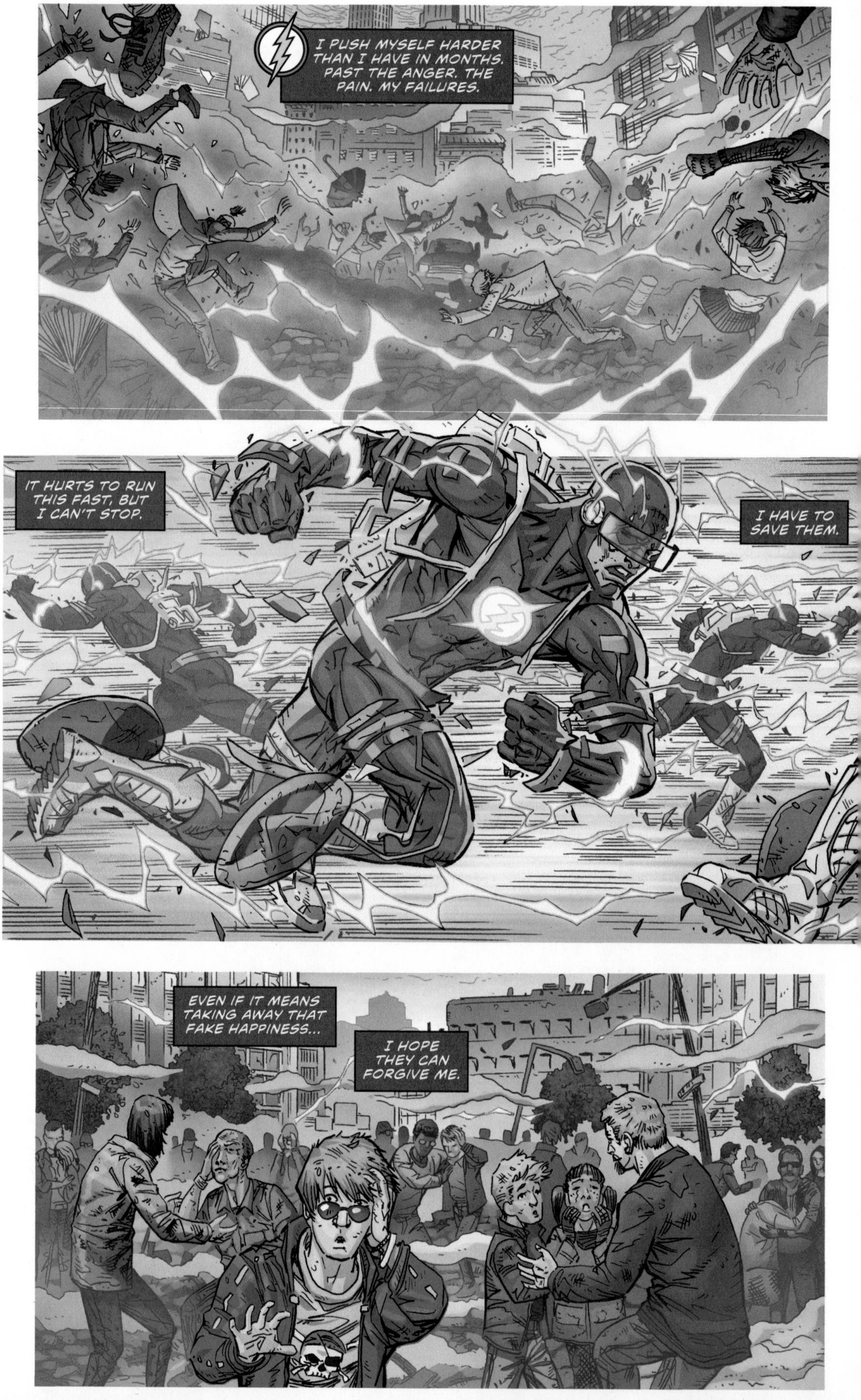
I PUSH MYSELF HARDER THAN I HAVE IN MONTHS. PAST THE ANGER. THE PAIN. MY FAILURES.
IT HURTS TO RUN THIS FAST, BUT I CAN'T STOP.
I HAVE TO SAVE THEM.
EVEN IF IT MEANS TAKING AWAY THAT FAKE HAPPINESS...
I HOPE THEY CAN FORGIVE ME.

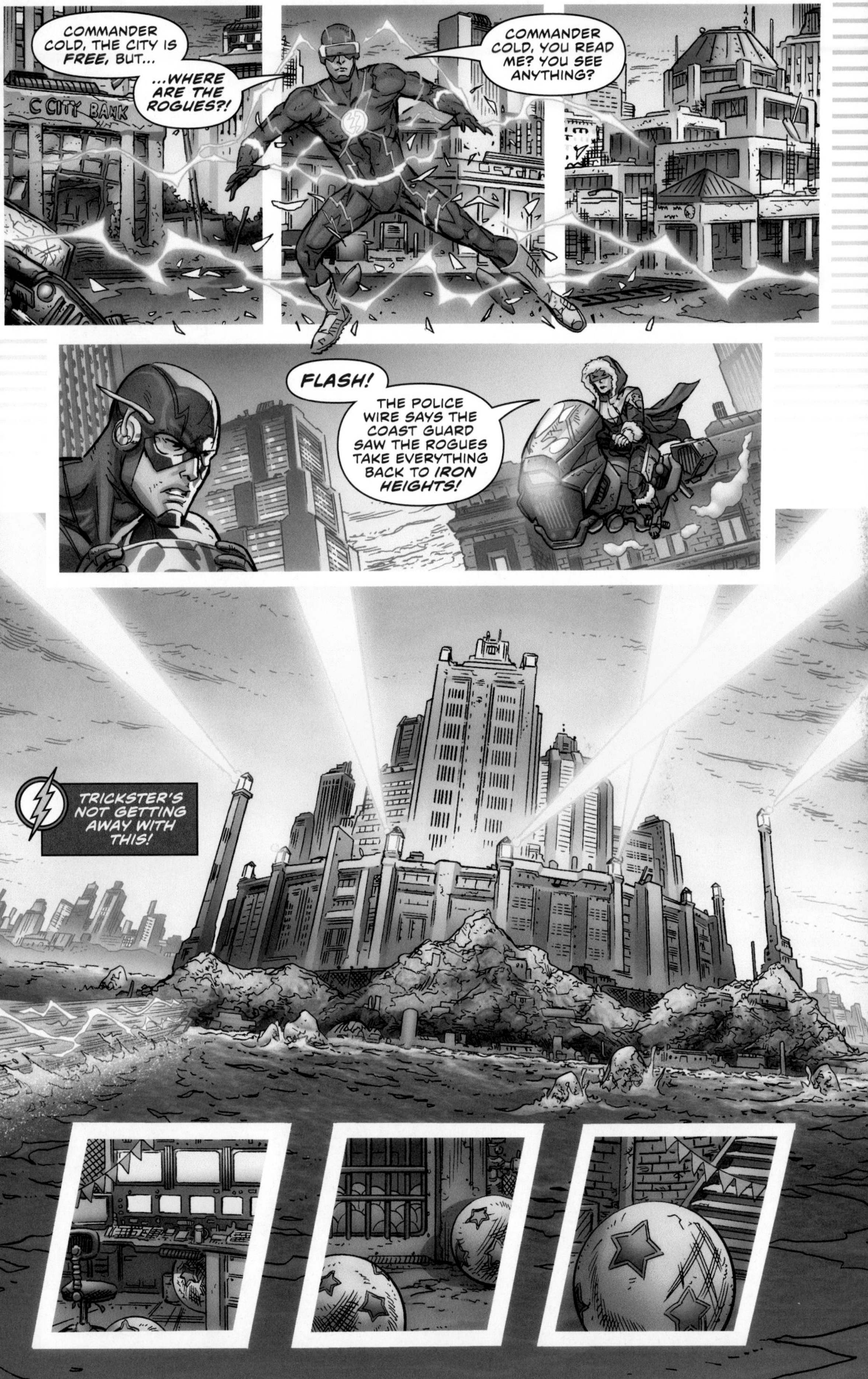
COMMANDER COLD, THE CITY IS FREE, BUT...
...WHERE ARE THE ROGUES?!
COMMANDER COLD, YOU READ ME? YOU SEE ANYTHING?
C CITY BANK
FLASH!
THE POLICE WIRE SAYS THE COAST GUARD SAW THE ROGUES TAKE EVERYTHING BACK TO IRON HEIGHTS!
TRICKSTER'S NOT GETTING AWAY WITH THIS!

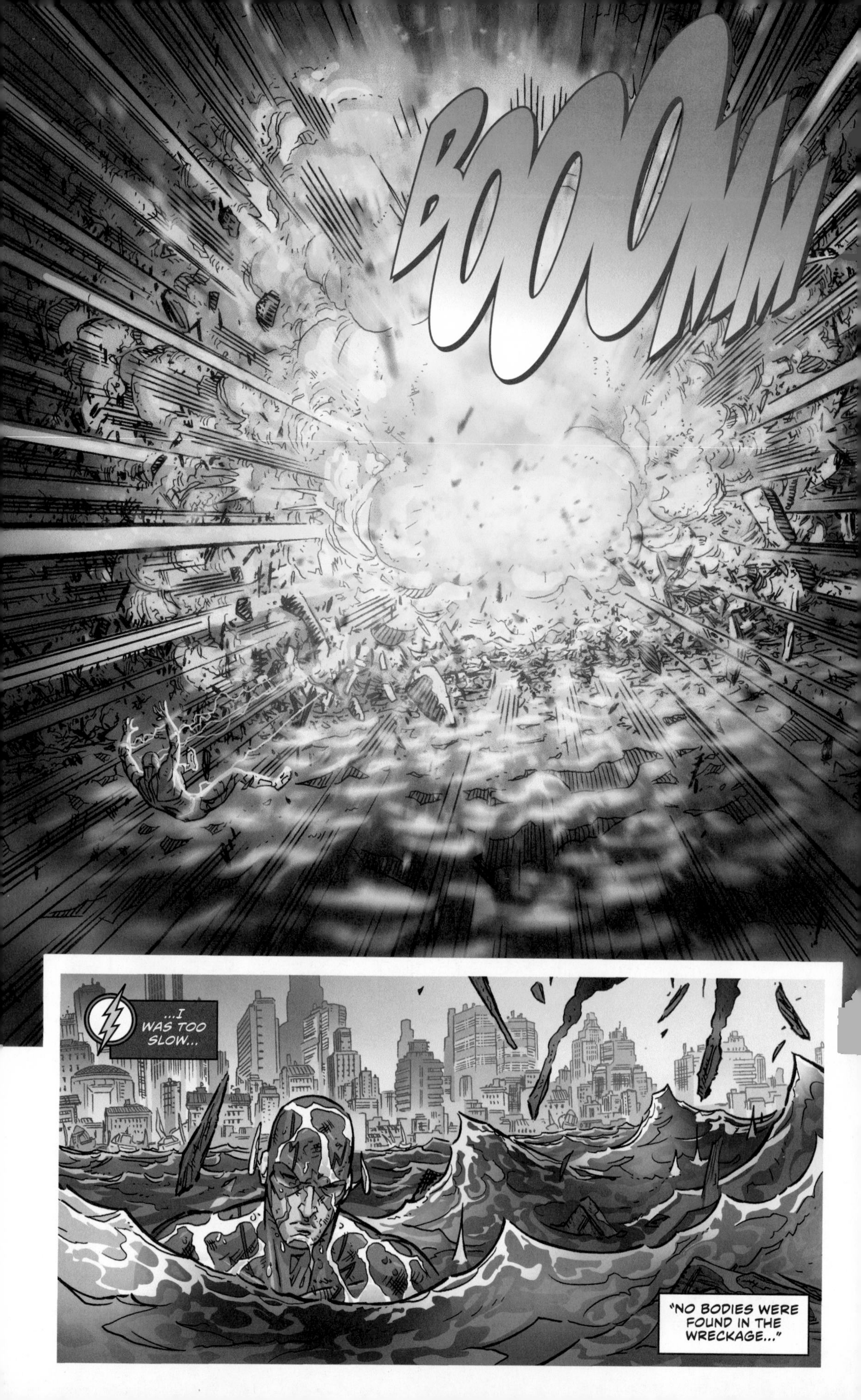
BOOOMM
...I WAS TOO SLOW...
"NO BODIES WERE FOUND IN THE WRECKAGE..."

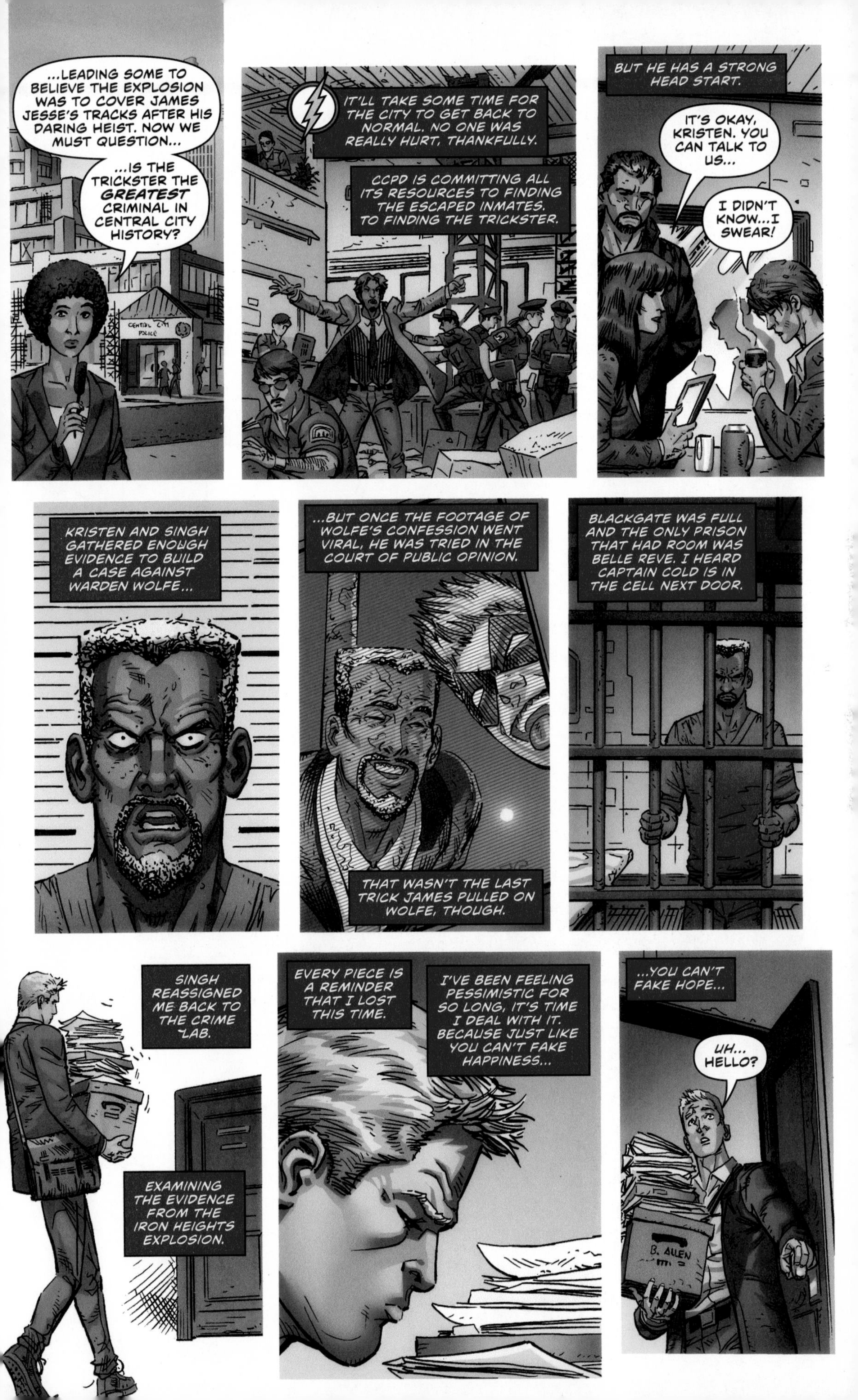
...LEADING SOME TO BELIEVE THE EXPLOSION WAS TO COVER JAMES JESSE'S TRACKS AFTER HIS DARING HEIST. NOW WE MUST QUESTION...
...IS THE TRICKSTER THE GREATEST CRIMINAL IN CENTRAL CITY HISTORY?
CENTRAL CITY POLICE
IT'LL TAKE SOME TIME FOR THE CITY TO GET BACK TO NORMAL. NO ONE WAS REALLY HURT, THANKFULLY.
CCPD IS COMMITTING ALL ITS RESOURCES TO FINDING THE ESCAPED INMATES. TO FINDING THE TRICKSTER.
BUT HE HAS A STRONG HEAD START.
IT'S OKAY, KRISTEN. YOU CAN TALK TO US...
I DIDN'T KNOW...I SWEAR!
KRISTEN AND SINGH GATHERED ENOUGH EVIDENCE TO BUILD A CASE AGAINST WARDEN WOLFE...
...BUT ONCE THE FOOTAGE OF WOLFE'S CONFESSION WENT VIRAL, HE WAS TRIED IN THE COURT OF PUBLIC OPINION.
THAT WASN'T THE LAST TRICK JAMES PULLED ON WOLFE, THOUGH.
BLACKGATE WAS FULL AND THE ONLY PRISON THAT HAD ROOM WAS BELLE REVE. I HEARD CAPTAIN COLD IS IN THE CELL NEXT DOOR.
SINGH REASSIGNED ME BACK TO THE CRIME LAB.
EXAMINING THE EVIDENCE FROM THE IRON HEIGHTS EXPLOSION.
EVERY PIECE IS A REMINDER THAT I LOST THIS TIME.
I'VE BEEN FEELING PESSIMISTIC FOR SO LONG, IT'S TIME I DEAL WITH IT. BECAUSE JUST LIKE YOU CAN'T FAKE HAPPINESS...
...YOU CAN'T FAKE HOPE...
UH... HELLO?
B. ALLEN

THIS WINDOW IS WHERE IT HAPPENED, ISN'T IT?

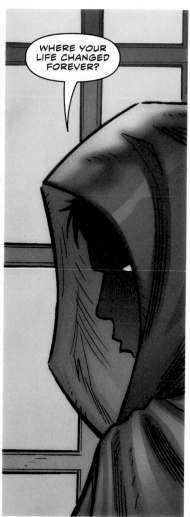

WHERE YOUR LIFE CHANGED FOREVER?

THIS...THIS IS AN OFF-LIMITS AREA OF THE CCPD.

I DON'T KNOW WHO YOU ARE, BUT YOU'RE NOT AUTHORIZED TO BE--

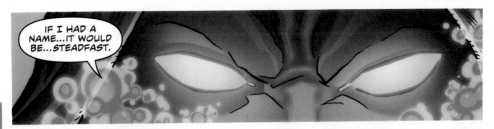

IF I HAD A NAME...IT WOULD BE...STEADFAST.

THAT ENERGY... THE STILL FORCE...?

I THOUGHT ONLY GRODD AND THE TURTLE HAD THE STILL FORCE. I WAS SEARCHING FOR--

I...I CAN'T MOVE...

YOU SHOULD NO LONGER GO FORWARD. YOU MUST GO BACK.

FOR THE MULTIVERSE TO SURVIVE WHAT IS TO COME, BARRY ALLEN...

FWOOOM

...YOU MUST REMEMBER...

"...SOMETHING YOU HAVE FORGOTTEN..."

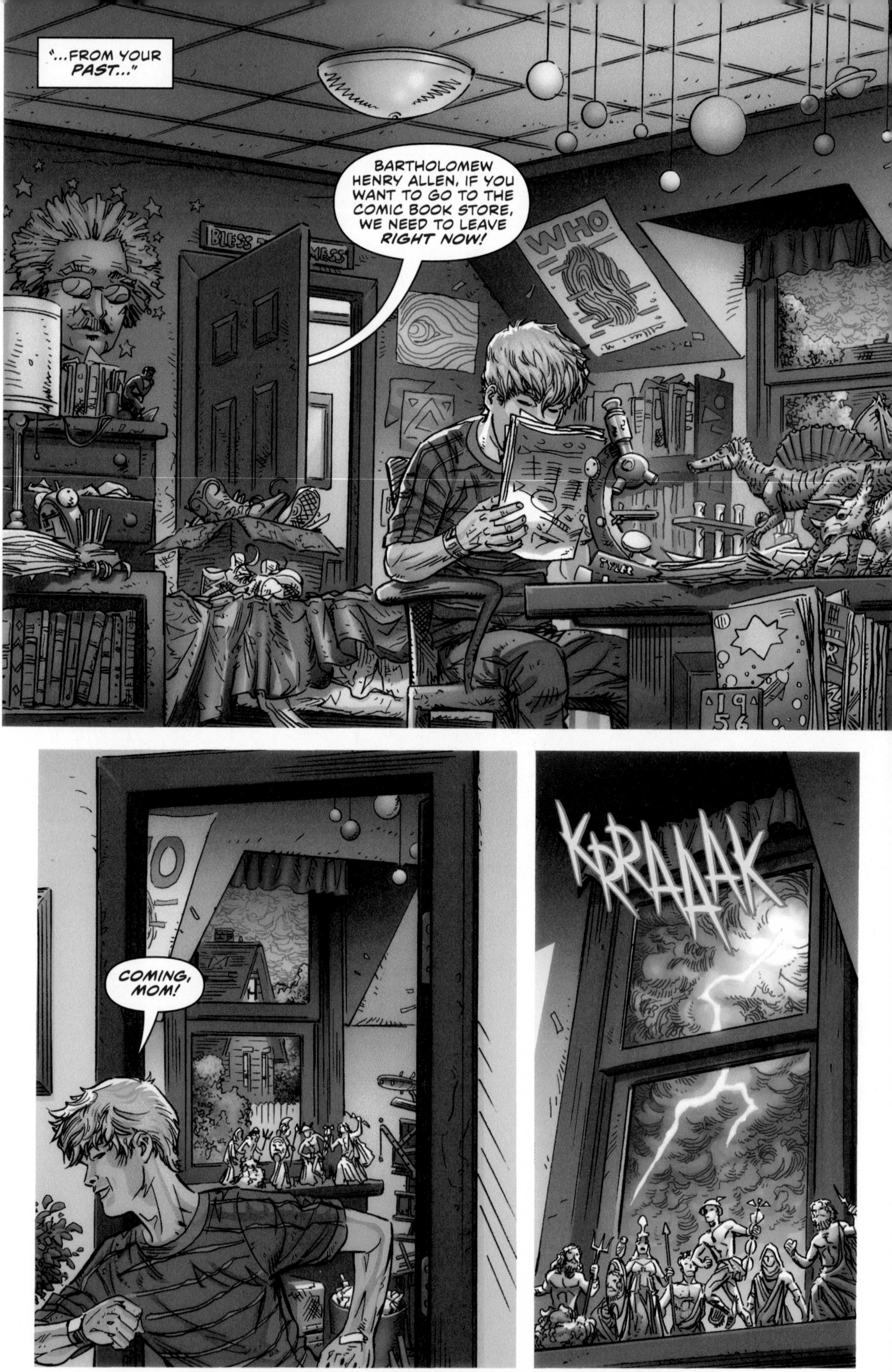
"...FROM YOUR PAST..."
BARTHOLOMEW HENRY ALLEN, IF YOU WANT TO GO TO THE COMIC BOOK STORE, WE NEED TO LEAVE RIGHT NOW!
WHO
COMING, MOM!
KRRAAAK

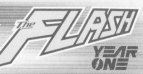

TO BE CONTINUED IN The FLASH YEAR ONE

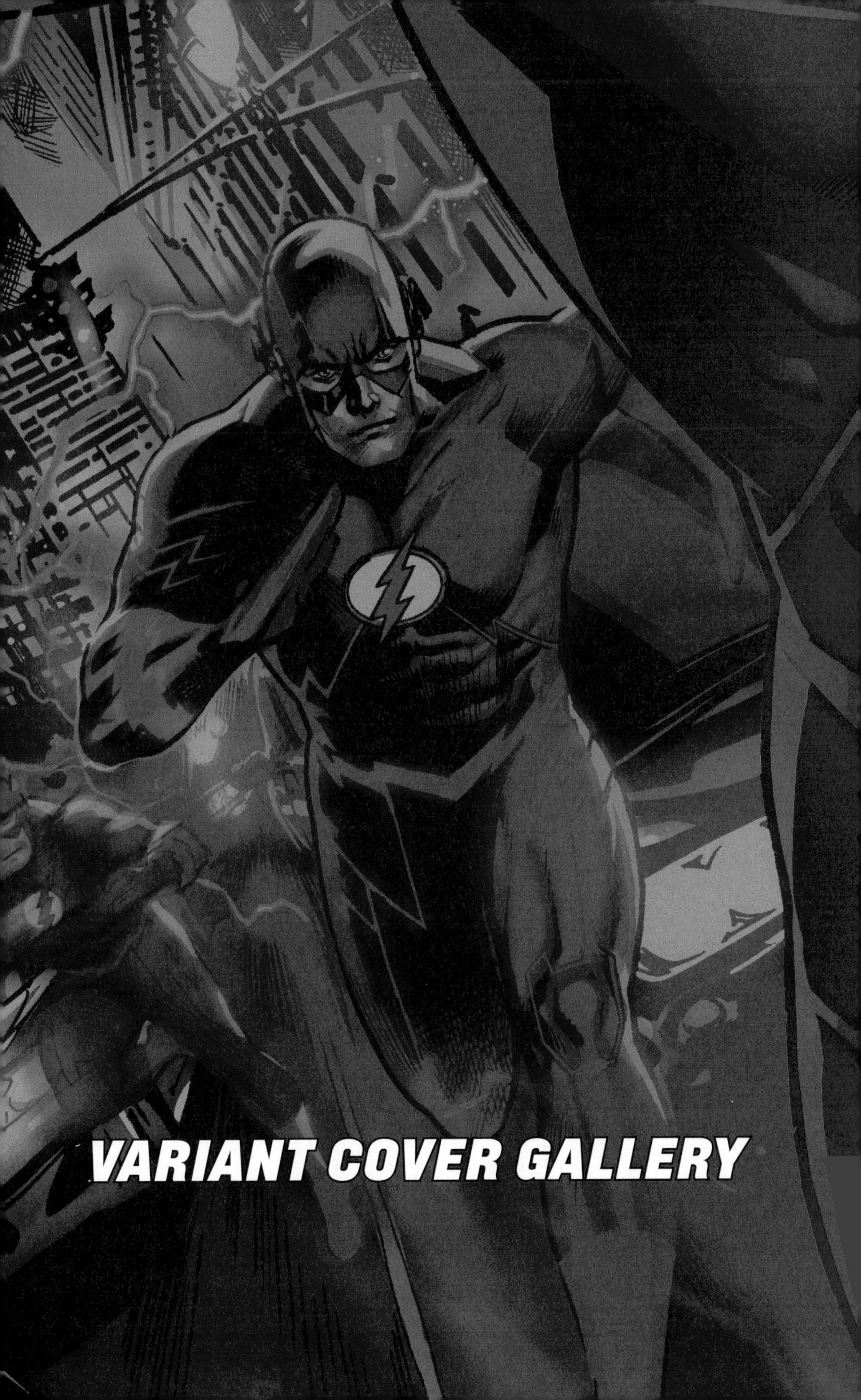

VARIANT COVER GALLERY

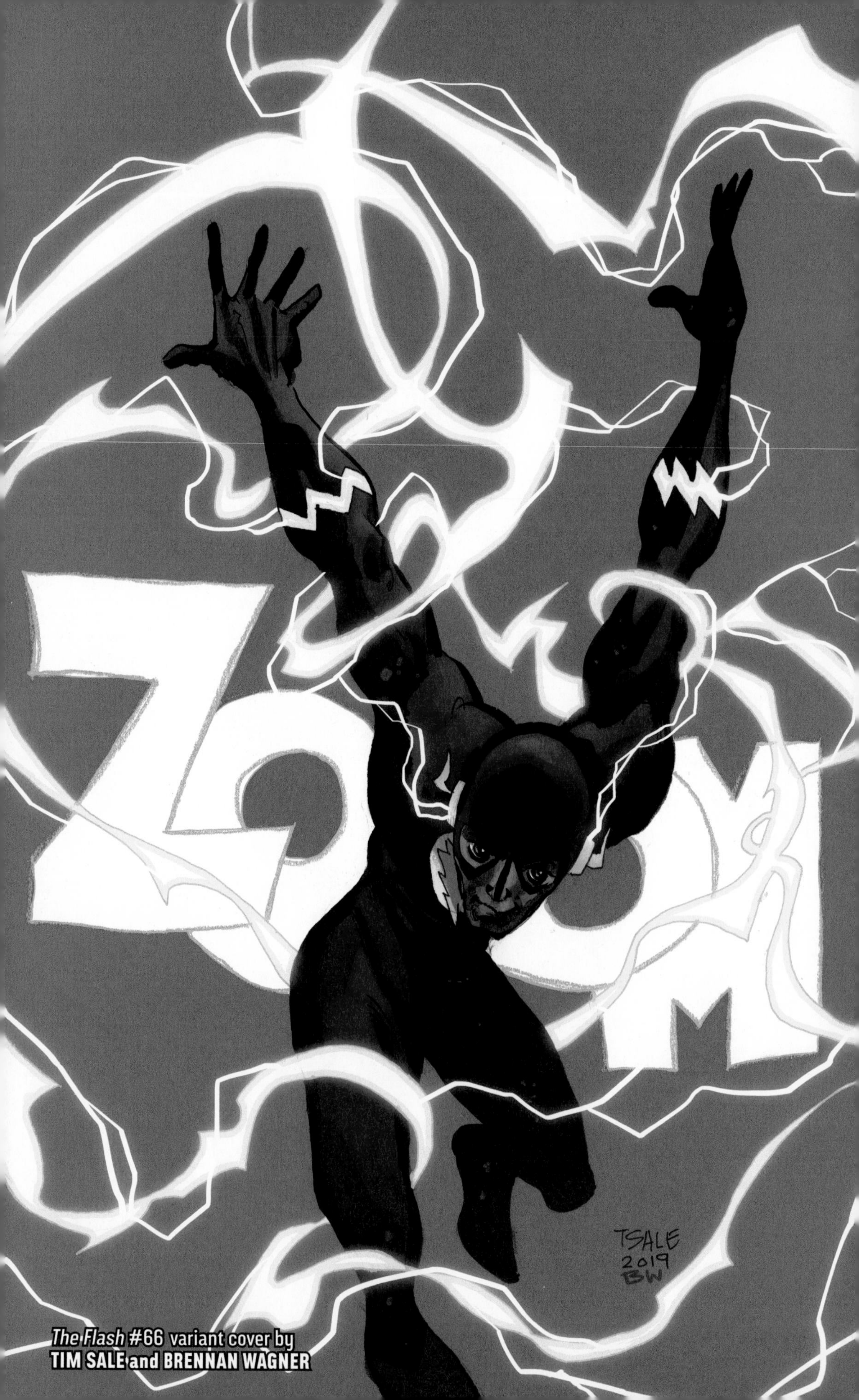
ZOOM
TSALE
2019
BW

The Flash #66 variant cover by
TIM SALE and BRENNAN WAGNER

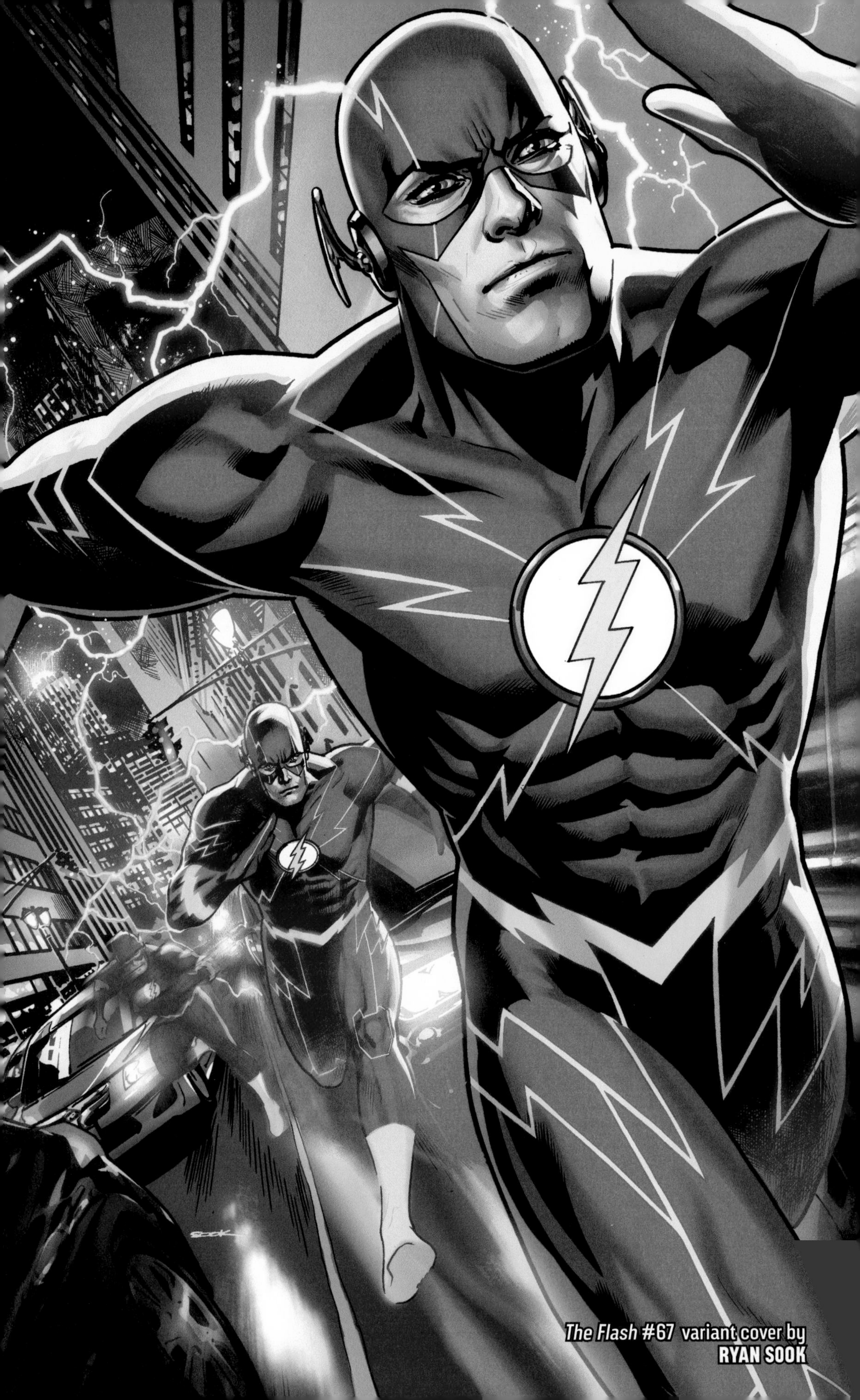

The Flash #67 variant cover by
RYAN SOOK

The Flash #68 variant cover by
MITCH GERADS

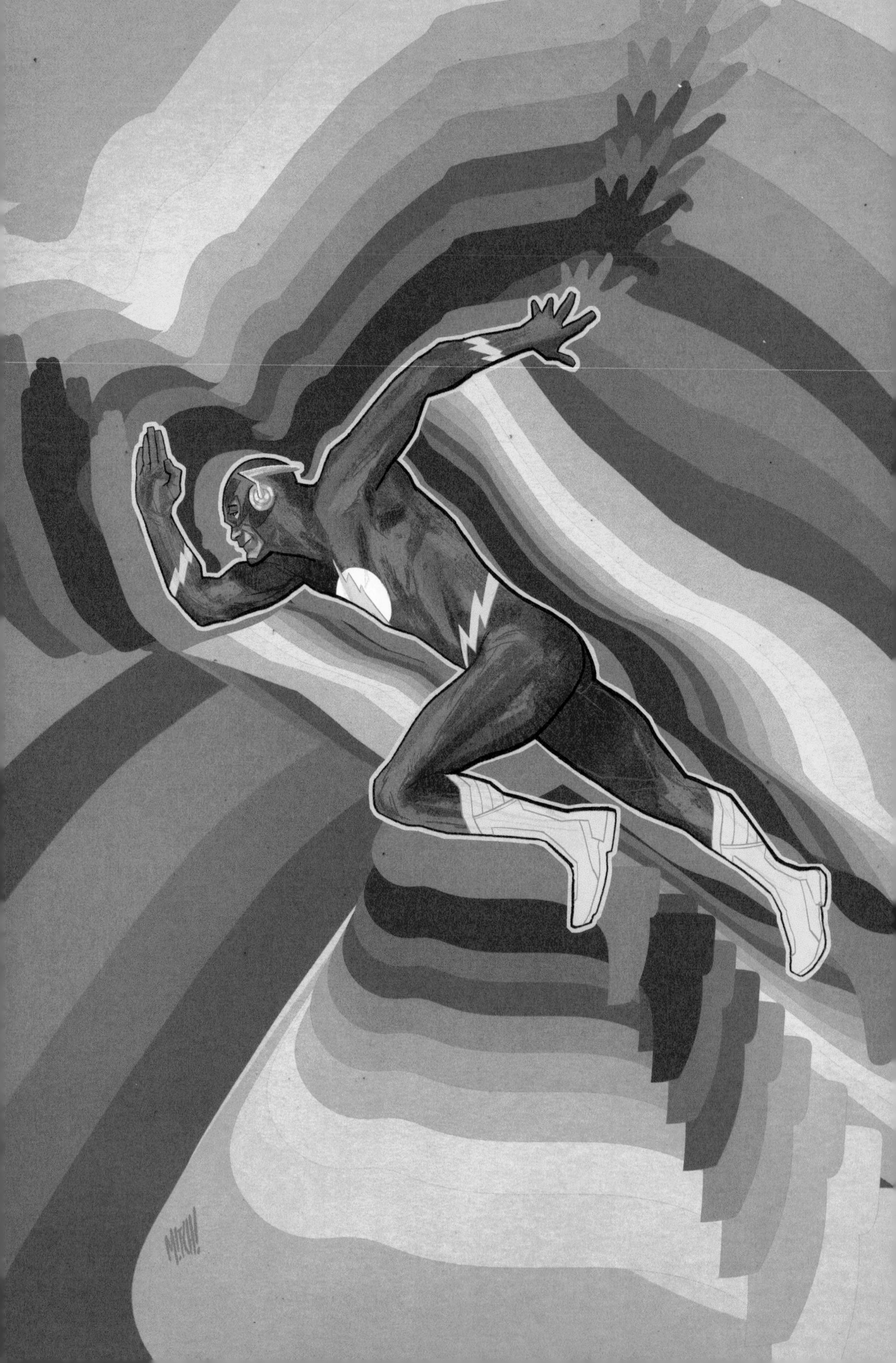

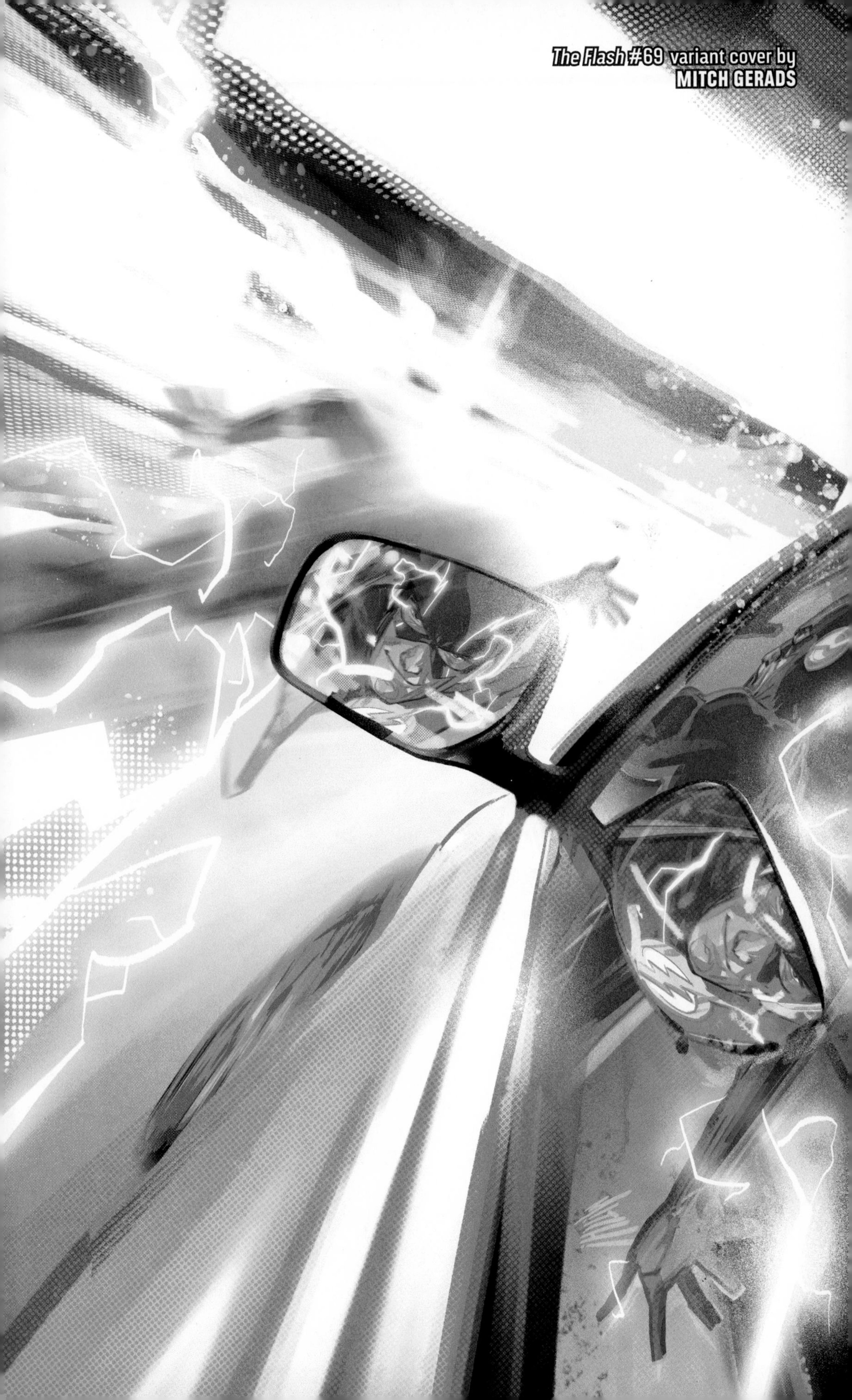

The Flash #69 variant cover by
MITCH GERADS

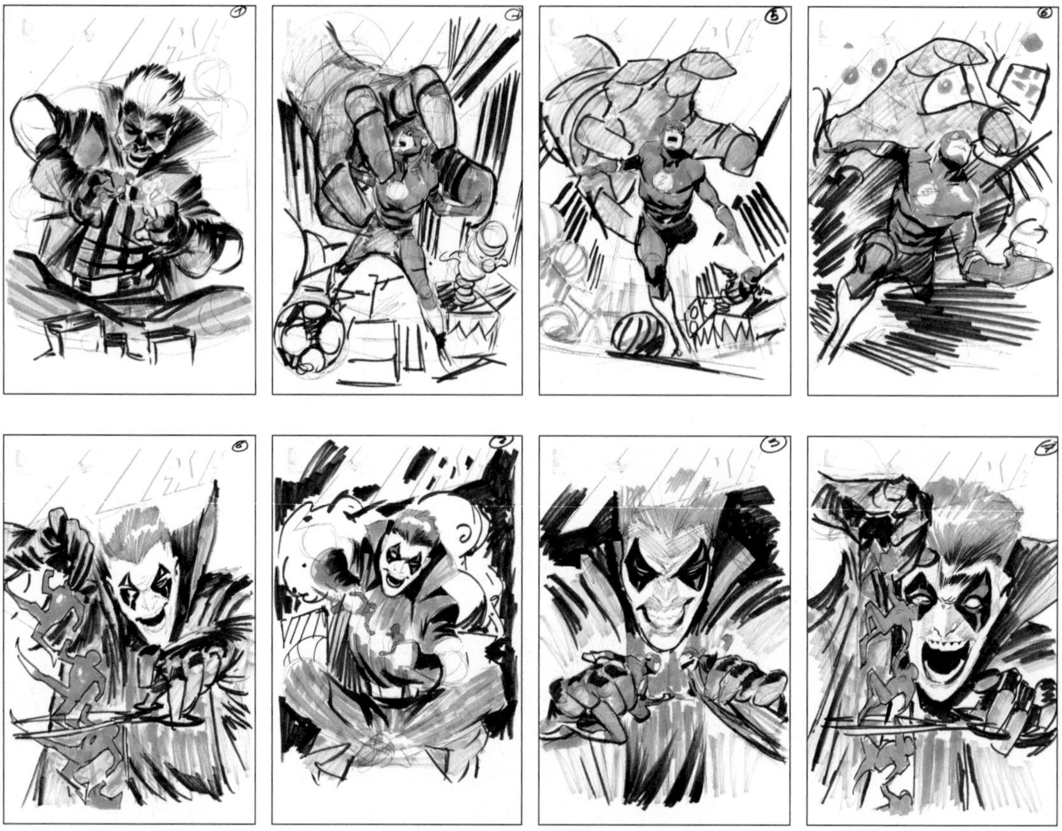

The Flash #66-67 cover sketches by
RAFA SANDOVAL

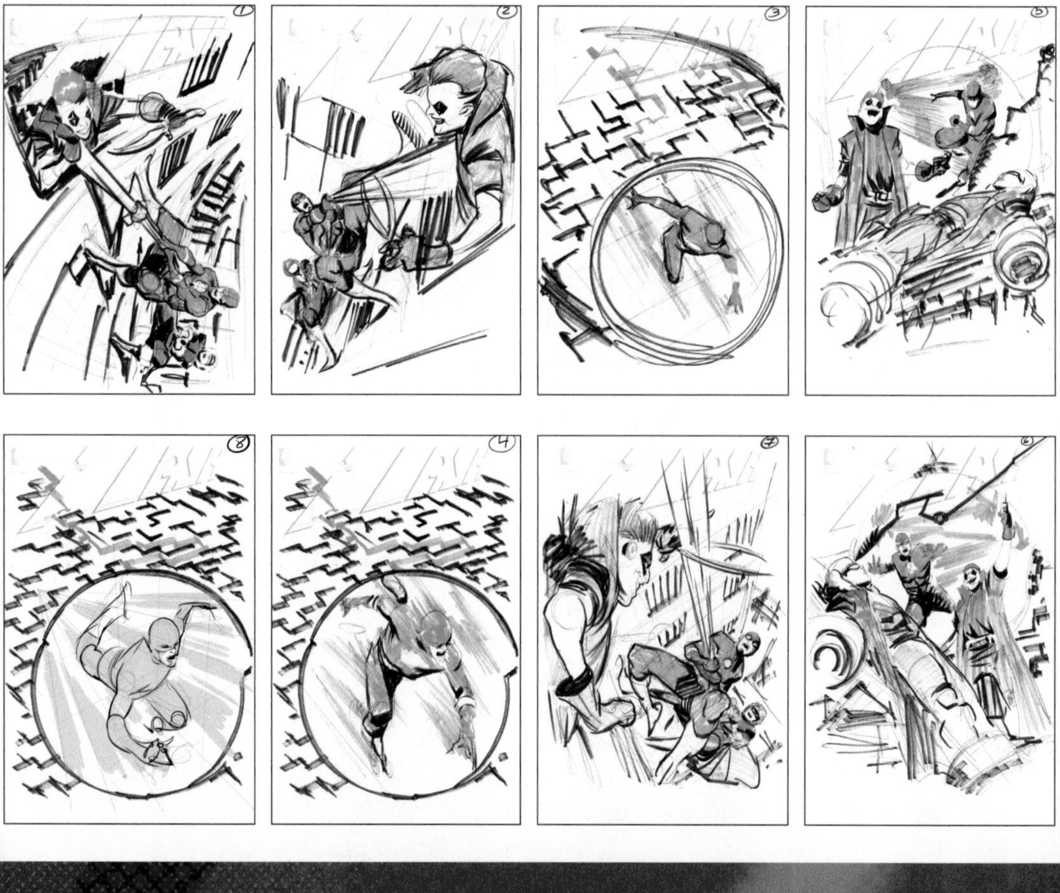

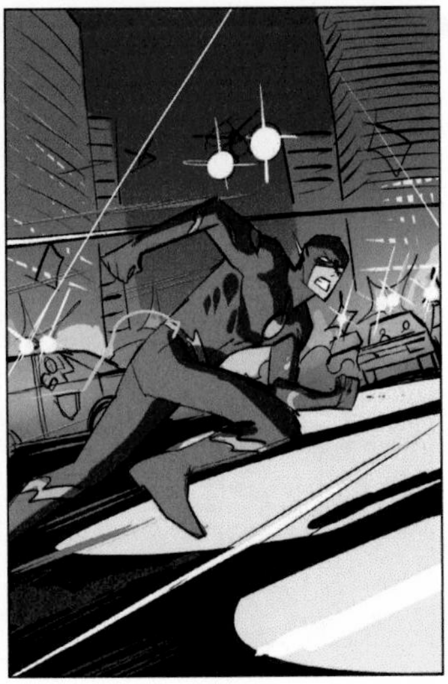

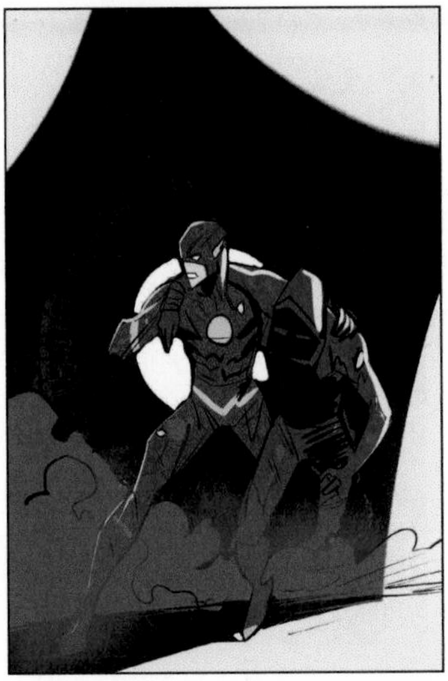

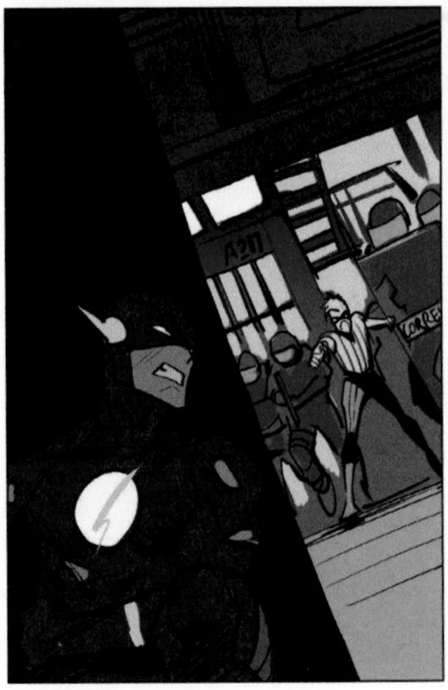

The Flash #68-69 cover sketches by
DAN MORA

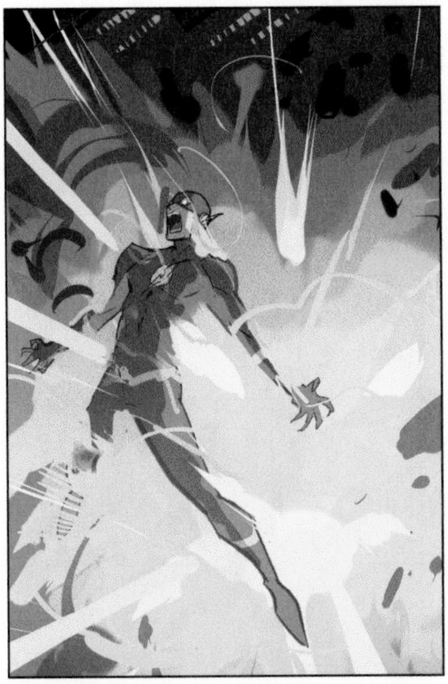

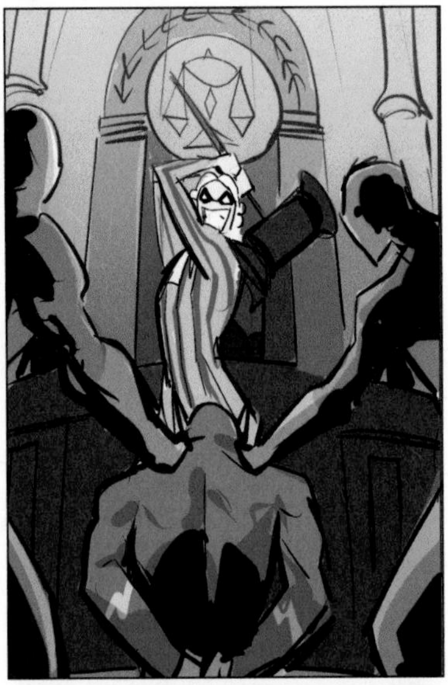

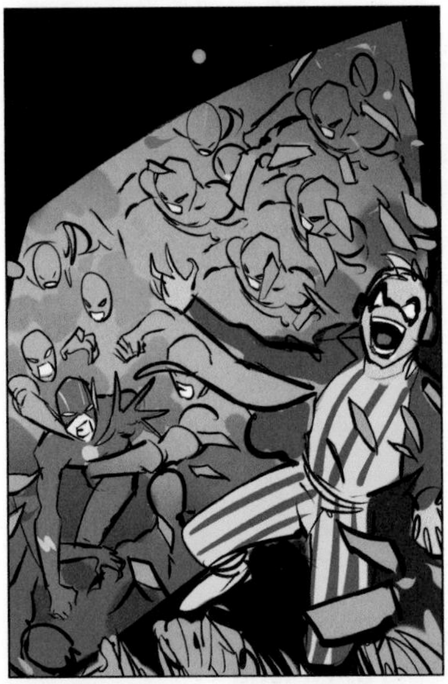

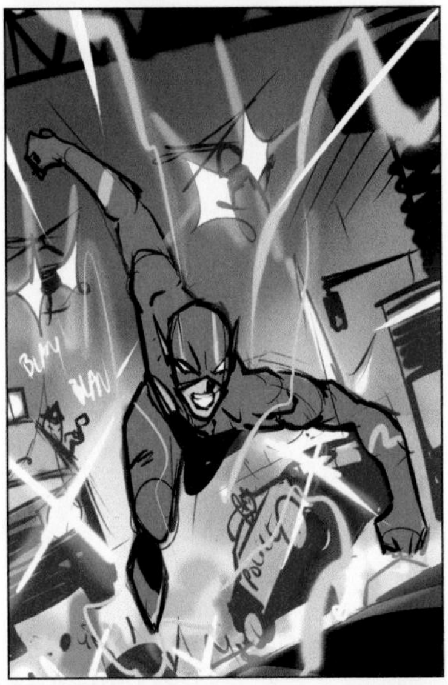

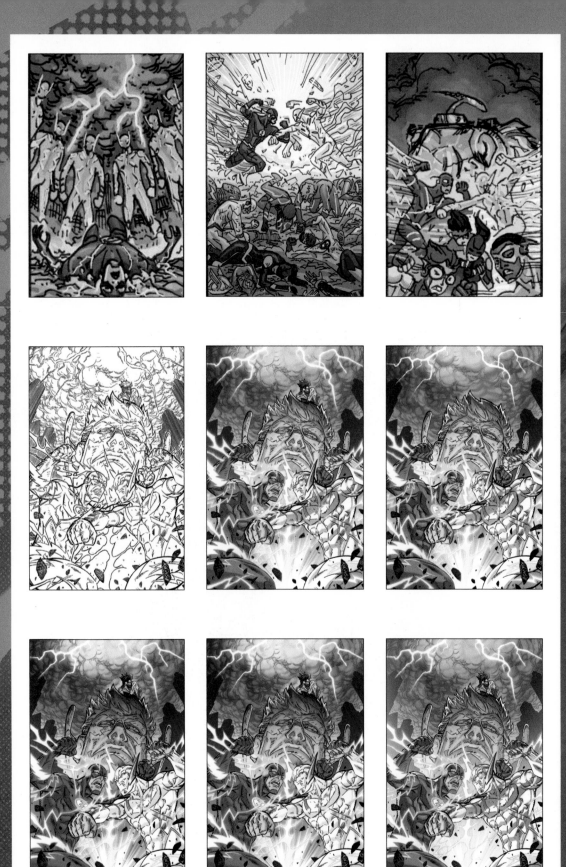

The Flash Annual #2 cover concepts and progression by
SCOTT KOLINS and LUIS GUERRERO

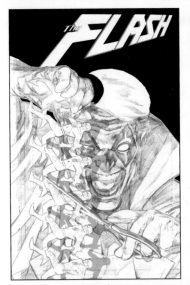

The Flash #66 cover progression by
RAFA SANDOVAL, JORDI TARRAGONA, and TOMEU MOREY

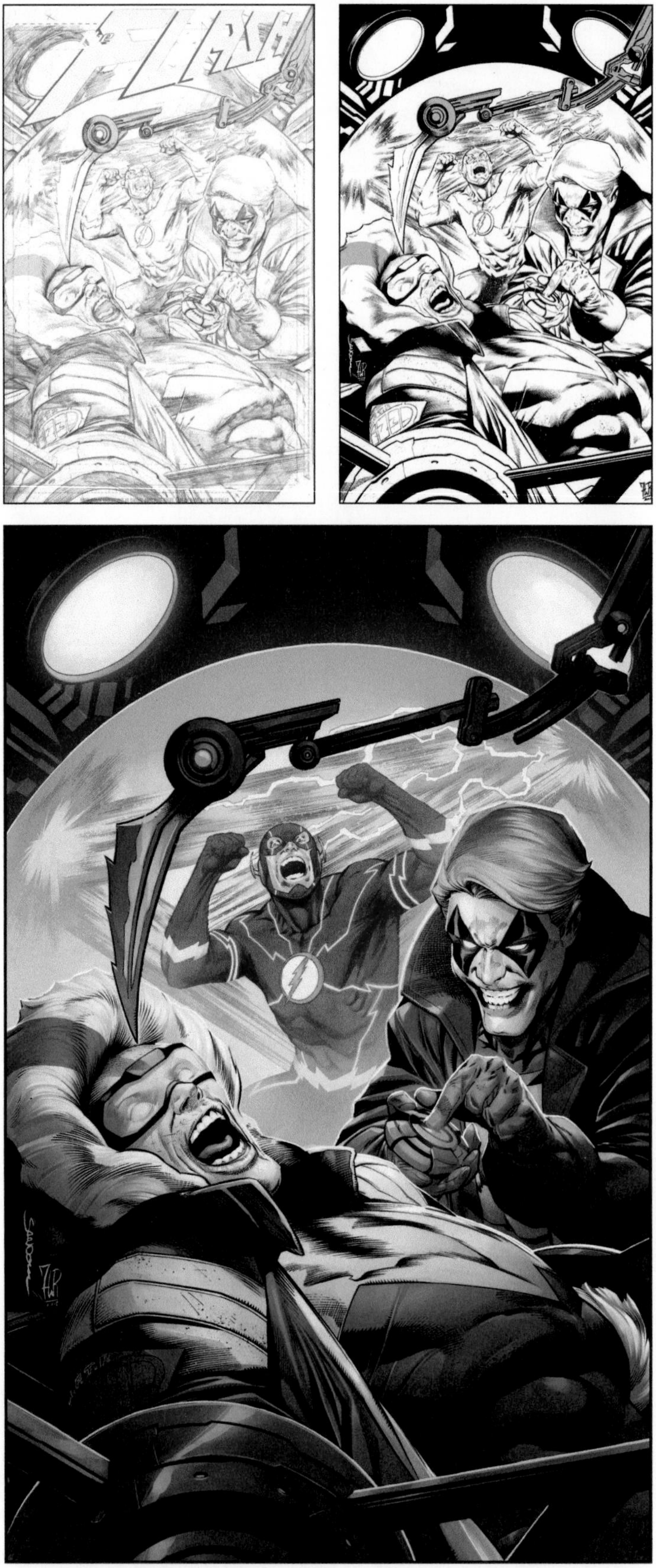

The Flash #67 cover progression by
RAFA SANDOVAL, JORDI TARRAGONA, and TOMEU MOREY

"Joshua Williamson's writing is on-point."
—NERDIST

"Plenty of action, emotion, and twists."
—NEWSARAMA

"As accessible as possible to new readers."
—CBR

THE FLASH
VOL. 1: LIGHTNING STRIKES TWICE
JOSHUA WILLIAMSON
CARMINE DI GIANDOMENICO

THE FLASH VOL. 2:
SPEED OF DARKNESS

THE FLASH VOL. 3:
ROGUES RELOADED

READ THEM ALL!

THE FLASH VOL. 4: RUNNING SCARED

THE FLASH VOL. 5: NEGATIVE

THE FLASH VOL. 6: COLD DAY IN HELL

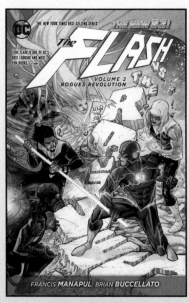